W9-ATR-204

This innovative new book seeks to contribute simultaneously to two different disciplinary fields: comparative political economy and Mexican history. It does so by attempting to explain why Mexico—contrary to the predictions of several dominant theories of economic growth—enjoyed a comparatively high rate of economic growth and development under the highly authoritarian dictatorship of Porfirio Díaz (1876–1911). By conducting a detailed political analysis of Díaz's rule, Armando Razo introduces network analysis to the study of institutions and growth and shows how dictators can maintain their power with credible growth-enhancing policies.

SOCIAL FOUNDATIONS OF
LIMITED DICTATORSHIP

SOCIAL SCIENCE HISTORY

Edited by
Stephen Haber and David W. Brady

SOCIAL FOUNDATIONS OF LIMITED DICTATORSHIP

Networks and Private Protection During Mexico's Early Industrialization

ARMANDO RAZO

STANFORD UNIVERSITY PRESS

Stanford, California

2008

WINGATE UNIVERSITY LIBRARY

Stanford University Press
Stanford, California

© 2008 by the Board of Trustees of the Leland Stanford
Junior University. All rights reserved.

No part of this book may be reproduced or transmitted
in any form or by any means, electronic or mechanical,
including photocopying and recording, or in any
information storage or retrieval system without the prior
written permission of Stanford University Press.

Printed in the United States of America on acid-free,
archival-quality paper.

Library of Congress Cataloging-in-Publication Data

Razo, Armando.
    Social foundations of limited dictatorship : networks and
private protection during Mexico's early industrialization /
Armando Razo.
        p.   cm. — (Social science history series)
    Includes bibliographical references and index.
    ISBN 978-0-8047-5661-7 (cloth : alk. paper)
1. Dictatorship.   2. Economic development—Political
aspects. 3. Industrialization—Mexico.   4. Mexico—
History—1867-1910.   5. Díaz, Porfirio, 1830–1915.
I. Title.

JC495.R39 2008
321.9—dc22   2007037713

Typeset by Publisher's Design and Production Services, Inc.
in 10.5/13 Bembo.

Published with the assistance of Indiana University.

Dedicated with love to
MSR,
DAR,
and MBR.

CONTENTS

Figures

Tables

PREFACE

This book has three audiences in mind. First, *Social Foundations of Limited Dictatorship* is addressed to students of the political economy of development, with its primary concern about the political foundations of growth in dictatorships. This book is embedded in the larger literature on institutions and growth, and builds upon that literature's canonical problem of making credible commitments, examining it in the understudied context of nondemocracies. To advance this literature, the book formulates a more general theoretical framework that examines policy credibility across regimes, and thus clarifies the conditions that enable dictatorships to promote growth successfully.

Second, *Social Foundations of Limited Dictatorship* is addressed to Latin American historians and political scientists with interests in authoritarian government, a recurrent concern in the political development of that region. In particular, this book examines the Díaz dictatorship in Mexico (1876–1911), a period that coincides with early industrialization efforts in both Mexico and throughout the region. Missing from the historical literature is a better account of political processes and the political foundations that enabled this early economic development. This book explains why the underlying policies of that early growth period were credible, while providing a historical context for the continuity of Mexico's political economy extending from that period into recent times.

Finally, *Social Foundations of Limited Dictatorship* will be of general interest to comparitivists and political economists interested in the interaction of formal and informal institutions. This book illustrates how a network-analytic approach, guided by theory, can shed light on research questions with a relational content such as business–state relations, crony capitalism, patronage and clientelism, corruption, and the role of social networks in development.

ACKNOWLEDGMENTS

This book builds on two previous projects: my dissertation and a co-authored book with Steve Haber and Noel Maurer. Both projects were completed while at Stanford University, and I have multiple people to thank. First, I want to thank the members of my dissertation committee for their advice and support. My main advisers, Steve Haber and Barry Weingast, provided expert advice at various stages of my research. I am especially grateful to Steve for introducing me to the study of Latin American economic history, and for the friendship and support that he has provided throughout the years. I have also learned a lot from the third member of my committee, John Ferejohn, during my first years in the program as his student and teaching assistant, and from the feedback and assistance he provided thereafter.

Other members of the Stanford political science department assisted me in various ways. David Laitin and Alberto Díaz–Cayeros participated in my oral defense committee and also provided a stimulating seminar environment for the study of comparative politics. Simon Jackman graciously provided technical assistance and sample computer code, which enabled me to complete important components of my dissertation's empirical analysis. I am grateful to Paul Sniderman, then chair of the political science department, for his support and the opportunity to teach related seminars the year after completing my graduate studies. Finally, I also want to thank Avner Greif of the Department of Economics for his willingness to chair my oral defense committee.

I was also fortunate to study among a cadre of graduate students with related interests in institutions and growth, who also provided useful feedback during the formulation phase of my dissertation project: Francisco Monaldi, Maite Careaga, and Norma Alvarez. Ian Read also provided excellent feedback on earlier analyses of relational data. Several staff members also deserve mention: Jeanette Lee-Ordeman, Eliana Vasquez, and Silvia Sandoval. I am also grateful to Jonathan Morgenstein and Albert I. Razo, who assisted with the collection of historical data.

I need to make special mention of a group of people whose work and friendship were particularly valuable during graduate school. First, I thank the staff of the Social Science History Institute, Marie Toney and Scott Wilson, and its director, Steve Haber, for the financial support that I received. The list of additional family members and friends who have supported me is too long to include here, but I want to mention a few people who made life for me and my family more memorable. These friends include Mark and Bonnie Smith, Jonathan Razo, Jovita Silvestre, Dan Ramirez, Scott Wilson, and Belinda Yeomans.

I have also benefited from useful comments from members of other institutions where I have presented my research. This list of people includes Randy Silverson, Keith Poole, Gary Cox, Sam Popkin, Donald Green, and Stephan Haggard. I also received very useful feedback from Michael Chwe and the Panel on Social Networks of the 2005 annual meeting of the American Political Science Association. James Robinson read the whole manuscript and provided very useful comments and suggestions.

Part of my research required me to travel to other institutions in search of data. I am grateful to the staff at the following institutions: the Hispanic Reading Room at the Library of Congress, the Benson Collection at the University of Texas at Austin, and the Bancroft Collection at the University of California at Berkeley. On the Stanford campus, I am in debt to Mary-Louise Munill and Christopher Harrison, who helped me obtain precious historical documents through interlibrary loans. The staff at the Lilly Library and Interlibrary Loans at Indiana University also helped me secure access to various historical documents. Indirectly, I also benefited from Roderic Ai Camp's extensive compilation of biographical data, which made possible the career and network analysis in this book.

More recently, I have benefited from the support of my colleagues in the Department of Political Science and the Workshop in Political Theory and Policy Analysis (The Workshop) at Indiana University. I thank Jeff Isaac, Elinor Ostrom, and Mike McGinnis for organizing a manuscript review session in April 2006. This event, sponsored by The Workshop and the Department of Political Science, and ably organized by Gayle Higgins, provided me with useful feedback to revise an earlier draft of this manuscript. Additional faculty and students who provided feedback include Lauren Morris MacLean, Abdulkadel Sinno, Tun Myint, Amos Sawyer, Brian Steed, Rob Holahan, and Frank Van Laerhoven. I am also grateful to Jeff Isaac, Alberto Torchinsky, Lin Ostrom, and the Office of the Vice Provost for Research at Indiana University for financial support toward the publication of this book.

I thank Norris Pope at Stanford University Press for the support given to this project. Emily-Jane Cohen was particularly helpful during the manuscript submission process. I am especially grateful to my production coordinator Denise Botelho for guiding me through the editing process, and to Catherine Ohala for her careful reading of my manuscript.

Last, but not least, I thank my wife and sons, whose continued love and support made the completion of this book possible.

SOCIAL FOUNDATIONS OF
LIMITED DICTATORSHIP

Chapter 1

Introduction:
The Puzzle of Growth
in Dictatorships

What factors determine the ability of countries to develop? Why do developing countries fail to sustain economic growth? Economic theory provides an answer with the identification of proximate causes such as investment and innovation, which are widely accepted as engines of growth. Economic historians and other social scientists have argued instead that the answer lies with institutions, which are the fundamental determinants of economic performance.[1] Based largely on the long-term success of advanced democracies, a consensus has emerged on the critical function of political institutions in providing the right incentives for investment and growth. Ultimately, countries fail to develop as a result of bad institutions (Acemoglu et al., 2001).

The link between institutions and growth works through the incentives of economic and political actors in balancing a tradeoff between the security of property rights and political authority. Economic actors will invest if there is an efficient legal framework to reduce transaction costs and to create national markets (North, 1990; North and Thomas, 1973). But the creation of such a framework requires fairly strong states to arbitrate disputes over property rights and to enforce private contracts (Root, 2001; Weingast, 1995). Concentrating political authority in a strong state is potentially problematic, however, because the state would also be strong enough to renege on its promises and prey on economic actors.[2]

The political foundations of growth thereby reside on finding a solution to the credible commitment problem of economic growth: Investors must believe that the government will not abuse its authority.[3] The political solution to solve this commitment problem in western economies was limited government (North and Weingast, 1989; Weingast, 1997a). Limited government is identified with a set of self-enforcing institutions that constrain the government to respect its own laws. Often associated with separation of powers or the existence of multiple veto points, limited government works via the established interests of other institutional actors that keep the government in check.[4]

The extant theory of institutions and growth goes a long way toward explaining the divergence of poor and rich countries. It is true that many developing countries have suffered, and continue to suffer, from lack of effective democratic constraints on their governments. It follows that in the absence of these constraints, economic actors would not trust their governments, and hence withhold from investing in long-term projects. Societies with inadequate or nonexistent formal political institutions to constrain government opportunism should then exhibit little, if any, growth. Again, the implication is that many developing countries are poor because they lack good institutions.

There exists ample evidence, however, that runs contrary to the conventional wisdom that formal political institutions, as found in advanced democracies, provide the necessary incentives for economic growth. In fact, a rich body of empirical literature in comparative politics and economic development has demonstrated that authoritarian governments can generate fast rates of economic growth over long periods.[5] Prominent among these case studies are the East Asian Tigers (Hong Kong, Taiwan, South Korea, and Singapore), but other relevant examples can be found in the larger Southeast Asian region, China, and some Latin American bureaucratic–authoritarian regimes, among others.[6] Cross-country statistical evidence also indicates the predominance of dictatorships among the fastest growing countries during a postwar period.[7]

This puzzling evidence is the main motivation for this book: If not limited government, what other explanation is there for growth and development in nondemocratic settings? Why would private actors trust their governments in the absence of democratic constraints? Why would dictators want to promote growth instead of using their authority to prey on society?[8]

The extant literature offers two competing images of dictators and their attitudes toward development: benevolent dictators and stationary bandits. On the one hand, benevolent dictators are assumed to choose optimal policies as a function of idiosyncratic traits that lead them to take decisive action for the betterment of their societies.[9] On the other hand, stationary bandits promote growth if they benefit from or have encompassing interests in economic activity, and if they intend to stay in office for a long time (Olson, 2000).[10] Dictators, according to Olson, thus promote growth when they *internalize* the costs of predation on their own welfare, which is contingent on future economic performance.[11]

The notion of a benevolent dictator reflects two complementary views about political authority. One view, which dates back to classical political theory, is that the concentration of political authority is desirable in the presence of enlightened leaders who are apt to choose optimal policies for their societies.[12] A second view is that concentration of political authority can facilitate coordination. Under certain conditions, a centralized solution with one decision maker (i.e., dictatorship) leads to more efficient outcomes than if multiple actors (i.e., democracy) were allowed to participate.[13]

Underlying each view is the assumption that the dictator is a perfect agent who is motivated to choose what is best for society. Indeed, extensive literature on the economic success of strong states highlights this role of dictatorships in facilitating decision making to help jump-start economic development. In the East Asian context, for example, and despite their distinct policy prescriptions, the competing bodies of literature of market-friendly and developmental states nonetheless shared a common underlying explanation for the economic success of authoritarian regimes. Governments used their monopoly of political power to take *decisive action* in the pursuit of some proposed set of growth-enhancing policies (Wade, 1990).[14]

Other related literature makes similar statements about relevant traits and abilities of authoritarian governments to enable growth. In Latin America, the economic success of some authoritarian cases has been attributed to bureaucratic–authoritarian regimes with certain ideological orientations that kept social discontent and worker demands under control so that capitalists and their allies could invest (Collier, 1979; Collier et al., 1979).[15] In the African context, it is not uncommon to find calls for "visionary leaders" or strongmen as a way to bring about progress (Gray and McPherson, 2001). The literature on patrimonial states sometimes also evokes the figure of (potentially) benevolent father figures to guide developmental projects (Martinussen, 1997, pp. 191–197, 217–236).[16]

Olson's (2000) conception of stationary banditry is more cynical. Dictators who are apparently benevolent are better perceived as former roving bandits or predatory actors. Under certain conditions, roving bandits can decide to settle down and switch from predation to investment in public goods to improve the economy, but they are not altruistic actors. Driven by their self-interest, they will become stationary bandits only if they have a stake in the economy, and if they expect to be in power for a long time. There is nothing benevolent about these growth-promoting dictators. If either condition fails, stationary bandits can revert to their old predatory ways.

Despite their relevance, both images of dictators provide incomplete accounts of economic growth under authoritarianism. For one, we know little about the conditions that enable the selection of "good" dictators. The focus in the literature has mostly been on identifying and proposing optimal policies, rather than explaining the political processes that generated and enforced those policies.[17] The fact that restrictions on democratic choices may be needed to enable collective action for the good of society does not by itself determine which specific restriction will be applied. There are multiple restrictions—in effect, multiple dictatorships—that can prevent incoherent collective choices, but not all lead to good outcomes. What guarantees the selection of a benevolent dictator? How do societies opt for stationary, rather than roving, bandits?

Moreover, we usually do not recognize cases in which dictators make credible commitments until sufficient economic development has taken place. At that point, classifying a dictator as either a benevolent or a stationary bandit is largely a subjective exercise. Based on observationally equivalent economic outcomes, the distinction between the two images also becomes moot. The real challenge is not to be able to apply a specific label after the fact, but rather to understand how dictators can become stationary bandits to *behave* like benevolent dictators.

Dictators have, of course, an incentive to proclaim themselves as benevolent promoters of development, regardless of their true intentions. But why should societies trust them? By definition, authoritarian governments have much discretion in the choices they make, and they will consistently choose policies that satisfy their own interests. Surely, they can take decisive actions that are conducive to growth, but as the record of economic performance clearly shows, not all dictators take those actions.[18]

Despite the presumed advantages of dictatorial decision making, we lack a good understanding of how politics interact with economics in nondemocratic settings.[19] One major reason is that descriptions of benevolent dictators or their decisive actions are typically devoid of politics.[20] In the case of stationary bandits, concomitant questions arise about the underlying political foundations that enable encompassing interests and long-term horizons. What are encompassing interests and how do they organize?[21] What do stationary bandits look like in practice? Under what conditions is stationary banditry likely to arise and persist?[22]

To be sure, we have specific explanations for the economic growth of selected cases, although the focus is not on the underlying politics or enabling institutions. For instance, we can explain the performance of some dictatorships with export-oriented economies like Singapore and Indonesia by identifying relevant external economic constraints. In these cases, access to foreign markets and capital mobility served to discipline authoritarian governments to prevent them from reneging on their commitments.[23]

The historical record shows, however, that the use of external mechanisms is very limited in practice. Even among those cases that eventually adopted successful export-oriented strategies, there was much variation over time in development strategies.[24] In fact, at one time or another, authoritarian regimes that were able to sustain fast rates in the twentieth century did so by relying on protectionist import–substitution strategies (Wintrobe, 1998, p. 148).[25]

Capital mobility can indeed serve as an enforcement mechanism, but its general applicability is limited if investors are heterogeneous. One crucial distinction exists, for instance, between foreign and domestic investors who are subject to different constraints and available mechanisms to protect their property rights. The former may be able to move their capital from place to place in search of safer economic environments. Domestic investors, on the other hand, have more limited options and are therefore more vulnerable to government predation. Hence, even if we can explain some commitments with capital mobility, it remains to be explained how some countries with dictatorial regimes were able to make commitments to domestic investors.

Another mechanism that receives attention in the literature is reputation.[26] Dictators can develop a reputation for maintaining benevolent governments, which in turn would lead to increased investment, especially from foreign investors. There are two problems with this mechanism. The first impediment is that reputation *takes time* to develop. In a certain sense, appealing to reputational mechanisms begs the question of credibility. In order for dictators to develop such reputations, they must have been credible to begin with, at least with respect to economic actors who first took a chance on an unproved dictator.

The second impediment is theoretical and is discussed in more detail in Chapter 2. The main point to be made here is that reputation is generally believed to enhance credibility because it acts as a reliable and *public* signal to encourage investment. The underlying assumption is that investors are homogeneous, or that they expect to receive the same treatment from the dictator given the latter's history of good behavior (presumably irrespective of investors' idiosyncratic traits). As I will argue in this book, however, dictators cannot make credible blanket promises to all investors, because investors themselves do not demand similar or equitable protection. It follows that dictators cannot develop reputations in the public sense in which we understand that term. At best, dictators can develop a good reputation (i.e., have a history of good behavior) with a limited set of actors, but that reputation is not informative for other actors whose interactions with the dictator have not been as amicable, or for new actors without prior interactions.

To advance our general understanding of commitments in dictatorships, we need to address a mismatch between the theoretical and empirical literature. On the one hand we have general theories that only fit certain cases, like the United States and England, but do not apply to authoritarian settings. On the other hand, the evidence from comparative politics and the developmental literature emphasizes economic policies, state capacity, and bureaucratic performance, with minimal attention to the underlying political institutions and incentives of relevant participants. By focusing on the right policies or conditions that enabled growth in fast-growing countries, however, the latter literature tends to be descriptive rather than explanatory, thus providing idiosyncratic rather than general explanations of growth.[27]

Despite our understanding of the importance of institutions for development, two key questions remain unanswered. First, there is the puzzle of growth under authoritarianism—the focus of this book: What conditions enable dictators to make credible commitments? A corollary question also arises about the great variation in the economic performance of dictatorships, especially regarding stagnation. Why are most dictators unable to promote investment and growth?

To answer these questions, we need a general theoretical framework to understand credible commitments under a wide variety of regimes, not just democracies, as has been the focus of the literature. Moreover, we need more empirical analyses of growth under authoritarianism, not just descriptions of successful cases to extract policy lessons, but explanations of policy credibility in different contexts. The following sections describe how this book moves the institutional literature along those two directions by building upon extant economic and political theories to inquire about the social foundations of growth in dictatorships as well.

My approach has three innovative features. First, I derive a theory of selective credible commitments and associated networks of private protection from first principles, firmly grounded on well-established tenets and economic models of individual behavior. I extend the literature by looking at networks as an enforcement mechanism brought about by the collective behavior of self-interested individuals. Hence, my theory is microanalytic and minimalist, and does not require specific organizational assumptions or the existence of some given group capacity, like social capital, which automatically enables collective action.

Second, I introduce social network analysis (SNA) into the study of the political economy of development and policy-making processes in *nondemocratic* settings. It is known that in the absence of reliable formal institutions, people rely on informal institutions (Elster, 1989, pp. 113–123, 147–158; North, 1990, pp. 36–45). The study of informal institutions is disparate, however, and there is no consensus on the best way to define or study informal institutions.[28] SNA provides a well-established methodology to study networks, thus providing a natural and systematic methodology to map and examine the nature and context of informal institutions.

Finally, not only do I provide a systematic methodology to study informal institutions with a network–analytic perspective, but I do so in an integrated way with existing approaches such as modern political economy and historical analysis. To date, students of formal political institutions (e.g., legislatures, constitutions, and separation of powers) have largely ignored informal institutions in their empirical analysis. Likewise, researchers who emphasize informal institutions (e.g., norms, networks, and related concepts like social capital) have for the most part ignored the study of formal institutions. This book considers *both* formal and informal institutions.

1 Relational Perspective on Dictators' Commitments

In this book I propose a *network theory of private protection* that explains how dictators can become *credible* stationary bandits with incentives to forgo predation.[29] Not only do I uncover the institutional arrangements supporting stationary bandits—that is, what stationary bandits must look like in practice—but I also predict what types of policies they can pass. Contrary to Olson's (2000) theory, I will argue that stationary bandits can credibly commit only to provide private rather than public benefits, so the commitments made by dictators will be qualitatively different from those of democracies.

I build my network theory of private protection by positing that there are two fundamental institutional differences between democracies and dictatorships.[30] First, I assume that dictators have greater discretion or influence on policy-making processes, meaning that they can either formulate or greatly influence policies.[31] Second, because of the lack of institutional constraints on dictators, policy implementation will be more difficult due to limited or nonexistent public enforcement.[32]

One major implication of a dictator's discretionary authority is a greater ability to offer lucrative policies to private economic actors (Wintrobe, 1998, p. 113). To characterize these selective commitments, I borrow from Bueno de Mesquita et al. (2001) the notion of private and public benefits or policies. The ability to formulate private policies, however, will give rise to a situation that I characterize as a *governability dilemma*: With greater discretion comes greater demands and a greater complexity in the exercise of authoritarian government. To ease the task of governing, the dictator will have incentives to be selective. Moreover, dictators are likely to benefit directly from selective commitments through the sharing of rents, so they will also prefer private policies that accord narrow benefits, as opposed to public policies that benefit society more generally.[33]

Private actors will also have an incentive to seek private rather than public policies, because the former increase profits. As noted by Haber et al. (2003), the assumption in the extant literature that economic actors condition their investment on the existence of universal protection is unrealistic. Recent evidence corroborates the claim that economic actors care primarily about their own property rights (Do and Levchenko, 2006). Theoretically, the reason is not hard to fathom: Selective protection also entails selective exclusion, so protected actors can gain at the expense of excluded competitors.

Because both dictators and protected actors stand to gain from selectivity, the outcome will be a predominance of private policies under dictatorships. Thus, one critical difference between growing democracies and dictatorships is that dictatorships grow based on selective rather than universal commitments to protect property rights.[34] This distinction will have major implications for the types of economic activity that can be sustained in dictatorships: Markets will be more concentrated than in democracies.

A second implication is that these private policies will be enforced differently than under a democratic setting. Private policies, however lucrative they may be, still require protection, but cannot rely on political institutions to provide public enforcement. What is more, policy credibility is no longer an issue of guaranteeing one public policy or social contract, but multiple private policies. All things being equal, the conditions for policy credibility in dictatorships will then be even more stringent than in democracies, because of the need to guarantee various concurrent but separate selective commitments. This situation exacerbates the dictator's governability dilemma.

How do dictators manage to make multiple credible commitments? Although they focus on instability, Haber et al. (2003) have advanced a general argument that economic and political actors will have an incentive to merge their interests when formal institutions do not work. Economic actors will seek to define economic policy and partake in the exercise of government, whereas political actors will be either directly engaged in or otherwise share the profits of economic activity. Both economic and political actors thus develop a shared stake in the fulfillment of various policy commitments.

I build on Haber et al.'s (2003) notion that credible commitments in this situation are contingent on the existence of a critical mass of third-party enforcers who can punish governments that renege on their promises. Because the political system cannot offer protection, investors will have to buy their own private protection. But the ability to buy private protection will depend on the availability of third parties (private enforcers) with the capacity to punish the dictator. The pool of private enforcers can include powerful politicians, public officials, military officers, or even private citizens with enough economic or political power to inflict punishment on the dictator. When these enforcers are absent, private policies cannot generate sustained economic growth because the dictator can change his or her mind and reallocate privileges at will.

I argue that these enforcers constitute the encompassing interests in Olson's (2000) theory of stationary banditry, but we need a better characterization of these interests and the underlying incentives to fight off predation. One major limitation in the theory of the stationary bandit is that it leaves unspecified the nature of encompassing interests, which is crucial for that theory. As a practical matter, dictators have varying levels of encompassing interests in the economy, and it is hard to imagine any dictator owning such a high share of the economy to give him or her an encompassing interest that would constrain predation in the short run.[35] In fact, what we often see is that the dictator is not the only beneficiary of concentrated authority. A larger set of cronies and political actors who support the dictator benefit from special privileges as well.[36]

The first critical step in characterizing encompassing interests is to recognize the inherently *relational* component to these favors, because connections to the dictator are crucial to obtain benefits (Kang, 2002, pp. 74–76; Khan, 2000a, pp. 89–103; Thompson, 1994, p. 216; Vatikiotis, 1998, p. 30). Dictators make selective rather than universal commitments, but they do not do so randomly. Commitments are explicitly selective, and social networks are likely to influence the selection of beneficiaries (Khang, 2000a; Thompson, 1998). Indeed, the value of personal connections has been widely recognized in the literature, and is often described in terms of clientelistic or patron-client relations, and also condemned as evidence of corruption (Campos, 2002). Missing from the literature, however, is the question of what makes these relational favors credible. After all, if dictators can prey on society, surely they can prey on isolated actors.

The possibility of isolated or selective predation highlights another major distinction between democracies in dictatorships. In the former, commitments have a more universal nature. Hence, it is sensible to formulate theories in terms of aggregate outcomes, as in explaining lack of growth resulting from the absence of universal protection. In dictatorships, however, the basic unit of analysis is an individual selective commitment or one private policy rather than a societal commitment.

Inquiring about whether dictators can credibly commit to promote growth therefore masks the more stringent requirement to honor *multiple*, concurrent commitments to bring about desirable aggregate developmental outcomes. But aggregate outcomes are our ultimate interest, so we need to find a way to move to a higher level of analysis that explores commitments from a societal perspective.

A relational or network perspective can facilitate the required multilevel analysis. The dispensation of special favors—however narrow and selective they may be—inevitably creates a complex web of related interests, depending on the various connections that may exist among beneficiaries, with potential aggregate outcomes.

Do connections affect the overall distribution of privileges in systematic ways? Do social structures make a difference in the collective ability of private actors to defend their property rights? Answering these questions requires a better understanding of the social foundations of policy making in dictatorships. More precisely, we need an explicitly network–analytic approach that recognizes the social context in which private protection is embedded.

But although network analysis can enable a more realistic analysis of policy making in dictatorships, it also presents two major challenges. First, there is the need to specify an explicit relational mechanism that goes beyond vague descriptions or metaphorical references to social connections.[37] The second challenge is that social networks exist everywhere, so our theories must carefully identify relevant networks.[38]

To circumvent those challenges, both my theory and empirical analysis are guided by SNA, which provides a well-defined set of concepts and methods to study networks (Scott, 2000; Wasserman and Faust, 1994). SNA helps with the operationalization of networks by defining them as a collection of nodes (either people or other relevant entities), that are connected in *one* particular way.[39] The identification task is therefore accomplished by formulating a minimalist network theory that clearly specifies overlapping private protection as the fundamental relation among influential political actors who can punish the dictator: The network that matters is that of private enforcers and their vested interest in the protection of multiple firms.[40]

My network theory is built around the problem of making selective commitments. Starting first with the enforcement of one private policy, I demonstrate that rents are crucial to induce third parties to deter predation. I then propose two relational mechanisms that enable private protection to be "scaled up" beyond the protection of an individual firm. First, when private enforcers share the protection of multiple firms, an isolated attack *propagates* the risk of predation to multiple firms. Networks thus matter because they make firms more vulnerable, even when their own property is not directly attacked, and despite the fact that they only care about their own property rights.

The second mechanism is collective retaliation. The dissipation of rents across various firms and private enforcers affects the latter's incentives to defend the network. If private enforcers are connected to various firms, they will be affected by the actions of other enforcers. If the prospect of eventual predation on one firm reduces the rents accrued to private enforcers not directly responsible for defending an attacked firm, these actors will have an incentive to punish the dictator. Not all actors may have such an incentive, depending on their placement within the network. But if a critical mass does exist, selective predation can be deterred by a collective response aimed at protecting the network. Again, this collective response occurs despite the self-interested nature of network participants.[41]

My resolution of the paradox of economic growth in dictatorships is that successful dictators will rely on an *exclusive* network of private protection with the collective capacity to punish predation. The success of this network will depend both on the existence of a pool of private enforcers and on the structure of the network. Social networks can greatly enhance the effectiveness of private protection by creating opportunities for shared stakes in preserving a network of protected interests. The reason is simple: If dictators prey on any network member, the dictator effectively attacks the whole network because of the interlocking interests of private enforcers. For that reason, I refer to cases in which a dictator restrains from predation as a *limited dictatorship*, not just because of observable behavior, but because the dictator's choices are effectively constrained, albeit by informal arrangements.

For selective protection to work, however, dictators cannot have absolute political control over society. Successful commitments require the dictator to depend on the political support or economic resources of protected special interests, or otherwise to be vulnerable to social pressures. If any of these conditions fails in a particular dictatorship, because the dictator is not powerful enough to offer private policies, or because economic actors cannot buy reliable private enforcement, then we would not expect to see growth.[42]

It is important to note that networks of private protection need not be created deliberately. The underlying force behind the political economy of dictatorships is the generation of rents or distribution of special privileges. Dictators will, of course, have a say in determining the recipients of privileges, but their ability to influence network structure will be somewhat limited. Participants may bring with themselves relevant social relations that activate either the propagation of risk or mutual assistance. These ties cannot be easily severed by dictators. Alternatively, enforcers may simply try to protect as many firms as possible to increase their own rents, and network connections will arise unintentionally. Patterns of overlapping protection are thus better understood as emergent social structures that arise from the decentralized and self-interested behavior of actors who want to enrich themselves, but whose fate becomes connected through the resulting network.

As a final requirement, it does not suffice that the required network structure exists to constrain the dictator at a given point in time. If networks are to sustain growth, they must enable long-term selective commitments. Despite not having complete control over network structure, dictators must nonetheless provide a way to enhance the durability of the network, especially the availability of third-party enforcers. This requirement is equivalent to Olson's (2000) condition that a stationary bandit has a long-term horizon.

For dictators to offer long-term commitments, they must credibly signal their own longevity. Thus a process of institutionalization is required, but it will be exclusive by design. In my theory, formal political institutions are not prominent because they do not directly enable dictators to make credible commitments, but they are no less important because they serve two supporting functions: First, they help ratify private policies that are negotiated within formal governance structures,[43] or within informal ones (such as social networks); and second, they provide a pool of private enforcers, public officials, or influential political actors that can punish dictators for reneging on their (private policy) commitments. Formal political institutions may give the appearance of inaction or passivity, but this is only because their contribution is kept out of the public eye and is restricted to a few participants.[44]

2 Mexico's Early Industrialization Under Porfirio Díaz

The purpose of this book is to provide not only a theory that can help explain growth in dictatorships, but also to complement it with evidence. The network theory of private protection makes a general argument about the importance of informal mechanisms for the enforcement of exclusive policies. A careful examination of relevant social structures in various contexts is therefore necessary to gauge the impact of *networks and institutions* on economic performance.

This book makes an empirical contribution with a careful examination of a canonical case of growth under authoritarianism: Mexico under Porfirio Díaz (1876–1911), one of the longest dictatorships in modern Latin America.[45] Díaz came to power in 1876 after a long period of economic stagnation in nineteenth century Mexico. Mexico's economy lay moribund at the onset of its independence from Spain in 1821 and faced major challenges to reactivate it. Upon assuming power, Díaz gradually established a dictatorship and passed a series of institutional changes aimed at promoting economic growth. The institutional changes of the Porfiriato set the foundations for Mexico's early industrialization. Economic policies encouraged massive foreign investment in infrastructure and capital-intensive industries, as well as domestic investment in various other industries, thus transforming the predominantly agrarian society with the creation of relatively modern manufacturing and banking sectors (Beatty, 2001; Haber, 1989; Maurer, 2002).

As one of the longest dictatorships in Latin American history, the Porfiriato has received much attention from historians concerning various social and political questions. There is a vast historical literature on the Porfiriato, which is intimately tied to the fall of the regime. The concentration of political and economic power led to the watershed event in the history of modern Mexico: the Mexican Revolution of 1910.[46] This revolution has been hailed as one of the major social revolutions of the world, because it sought to remedy the injustices of the Porfiriato. With the assistance of peasants and workers, discontented elites forced Díaz into exile in 1911, thus ending a dictatorial regime, and ushering in the hope of a more equitable and democratic nation.

Missing from the historical literature, however, is an explanation for the ability of the Díaz government to implement economic policy successfully.

To restore economic activity, especially the infrastructure required to jump-start the economy, investors in Porfirian Mexico needed assurance that the commitments they received were credible. Díaz's policies should not have been credible, however, because investors knew that he could use his political and military might to confiscate and redistribute assets, and engage in repression more generally.

Moreover, Díaz could not base the credibility of his policies on an established, good reputation. Mexican governments in the nineteenth century had a long history of reneging on their commitments. Throughout the nineteenth century, property owners had been subject to arbitrary behavior and recurrent government raids on property rights. Indeed, just a few years before, liberal governments that dominated the period had reneged on their debts and confiscated the property of the Church and other private actors. Potential investors had no reason to believe that Díaz, also a liberal, would act differently than previous governments.

The literature also lacks a systematic study of political institutions during the Porfiriato, which could help us understand the institutional setting that enabled Díaz to restore order and to implement his policies effectively. Simply classifying Díaz as a dictator does not tell us much about the politics of the period. Indeed, Díaz was able to restore political order by concentrating power. The existence of competing political groups during the nineteenth century brought conflict and disorder. By becoming a dictator, Díaz ameliorated these problems, but why did not previous governments recognize this option and establish similar dictatorships to suppress competition?[47]

What is more, Mexico's political system at the time had peculiar features that raise puzzling questions about the nature of Díaz's dictatorship. When Díaz came to power, he inherited an institutional framework that included both elements of checks and balances—with a relatively strong legislative branch as well as a federal structure, partly derived from a historically segmented polity with strong regional leaders. If Díaz was a dictator, why was there a Congress? Why were there governors? Moreover, these political features remained intact throughout the period. How was a dictatorship established without major political changes in the underlying formal institutional environment?

It may have been that political institutions were merely symbolic, but this begs the question about the actual source of political stability, which required some measure of state capacity and stable political organization. When Díaz came to power, the administrative structure of the state (to the extent that there was any) was weak. Setting up any type of structure was a costly endeavor, and the federal government lacked the means to collect and administer resources (Maurer, 2002, pp. 2–3). Another noteworthy feature of modern Mexico is that for its first hundred years of independence until the late 1920s, it lacked established political parties that could provide a stable environment for political activity. What institutions or organizations enabled governance during the Porfiriato? Moreover, if there was a legislature, why were there no political parties during the Porfiriato?[48]

We have a better, albeit incomplete, understanding of economic policy and development during the Porfiriato.[49] We know that Díaz was able to deal successfully with the problem of economic stagnation by encouraging industrialization with the passage of apparent market-friendly policies and the encouragement of foreign investment (Beatty, 2001). Historians typically explain these policies in terms of the positivist ideology that characterized many Latin American elites in the late nineteenth century. But ideological explanations neither explain commitment nor address the fact that economic progress took place against the backdrop of authoritarian government and an unequal distribution of economic rewards. Why did self-proclaimed liberal governments, like Díaz's, which professed an interest in protecting individual political and economic rights, nonetheless promote growth on the basis of very exclusive policies?[50] Who received preferential treatment from Díaz's policies and why?

The attention to the underlying institutional environment in which economic development took place has been limited, and has not systematically addressed the interaction between politics and economics. Why was Díaz successful when attempts by previous governments had failed? Was there something unique about the politics of the Porfiriato, or the interaction of politics and economics during that period, that assured investors that their property rights would be secure?

Recent works such as that by Maurer (2002) provide compelling evidence of strong connections between political and economic actors, thus paving the way for more detailed studies of political institutions. Haber et al. (2003) go further by claiming that the political economy of the Porfiriato rested on a set of informal arrangements enabled by a political process defined as *vertical political integration* (VPI), which blurred the distinction between economic and political actors. VPI accurately depicts the fact that economic and political actors during the Porfiriato found it in their interest to cooperate, but there remains to uncover the microlevel mechanisms that enabled cooperation or integration.

This book expands on this new line of research by providing a comprehensive study of political institutions during the Porfiriato, with an explicit analysis of the interaction between politics and economics, formal and informal institutions, and a focus on the credibility of Díaz's promises to protect property rights. Coatsworth (2005) notes that the VPI mechanism proposed by Haber et al. (2003) does not address time horizons. In *The Politics of Property Rights*, my co-authors and I note the robustness and the persistence of the political economy of the Porfiriato beyond the dictator's exile and the Mexican Revolution of the 1910s. Evidently, Porfirian institutions proved to be a durable arrangement, but we did not explicitly theorize about factors underlying the longevity of informal arrangements. *Social Foundations of Limited Dictatorship* addresses the question of durability, and specifies the underlying political and *social* foundations that elongated the time horizons of the informal arrangement between Díaz and protected economic interests.

To delineate my analysis, I examine three main testable implications of the network theory of private protection. First I evaluate whether there was a predominance of private policies or selective protection. This analysis is carried out at two levels: the interaction between private firms and the government, as well as between government and industry groups. A second hypothesis has to do with the organization of private protection. My theory predicts reliance on a network that spans the interests of individual firms and enforcers to care about the protection of the whole network.

Third, the enforcers need to be reliable and the pool of private enforcers should be distributed according to the need for protection of various asset holders. Sectors that are more vulnerable should have a higher concentration of public officials than other sectors with alternative sources of private enforcement. In the case of Mexico, the vulnerable sectors were banking and manufacturing. Without recourse to foreign governments to protect their property rights, asset holders in these sectors were subject to changes in government policies that reduced the security of their property rights. In contrast, those sectors that did have access to external enforcement, such as mining and the oil industries, would be expected to have a lower number of public officials on board.

My empirical analysis has an explanatory as well as an exploratory goal. First, I provide a specific explanation for the credibility of economic policies in a particular dictatorship. Second, I show how the use of a network–analytic approach can enhance our understanding of the link between institutions and growth. Social networks exist everywhere and their study can be inherently complex, so one must be careful to ascertain the limits of network explanations. Some guidance will come from theory, but we need many empirical studies such as this one to illustrate network analysis, and to explore and identify good instruments for eventual comparative work.

Studying the Porfiriato can also inform our understanding of growth under dictatorships because we can isolate the question of commitment in a more simple setting without confounding variables. By confounding variables, I refer to the explanations advanced in the literature on growth under authoritarianism, which point to factors that accelerate economic performance: choosing the right economic policies or technologies, having expert bureaucracies, and enhancing state capacity. I do not dispute that these factors cannot play a role in economic growth, but they are surely not conditions for policy credibility. Most important, these conditions cannot explain the case of the Porfiriato, in which (1) there existed no technological sectors to promote; (2) there could not have been a recourse to expert bureaucracies because public administration was incipient, if not nonexistent; and (3) state capacity was severely limited because the nineteenth century had been a period of major instability that gave rise to a relatively weak state. The question of credibility thus remains unanswered: How could Díaz promote growth at all without recourse to either reputation or the other favorable conditions advanced in the literature?[51]

2.1 EVIDENCE AND NETWORK ANALYSIS

My empirical analysis entailed the construction and analysis of an integrated database of political and economic variables from various historical documents. The purpose of the database was to examine political and policy-making processes, as well as to identify relevant connections between public officials and economic actors.

My database included information on (1) 149 of Mexico's major companies in the early 1900s, which included corporate information such as listings of boards of directors and capital; (2) a government registry of 5071 firms for the period 1886 to 1907, which includes corporate types (e.g., corporations, cooperatives, partnerships, sole proprietorships), ownership data, and government concession terms for firms in various industries; (3) 1691 career profiles of all major politicians at the federal and state levels for the period 1876 to 1911; (4) decree information for the period 1890 to 1898 involving all laws and legislation passed by the federal government; and (5) various indicators of legislative activity for the period 1876 to 1911, including congressional roll call data for the period 1876 to 1888. I also collected data on the political connections of major corporations during the period 1907 to 1910.[52]

This information encompasses the universe of major economic activity during the period, and enabled me to ascertain the structure of protection at the national level, as well as the centrality of particular network members at an aggregate level.[53]

Analyzing the composition of corporate boards is important for two reasons. First, we would expect a large number of public officials on these boards to mitigate policy conflicts between the government and private actors. That is, the more public officials on corporate boards, the more likely it would be that the government shares the policy preferences of economic actors. The underlying reason for consensus on policies is that government actors have a stake in the welfare of the corporations in which they participate. Second, more public officials on corporate boards reflects a higher degree of integration between political and economic actors. That is, the distinction between political and economic actors gets blurred within the confines of their informal coalition.

One of the methodological contributions of this book is to study connections between politicians and companies with an explicit network–analytic approach. SNA is especially useful because it allows me not only to identify the governance structure required by my theory, but also to map the encompassing interests that motivated Díaz to commit to promote growth credibly. With SNA, I am able to study the social aspects of the informal coalitions that dominated policy making during the Porfiriato in a systematic way that can be replicated in other settings.[54]

As the Díaz government became less democratic, and therefore could rely less on formal institutions, there was greater room for selective protection and private arrangements. SNA of information on corporate connections and political careers provides an additional perspective about the nature of existing political–economic networks, and the centrality of key players who provided key enforcement and monitoring roles.

Until recently, SNA focused largely on descriptive and mathematical analyses of network structures. Recent advances in the statistical analysis of networks, however, have paved the way for quantitative studies within an inferential, not just descriptive, framework (Carrington et al., 2005). I show how one can use these new methods to examine specific hypotheses about network structure.

2.2 EXPLAINING THE SUCCESS OF DÍAZ'S POLICIES

To restore political order, a series of developments took place that increasingly gave Díaz dictatorial powers and suppressed political competition. These developments were part of a twofold process. Initially, Díaz relied on repression, but he also depended on influential political actors who willingly and knowingly deferred their political power to the executive government. In other words, Díaz was not always a dictator, and he became a dictator thanks to constitutional changes that were ratified by other actors.

When his stay in power was secure, Díaz courted investors with favorable economic policies. These policies were very profitable, but the prospects of high profits alone did not make those policies credible. I argue that Díaz's policies were credible because he was a limited dictator. Certainly he had political and economic influence, but this influence was kept in check by other political and economic elites. In fact, these elites deliberately allowed Díaz to become a dictator in exchange for lucrative policies. To ensure the credibility of Díaz's policies, elites relied on informal arrangements that gave influential participants a stake in protecting the rights of an exclusive network of beneficiaries. These informal arrangements had a critical role in keeping the dictator in check.

Along with selective commitments, investors also required long-term stability. For the network to sustain long-term investment, it needed a persistent governance structure. Although the exclusive network of private protection was the primary mechanism to induce credibility, it did not operate in an institutional vacuum. Formal political institutions enhanced the longevity of the network by providing an easily accessible, and long-lived, pool of private enforcers. Formal institutions were reliable because they were populated by elites with long-term interests in maintaining the status quo.

3 Plan for the Book

Chapter 2 presents my network theory of private protection. First, I establish the predominance of private policies and selective credible commitments in dictatorships. Second, I examine how private policies can be protected in the absence of public enforcement mechanisms—as would be the case in a democracy. To understand the underlying incentives of relevant political and economic actors, I present a series of game-theoretic models that elucidate the logic of private protection under a variety of simple social structures. I discuss further how existing and emergent social networks enable dictators to select beneficiaries under conditions that make selective commitments credible.

Chapters 3 through 6 are empirical chapters that examine the political economy of growth under the Díaz dictatorship. Chapter 3 provides relevant historical background along with a review of the instruments that Díaz used to stay in power. The first half of his tenure ends with two outcomes that provide the backdrop against which subsequent economic growth was to have taken place: First, by the early 1890s, Díaz had restored order to a country that had experienced instability for much of the nineteenth century; second, Díaz's ability to reelect himself repeatedly and dominate policy-making processes effectively gives rise to a period of consolidated dictatorship.

In Chapter 4 I demonstrate the use of private policies to reward network participants. Historical evidence establishes that the political economy of the Porfiriato was driven by selectivity and the generation of rents. Moreover, historical evidence also shows that the exercise of an authoritarian government under Díaz conformed to my theoretical prediction about the predominance of private policies in nondemocratic settings. Statistical analysis clearly indicates that both concessions and survival were driven by rent prospects.

It was in this setting of political stability and dictatorship that the transforming economic policies that characterized the Porfiriato were proposed and implemented, so the question of policy credibility was paramount. Even if the dictator offered lucrative opportunities to economic actors, there were no formal enforcement mechanisms to make such policies credible. I therefore demonstrate in Chapter 5 the existence of a long-lived pool of enforcers, powerful enough to mitigate government opportunism. I do so by analyzing career and political mobility patterns, as well as connections to elite networks, to ascertain the influence and incentives of third parties to participate in a network of private protection.

Chapter 6 is the core empirical chapter of this book, where I provide a more detailed examination of the network of private protection that made Díaz's policies credible. SNA indicates strong linkages among major companies and influential public officials. Moreover, a statistical analysis of network data indicates the important role that public officials had not just in formulating and enforcing public policies but in shaping the network. I further establish that the network was populated by actors who could credibly punish the dictator if he chose to prey on protected firms.

Chapter 7 concludes the book with a return to the general question of how nondemocratic institutions affect economic development. I discuss the implications of my theory and empirical study for the varied economic performance of other dictatorships, addressing successful cases of growth as well as the more typical cases of economic stagnation. I conclude with a discussion of the long-term implications of my theory for the trajectory of countries that develop on the basis on private protection. My main claim is that early industrialization will provide severe constraints on subsequent economic and political liberalization.

Chapter 2

Network Theory of Private Protection

What types of credible commitments, if any, are dictators expected to make? Because dictators are above the law by definition, they cannot resort to formal political institutions as a way to make credible commitments. What, then, are the mechanisms that dictators use to add credibility to their commitments? How are these credible commitments different from those of democracies?

To make the interaction of politics and economics explicit, I assume that dictator and economic actors come together through an exchange of policies for economic benefits.[1] We can think of a government's policy commitments as policy contracts. For my purposes, I use a general definition of *policy* as any variable of the government's choice that affects the behavior of some members of society. Policies affect various types of private decisions, but my focus is on investment decisions.

Thinking of policy commitments as contracts is a natural depiction of policy-making processes. The study of contracts involves (at least) two phases: a definition phase and an implementation phase.[2] A policy proposal by the government corresponds to the definition phase of a policy contract. It is just a promise that remains to be implemented.

The credible commitment problem of growth can be formulated in terms of the enforceability or implementation of policy proposals. The basic transaction that takes place is one in which a dictator enacts a protection policy, which enhances the value of investments for an asset holder, in exchange

21

for some economic benefit (either through taxation or direct transfers to the dictator).[3]

As a first step in their interaction, the dictator offers a policy contract stating the government's choice to protect property rights of investors. Second, the asset holder accepts or rejects the contract proposal. If the contract is rejected, the interaction ends and there is no investment. Otherwise, the asset holder makes an investment to produce some level of economic goods. Finally, the dictator decides to implement the original policy during the fourth stage by not abrogating the asset holder's property rights.

The sequence of this interaction gives rise to a fundamental problem known as the *sovereign dilemma problem* (Alston et al., 1996, pp. 129–133; Weingast, 1995, pp. 1–2). A dilemma arises because the government's strength diminishes the credibility of policy proposals. The reason is that during the final stage, dictators have no constraints on their ability to seize all assets or profits from production. The asset holder can, of course, anticipate future predation, and choose not to invest in the first place.

The inability of governments to make credible commitments to restrain themselves from abusing their position is well-known in the social science literature. The credible commitment problem is a specific instance of the general managerial or vertical dilemmas that superiors face in organizations (Miller, 1992). In policy contexts, Barro and Gordon (1983), for instance, have shown that a government's inability to commit to a monetary rule may lead to excess inflation. Shepsle (1991) also highlights the general trade-off that governments face between discretion and optimality.

The solution to the commitment problem requires self-restraint by governments not to abuse their position. Root (1989), among others who have conducted historical analyses of industrialized countries, has demonstrated that institutions in which sovereign states "tie their hands" help bring about the desired credible commitment. In particular, students of the political foundations of economic growth argue that limited governments work best in providing the necessary incentives for economic activity. For instance, North and Weingast (1989) argue that limits to government brought about by the Glorious Revolution in England enabled new governments to commit credibly to upholding property rights. This led to a surge in financial activity and otherwise created incentives for enhanced economic performance.

Although limited governments are normatively attractive, their existence is not guaranteed, as cautiously noted by Weingast (1997b). Limited government does not come automatically, and it carries the stringent requirement of a widely shared set of beliefs among private citizens on what the appropriate limits to government should be.

What is more, often there are redistributive effects to a government's predatory behavior: A government may transgress the rights of one group and share the spoils with another group. The beneficiary group will not have an incentive to request that the predatory behavior be restricted. In such a case, the outcome will include both selective protection and selective predation.[4]

This chapter advances a theoretical argument that there is indeed a systematic difference in policy-making processes and outcomes between dictatorships and democracies. I argue that dictators' relatively greater powers in policy formulation and implementation create incentives for both political and economic actors to pursue private policies that provide selective benefits to particular economic actors (as opposed to public policies with universal application that indiscriminately benefit a larger group of people).

Second, I argue that because these private contracts are meant to be as profitable as possible for economic actors, the nature of policy making in dictatorships has observable implications for the market structure sustaining economic growth in dictatorships. Namely, economic activity in dictatorships will be based on clusters of protected and concentrated markets, and market power is determined politically via private rather than public policies.

The organization of private protection matters a great deal for the exercise of authoritarian government and the credibility of private policies. Although private policies may be very profitable for the dictator and protected economic interests, relying on private policies has some negative effects as well. For the dictator, a heavy reliance on private policies increases the complexity of government. For economic actors, selective protection also entails selective exclusion, so widespread use of private policies increases the need to monitor other private contracts, not just their own.

Dictators who are able to make selective credible commitments will need to rely on governance structures that mitigate the added burden of discretion. In addition, dictators must address the concern of protected economic groups regarding future competitors who desire private protection. Put together, these two incentives will lead both the dictator as well as economic actors to create an exclusive network of protected interests.

Social networks enable selective credible commitments on multiple private policies by aligning the incentives of powerful political actors with the interests of economic actors.[5] More specifically, by linking the interests of various economic groups, the structure of social networks greatly enhances the encompassing interests of political actors acting as third-party enforcers for asset holders. As Olson (2000) predicts, greater encompassing interests create added incentives for dictators to promote economic growth.

The rest of this chapter is organized as follows. The first two sections lay out my theoretical argument, beginning with my general assumptions. "Private Policies and Network Enforcement" makes an argument for the prevalence of private policies in dictatorships. It also discusses the role of social networks in facilitating the enforcement of private policies. "Strategy of Private Protection" presents a series of game–theoretical models that formalize the argument of the previous sections. Readers can choose to skip the models at first reading and proceed immediately to the empirical chapters, and come back to this section as needed to examine further the conditions that make private protection work. The final section contains my concluding remarks.

1   General Assumptions

I.I GOVERNMENT BEHAVIOR

I assume that dictators are self-interested and are driven by two major motivations. First, dictators want to increase their own income.[6] Second, dictators want to stay in power. Arguably, these motivations are observationally equivalent in light of the evidence that dictators often use public office to enrich themselves, but my distinction is useful to draw a conceptual difference regarding the use of money and power. Money can certainly be used to enhance a government's stay in power, and that power can be used to get more money. But power also enables dictators to impose their will on society. A dictator can, for example, impose a particular ideology on society that produces no income, but nonetheless can give the dictator much satisfaction. Power then provides additional benefits that cannot be directly translated into monetary terms or to increase private consumption.[7]

Whether motivated by money or power, dictators will have incentives to lengthen their stay in power. The implication of these assumptions is that self-interested dictators will want to promote economic growth only when this improves their private income and survival prospects. In other words, dictators care primarily about durable privileges.

I.2 ECONOMIC BEHAVIOR

From a cross-country perspective, systemic differences in the protection of property rights are important determinants of a favorable environment that promotes investment. Consistent with this aggregate perspective, the extant literature implicitly assumes that there is an intrinsic interest in the universal protection of property rights—the supply of protection as a public good—but without further inquiring about the individual prefer-ences of private actors. I take a different approach, which inquires about the demand side as well. Instead of asking how the political system can change government incentives to protect or prey, one should also inquire about the conditions that would induce economic actors to invest in the first place. Answering this second question prompts a more careful exami-nation of economic behavior and preferences than has taken place in the extant literature.

I make two assumptions regarding the behavior of economic actors or asset holders. First, they seek to maximize the profits from their economic activity. Second, I borrow from Haber et al. (2003) the assumption that eco-nomic actors care primarily about the security of their own property rights. As long as economic actors perceive their own property rights to be secure, they will engage in economic activity for private gain, regardless of the pro-tection that other asset holders may or may not be receiving.[8]

Given my assumptions about profit maximization and self-interest, from an economic actor's point of view, whether property rights are protected universally and impartially (as would be the case under the rule of law) is ir-relevant as long as their own property rights are secure. In fact, faced with a choice between selective and public protection, my assumptions imply that economic actors will provide the former if profits are higher. More specifi-cally, if private policies offer economic actors market power or some other advantage over competitors, economic actors will find selective protection more attractive than universal protection.

1.3 POLITICAL CONSTRAINTS

How is individual behavior affected by the political institutions or political organization of dictatorships? We do not yet have an adequate answer to this question for two reasons. First, systematic studies of political institu-tions have largely been confined to democratic settings.[9] Second, dictator-ships exhibit a wide variation in terms of underlying political institutions and organization. Many dictatorships have legislatures, bureaucracies, and other types of political organization, but there is no typical organization that characterizes all dictatorships.[10]

I therefore draw on the extant literature on authoritarianism to make general assumptions about the nature of political institutions in dictator-ships.[11] In particular, my assumptions about the institutions of dictatorships are informed by Linz's seminal work on authoritarian regimes.[12] This book does not cover all aspects of authoritarian regimes.[13] For my purposes, I concentrate on two of Linz's four dimensions of authoritarianism that are most relevant to the analysis of policy credibility under dictatorships. The first dimension is limited pluralism, which imposes political constraints on dictators because it captures the collection of represented interests among supporters of an authoritarian government.[14] The second dimension is discretion. Linz actually phrases this dimension differently, in terms of informal, yet predictable, rules that govern the interaction among the small group of people in power in authoritarian regimes (Linz, 2000, pp. 159–166).[15] These rules, however, will determine how much flexibility dictators will have in choosing their desired policies.

Higher values on either of these two dimensions imply a more authoritarian or dictatorial government. Extremely limited pluralism implies that the government will be free to choose its most preferred policies because its supporters do not impose heavy demands for some reason. Likewise, if the interaction rules among powerful political actors are not very restrictive, the government will have much discretion to deviate from the policy directives of its supporters.[16] In other words, with more authoritarianism, we would expect to find more arbitrariness or greater discretion than in democratic settings, depending on the dictator's preferences (Linz, 1964; 1975).[17]

If dictators have more discretion in their exercise of power, then it follows that the policy-making powers of dictators will be greater than those of democratic governments. In democratic settings, it is often the case that government powers are divided or shared among different political actors. For example, policies get formulated in legislative bodies and are implemented separately by an executive government or executive agencies.[18] In contrast, I assume here that the dictator has the prerogative of acting not just as an executive government (to implement policies), but also as a legislator, with wide discretion in defining and proposing policies.

That the government participates actively in legislative processes is certainly not unique to dictators, but the reason why dictators participate is different. Dictators' discretion reflects their greater ability to *restrict access* to the exercise of executive and legislative powers, which will not be as widely available to other political actors as would be the case in democracies (hence the limited pluralism).[19]

Another characteristic of dictatorships is the absence of an independent judicial power that could punish the dictator if policies are not implemented as expected. In democracies, when policies are passed, there are formal mechanisms that ensure the application of those policies in a universal and nondiscriminatory manner.[20] This means that governments and *any* asset holders who rely on the rule of law need not worry about providing their own enforcement. In contrast, dictators do not have access to this automatic public enforcement mechanism. What is more, the enforcement of policies will also be at the discretion of the dictator. This last statement captures the conventional view of dictators as being above the law.

1.4 INSTITUTIONAL DIFFERENCES BETWEEN DICTATORSHIPS AND DEMOCRACIES

Taken together, my assumptions about the constraints that dictators face have important implications for the nature of the credible commitment problems that democratic governments face. With greater powers to formulate and implement policies, dictators, unlike democratic governments, are not restricted to a binary choice between offering universal protection to everyone and offering no protection at all. The scope of government action in dictatorships is effectively expanded from that binary choice to a wider range of possibilities in which the dictator protects some, but not all, asset holders.

This increased flexibility reveals an irony behind excessive power. Dictators may have more power, but the lack of democratic constraints does not ease the task of governing, as dictators can—and indeed are expected to—do much more than democratic governments. Moreover, instead of committing to a universal policy, dictators must guarantee each individual commitment they make. That is, each asset holder must find its own selective policies to be credible, recognizing that just as dictators can offer selective protection, so can they engage in selective predation.

Overall, the exercise of authoritarian government is more demanding relative to democracies—a different problem than those identified by Wintrobe (1998) regarding insecurity and Weingast (1995) regarding credibility. To the best of my knowledge, this irony has not been addressed in the literature on dictators, and so I will denote it as the dictator's *governability dilemma* to reflect the tension that exists between attaining greater discretionary power and the concomitant increase in the complexity of authoritarian government. A fuller characterization of a dictator's dilemmas would then include three ironies of excessive power: Dictators are more insecure, less credible, and also face a greater workload with higher expectations.

My assumptions about economic behavior also approach the credible commitment problem from a new perspective. Finding a solution to the commitment problem actually depends on which of two questions we ask. We could ask, for instance, what a society can do to prevent government predation. In addition, because government behavior is partially determined by political institutions, a natural question for us as political scientists is to inquire about the political institutions that can deter predation. From that angle, solving the commitment problem is a question of institutional design regarding a choice of political institutions that will limit government behavior.

Indeed, the extant literature on political foundations has mostly concerned itself with this institutional design question. The Rise of the West was characterized by a concurrent expansion of political and economic liberties. In that context, it is reasonable to assume that investors had clear preferences for both economic liberties (freedom from government predation) and political liberties (less restrictions on political rights, or greater political influence). Hence, the protection of individual property rights required a concomitant institutional change.[21]

Viewed from a long-term historical perspective, the implications for institutional design are clear. If less developed countries had been able to devise similar political institutions—whenever they had a choice—they would have been able to sustain economic growth and, thus, be more developed (North, 1989; Haber, 1997). To be sure, scholars in this tradition do not claim that societies are always in a situation in which they can easily change their political institutions. North (1989), among others, recognizes the persistence of institutional arrangements that are not conducive to growth. Nonetheless, when examining the trajectories of advanced economies, there is an unstated assumption that democratic political institutions, as found in advanced western economies, provide the political foundations for economic growth because economic investors would not invest unless governments offered to protect everyone.

Societies governed by the rule of law may, in fact, demand universal protection, but as Weingast (1997b) notes, the underlying shared beliefs for universality may not be present in all societies. Moreover, whether a good is public depends partly on technological constraints. If the government were unable to exclude access to the benefits of secure property rights, then the implicit assumption of the extant literature would be warranted. Given my assumptions about the discretion of dictators in formulating and implementing policy, dictatorships do indeed possess the ability to offer protection on a selective basis. Hence, property rights in dictatorships are not likely to be offered as a public good because the dictator will find it more profitable to offer protection as a private good.[22]

2   Private Policies and Network Enforcement

If policies can be thought of as contracts, what types of contracts do dictators offer? There is an important distinction that should be made about the policies that governments can generate. I posit two basic types of policy contracts, public or private, that governments can offer to economic actors. This distinction stems from examining the nature of the policy along with the mechanisms used to implement it. I define a *public policy* as one that is debated (enacted) in a public forum (and thus can be seen as a sort of a public or social contract), is readily available in a nondiscriminatory way, and is enforceable by a public enforcement mechanism. If any of these three conditions fail, then the policy in question will be denoted as a *private policy.*

The purpose behind my distinction between public and private policies is to characterize better the nature of the policy commitments that dictators make. When we talk about policies, we generally think of them as being public policies because they are defined in the context of formal political institutions (thus the policy is publicly known), are defined for the public interest (i.e., are meant to affect everyone in society), and rely on formal political institutions to enforce them (i.e., there are publicly known enforcement mechanisms that guarantee their implementation). It is exactly in this public sense that the protection of property rights has been analyzed in the literature on institutions and growth.[23]

To be clear, my distinction between private and public policies focuses on *procedural* differences regarding policy design and implementation, and should not be confused with a related distinction between private and public goods. A good is public if it is nonexcludable and nonrival. An example of a policy that creates a public good is the choice of national defense along a country's borders. By protecting the borders, the government effectively protects everyone within the national territory. The "consumption" of national security by one private actor within the country's boundaries does not affect the consumption of other actors within the same territory. Although some public policies benefit all members of society (i.e., have universal application), there are others that have more limited application. For example, a central bank's choice of an interest rate will only have a direct effect on the behavior of lenders and borrowers in society.

Because private policies are enacted in opposition to or at the margins of the public interest, there are profound implications for their implementation, and herein lies the difference that fully characterizes private policies and makes them distinct from the concept of private goods. Private policies are not defined solely by favoritism. Indeed, one could argue that this tension between the private and public interest is present in all policy proposals irrespective of political system. The crucial distinction lies with the institutions that are expected to enforce such policy. Policies that afford narrow benefits, but that also lack public enforcement, will be denoted as private policies because their implementation either explicitly avoids or otherwise recognizes the lack of a public enforcement mechanism.

The distinction between private and public policies is thus particularly useful to distinguish between dictatorships and democracies. During the first stage of policy definition, dictators have a greater choice to limit or broaden the application of a certain policy than democratic governments, which must be more attentive to the interests of society. To the extent that policies are targeted at specific actors (have more limited application), these policies will be less available to any anonymous actor in society. The nature of a given private policy is thus more personal, so the policies will be private and exclusive rather than public, universal contracts. Moreover, because dictators lack an independent judicial power to constrain their behavior, during the second stage of policy implementation dictators will have to rely on informal enforcement mechanisms to make credible commitments.

What determines the mix of private and public contracts that dictators offer to economic actors? I argue that private policies should be the norm in authoritarian government because both the dictator and the economic actors will have strong incentives to pass private policies. The basic logic is as follows. We know that economic actors are self-interested and motivated by profit maximization. Economic actors know that the dictator's discretion can serve to increase their own profits. For example, private policies that provide economic actors with selective benefits such as market power or special protection will increase the income of economic actors. But we also know that dictators promote economic growth for private gain only. Faced with a choice between a public policy and a private policy, all things being equal, a dictator would prefer a private policy that generates more invest-ment profits and thus more income for the dictator. The potential rents of private rents or selective protection therefore lead both the dictator and economic actors to generate as many private policies as possible.

2.1 ROLE OF SOCIAL NETWORKS

A dictator's ability to offer rents will generate much demand for private protection. Indeed, a common characteristic of dictatorships entails the recognition by other actors in society that they can use the dictator's au-thority for their private gain (Campos, 2002; Chehabi and Linz, 1998a).[24] The actual award of special privileges hinges on three factors. Foremost, dictators must find a way to benefit their core supporters, as noted by Bueno de Mesquita et al. (2001).

Besides that general political constraint, dictators face two additional countervailing considerations. On the one hand, dictators will want to in-crease the number of commitments to increase revenue and sources of rent. This desire may be motivated either by wanting to increase private consumption or, if we assume that governing is costly, to cover the cost of government, which is not likely to be met by just one asset holder.

On the other hand, the dictator must limit the number of beneficiaries to manage the governability dilemma. Too many multiple commitments make it difficult to govern, so the dictator must be somewhat selective, recognizing as well the need to make individual guarantees to each private policy. Decisions about the identity and number of protected interests is a strategic choice that is not modeled here. To focus on credibility, I will proceed under the assumption that the dictator has already solved this selection problem. I will note, however, that the empirical literature indicates that dictators rely heavily on personal connections to award special privileges. Hence, we know that some social networks play a major role in the selection of beneficiaries. Of course, social relations do not preclude other mechanisms through which potential beneficiaries may get access to the dictator, but networks cannot be readily dismissed either.[25]

The role of networks that is more relevant to my theory deals with the enforcement of concurrent, selective commitments. What are the implications for policy credibility when dictators make selective commitments to multiple firms? First, private protection enlarges the set of predation opportunities for the dictator, who is no longer restricted to a binary choice between universal protection or universal predation.[26] When we allow governments to exercise discretion regarding which types of policies they can offer, the focus on *one* interaction alone is no longer sufficient to assess the overall credibility of the government, because there is not a single policy contract to be honored.

Protected firms do not, in fact, demand universal protection because the logic of private protection simply requires that each and every instance of private protection be individually defendable. Firms will have to rely on third parties for the enforcement of their policy contracts.[27] As long as a firm is not directly attacked, selective predation on other firms does not affect accrued rents within the context of that firm's particular agreement with the dictator.

Most important, the conditions for policy credibility will also depend on how firms relate to one another. Firms can be connected in many ways: through social or business relations, or through some other common characteristic (e.g., a common ethnic identity). The relevant relation for my theory is overlapping protection because it embeds two complementary relational mechanisms that affect the enforcement of multiple policy commitments. First, predation on a firm increases the risk of predation on other connected firms, making firms more vulnerable. Second, networks can enhance the scale of private protection against predatory attacks. Being part of a network may enable a firm to enjoy better protection than if it relied solely on its own hired protectors.

Propagation of Predation Risk. The propagation of predation risk is one of two motivating factors behind the ability of networks to secure the property rights of their members. When participants understand that passivity with respect to predation on other firms can later decrease the security of their own property rights, "helping" others is a rational response against a common threat. In a nutshell, selective predation can cease to be an isolated attack when predation risk propagates to other beneficiaries of private protection. When this happens, otherwise disconnected actors will have a collective incentive to defend related firms.

To understand how networks link the fate of related firms, consider first the case of isolated firms, those disconnected from other firms. In such a setting, the logic of private protection predicts that firms will successfully defend their property rights when they hire willing and able private enforcers, regardless of what other firms do. In contrast, firms that lack private enforcers, or have unwilling or weak ones, would expect to be preyed upon if they accept the dictator's initial protection promise.

The difference between the isolated and the network cases hinges on the information conveyed by one act of predation. In the isolated case, each firm is in a class of its own in terms of vulnerability to predation. With multiple commitments, the dictator is in effect engaged in parallel but independent games of private protection. A dictator contemplating predation can judge each firm independently based on their capacity for private enforcement. Asset holders know that if they have a reliable enforcer, there is no reason to worry, even while others are being attacked. In this sense, selective predation is uninformative for unaffected firms because the dictator's action cannot be used to predict who will be preyed on next. This situation makes it clear why we cannot make a general appeal to reputation to credibly make societal commitments.

With connected firms, however, both the dictator and the asset holders can condition and interpret behavior in terms of network relations. For the dictator, it may be possible to classify vulnerable firms in terms of relevant shared relations, not just their individual capacity for private protection. Asset holders can also reason that if the dictator attacks some firm, there may now be a positive probability that they will be next, by virtue of their own connection to the attacked firm.

More precisely, the logic of private protection identifies a type of relation among firms that directly determines predation risk: overlapping private protection. A critical component behind private protection is that there be an independent third party that can effectively punish the dictator. If this third party is unreliable, the protected firm becomes vulnerable. Now consider a situation in which two firms share a common protector. If this protector is unwilling or unable to defend against an isolated attack on either firm, the unaffected firm now faces an immediate risk of predation.

To be sure, there can be various other types of connections among firms, and these can have an impact on the propagation of predation risk. For example, shared ethnicity could have been used by Indonesian investors to predict future predation if the late dictator Suharto targeted particular Chinese investors.[28] But private protection hinges on enforcement incentives, not social relations. If predation risk does propagate through means other than overlapping protection, there would be an even greater need for individual firms to recruit very powerful enforcers, but we would not necessarily expect private enforcers to respond to those external social connections. The following section makes the enforcement incentives more explicit.

Encompassing Interests and Collective Enforcement. I will use a simple graphical example (Fig. 2.1) to explain networks (defined by overlapping protection) that enable dictators to make selective credible commitments.

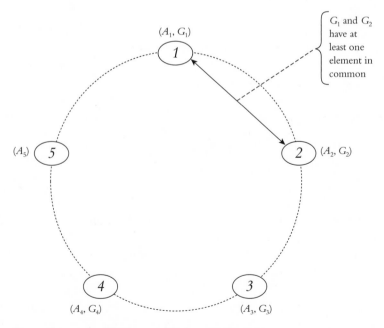

Figure 2.1 Asset Holders and Private Enforcers

Suppose that there are five firms or economic groups in society. Each firm *i* is owned by an asset holder (or an organized group of asset holders) denoted by A_i. Each of these firms requires that their individual property rights be protected.

A dictator *D* (not shown in this diagram) promises to protect property rights to induce asset holders to invest. Theory requires that the asset holders recruit third-party enforcers with the right incentives to ensure that *D* honors his commitment. The third-party enforcers on whom asset holders rely will be powerful political actors who can punish *D*, so I will refer generally to these enforcers as public officials. The set of enforcers for firm A_i is denoted by G_i. The incentives of these enforcers are aligned with those of asset holders by sharing the profits of the firm they protect.

In an authoritarian setting, firms without access to private protection are not expected to last. In Figure 2.1, for example, A_5 does not share profits with any government actor for some reason.[29] We can readily predict that A_5 will be preyed upon by the dictator by the nature of the credible commitment problem of growth. Whether A_1 through A_4 will obtain selective credible commitments from *D* depends on the ability of their respective private enforcers to punish the dictator if the latter ignores prior protection promises. If any of the G_i's is unable to impose a high enough penalty on reneging, then the dictator will prey on the corresponding firm owned by A_i.

Suppose, for instance, that A_1's group of enforcers, G_1, is not capable of deterring government predation. To avoid predation, A_1 would have an incentive to buy more protection—that is, remaining profits are shared with additional enforcers. The more vulnerable the sector, the greater the need for added enforcement.[30] We would then expect that, all things being equal, economic sectors that are highly vulnerable to predation will have a greater presence of government officials. These officials, as a group, have a greater encompassing interest in one firm as their number increases.

The crucial step in understanding the role of social networks is to analyze a situation in which the interests of A_1 and A_2 overlap. How does the connection between them affect their ability to protect their own property rights? The answer lies in the incentives of private enforcers, who obtain rents from both firms, to respond to predation on either one of these two firms. The encompassing interests of private enforcers naturally arise from the networked interests of protecting multiple firms as follows. Suppose, for example, A_1 and A_2 share one common official *G*. This actor *G* has an encompassing interest in both firms. For that reason, if the dictator were to prey on the first firm, the dictator is effectively threatening all of *G*'s assets—in this case, both firms.[31]

The networked nature of encompassing interests has clear implications for the protection strategies of asset holders. First, as I noted, asset holders will seek a group of enforcers who are powerful enough to deter predation. Second, asset holders can increase their protection by recruiting powerful actors who defend other economic interests as well. By recruiting these actors, a particular asset holder draws on the actors' encompassing interests beyond one firm to link his or her fate with those of other asset holders.

Clearly, as asset holders recognize the usefulness of this strategy, they may have incentives to coordinate—especially when the interests of asset holders themselves are scattered across various industries. It is important to note, however, that the protection strategy I analyze does not require coordination among asset holders to be attractive, because, as formulated, the emergent structure of the networks I propose is driven by decentralized and opportunistic behavior. An asset holder might not have any particular interest in protecting the specific policies that another asset holder obtains, but will recognize nonetheless that the common enforcer will protect both asset holders even if the asset holders are not on speaking terms.[32]

Public officials have strong incentives to accept proposals to protect multiple asset holders. The basic reason is that more protection opportunities directly increase the economic benefits that these officials obtain. The incentives of both asset holders and private enforcers thus reinforce each other in increasing the number of related firms. An increase in the number of relations, in turn, increases the density of the network. By definition, density equals the "number of [relations] in a [network], expressed as a proportion of the maximum number of lines [relations]" (Scott, 2000, p. 71). The density of the network offers a good approximation for the encompassing interests and effectiveness of the private enforcers who are scattered throughout the network. Density is a measure of connectedness, which ranges from zero to one. When network density is equal to zero, protected interests are isolated. Intermediate density values reflect various degrees of connectedness. In the extreme case, when density equals one, each private enforcer has an economic interest in all protected economic groups. Such a dense network would be very effective in deterring predation by the dictator, because all asset holders would share the exact same set of enforcers. Predation against one firm is predation against all.[33]

3   Strategy of Private Protection

This section formalizes the claims made earlier about the incentives of dictators to forgo predation, and the incentives of enforcers to defend private policies.

3.1 PLAYERS AND PAYOFFS

There are three players: an asset holder A_1 with productive resources, a dictator D, and a third party (denoted by either T or G). The government offers to protect the property rights of a particular asset holder. The asset holder is interested in securing investment profits. The third party enforces the agreement between D and A_1.

I do not explicitly model a firm's optimal investment choice. I assume that the asset holder has already calculated a profit-maximizing level of investment, which produces nonnegative amount rents, $R \geq 0$, and all there is left to decide for the purposes of this game is whether to carry out the investment project. In addition, recognizing an institutional environment without public enforcement, asset holders pay a positive protection fee $b < 1$ to each enforcer that they hire.

I also assume that the asset holder has a reservation value $v_1 \geq 0$, which determines the minimum payoffs that must be exceeded for A_1 to participate in this game. This reservation value represents the minimum payoffs that A_1 receives if he invested elsewhere. If A_1 could not redeploy his assets, perhaps as a result of sunk costs, then v_1 may be very close or equal to zero. The reservation value will be positive and will increase if A_1 is able to redeploy assets to alternate, more secure economic environments.

Dictators are self-interested and want to maximize their payoffs, which are proportional to rents. More precisely, in this game D obtains a fixed share t of rents as tax revenue, or tR, where $0 < t \leq 1$, in exchange for a policy that safeguards property rights. One plausible motivation for a tax rate is that there is a mutual understanding that the protection of property rights and the exercise of government, more generally, requires some public administration that is costly.

The dictator also faces an additional cost $C_D \geq 0$, which serves to model the dictator's own participation constraint. At the very least, the dictator must cover this cost to remain in office, but the cost is not derived solely from the internal functioning of government. This cost is also a function of other factors, such as the need to distribute rents to other supporters outside of this game. In fact, I interpret this cost function in this latter sense to reflect a dictator's vulnerability to social pressure. The greater the cost, the greater the need for the dictator to generate investment rents to remain in power.

To model predation, I allow dictators to increase their payoffs by taking a larger share of investment profits than the allotted tax rate. I denote these additional payoffs as *predation gains*, because they entail the confiscation of A_1's after-tax profits: $(1 - t)R$.[34]

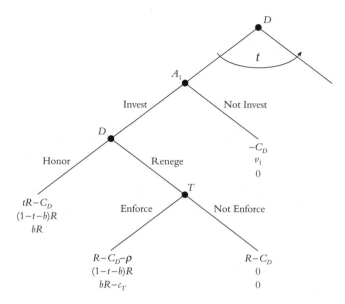

Figure 2.2   Private Protection Game with Isolated Firm

3.2 SEQUENCE

The sequence of the game is illustrated in Figure 2.2. Initially, D first offers a protection contract to A_1. The asset holder decides whether to accept the policy contract. If the policy is rejected, the game ends. If A_1 accepts, the game continues to an investment stage. After the investment, the dictator decides whether to honor his (or her) commitment or to act as a predator and confiscate all of A_1's rents. If D does not prey on A_1, the game ends with all parties sharing the rents enabled by D's proposed private policy. If D does act as a predator, then T is called upon to enforce the contract. If T does not enforce it, the game ends with D confiscating all rents. If T does enforce the contract, T imposes a punishment ρ on the dictator, but this is a costly activity reflected in a private, positive cost c_T.

3.3 PRIVATE PROTECTION AND RENTS

The game is solved using the solution concept of Subgame Perfect Nash Equilibrium (SPNE), which requires that players act optimally in all subsets of the game. Because this game is one of complete and perfect information, a SPNE can be obtained by backward induction—by analyzing players' optimal choices at each (sequential) node, working our way back from the last stage. At each stage, the relevant player's optimal choice will correspond to the best available option given the history of play and pre-dicted behavior of players in subsequent stages.[35]

To derive the equilibrium for this game, I will first derive T's optimal choice at the enforcement stage, taken as given A_1's earlier investment behavior and D's implementation decision. Let T's decision be denoted as $\sigma_T = \{E\}$, where $E = 1$ if T enforces and $E = 0$ otherwise. Second, I derive D's implementation decision denoted by H in $\sigma_D = \{t,H\}$: $H = 1$ if the dictator honors his commitment, and $H = 0$ if he reneges. Third, I derive A_1's investment choice denoted as $\sigma_{A_1} = \{I\}$, where $I = 1$ if A_1 chooses to invest, and $I = 0$ otherwise. Finally, I derive D's policy announcement strategy denoted by a tax t, with $t \in [0,1]$. The output of this backward induction exercise will be a SPNE denoted by the vector $\hat{\sigma} = \{\hat{\sigma}_D, \hat{\sigma}_{A_1}, \hat{\sigma}_T\}$, where $\hat{\sigma}_i$ represents player i's optimal strategy.[36]

Enforcement Stage. The analysis starts with T's enforcement decision. If the third party enforces, he obtains a protection fee bR minus a private cost of c_T. Without enforcement, the dictator captures all the rents, in which case T gets nothing. Hence, T will enforce if $bR - c_T \geq 0$. It will be useful to express this condition in terms of rents. Let $R_0^* = c_T/b$ be the value of rents that would make the third party indifferent to enforcing or not, given his own private cost and expected share of rents. T will choose $E = 1$ if rents are sufficiently high, an *enforcement condition* that can be expressed as follows:

$$R \geq R_0^* \tag{2.1}$$

The dictator will anticipate T's decision as he makes his own choice between honoring or reneging on his initial policy announcement. If D honors the commitment, he obtains tR minus the cost C_D of being in power. If he reneges, he obtains $R - C_D$ when T does not enforce, and $R - C_D - \rho$ when T retaliates to enforce the agreement.

To investigate further the conditions leading to a credible commitment, I consider the second case in which T does have incentives to enforce. Here, D will not act as a predator, provided that he is at least as well off as if he reneged and was punished by T, or $tR - C_D \geq R - C_D - \rho$. Letting $\rho_0^* = (1-t)R$ denote the penalty at which D would be indifferent, we can now state a *commitment condition* in terms of the imposed penalty ρ as follows:

$$\rho \geq \rho_0^* \tag{2.2}$$

The asset holder's optimal strategy depends on the proposed tax rate t and the expected implementation and enforcement decisions of the other players. Clearly, if T either does not have incentives to enforce or is not sufficiently strong to punish D, the optimal choice for A_1 is not to invest: $I = 0$.

For A_1 to invest, both the commitment and enforcement conditions must hold. In addition, the asset holder must perceive a gain from this private protection arrangement. In other words, the residual claim of private rents must be at least as large as the reservation value, or $(1 - t - b)R \geq v_1$. The relevant variable for this comparison is the initial tax rate proposed by the dictator, which affects the participation of A_1. The asset holder prefers lower tax rates because the rates increase after-tax rents. Moreover, if the tax rate is too high, A_1 would be better off deploying his assets elsewhere, so acceptable tax rates are contingent on the reservation value. Based on these considerations, the maximum tax rate that A_1 would be willing to accept is given by the following critical value, which makes the asset holder indifferent to investing or not:[37]

$$t_1^* = (1-b) - v_1/R \qquad (2.3)$$

The tax rate t_1^* is one of two participation constraints that D must take into account when providing private rents. The second constraint is that the dictator's own share of rents, tR, must cover his operating costs, C_D. Using this constraint, we can derive a minimum tax rate, as a function of C_D, that would make D indifferent: $t_D^*(C_D) = C_D / R$. The dictator's optimal choice, $\hat{t}$, will depend on the relationship between $t_D^*(C_D)$ and t_1^*. If A_1 has a sufficiently low reservation value or C_D is not too high such that $t_1^* \geq t_D^*$, then D will propose the higher rate; otherwise, D will propose t_D^*:

$$\hat{t} = \max\{t_D^*, t_1^*\} \qquad (2.4)$$

Proposition 1 on Rents and Private Protection. If $t_D^*(C_D) \leq t_1^*$, private protection is mutually beneficial for D and A_1, and there is a unique SPNE determined as follows:

1. If $R > R_0^*$ and $\rho_T > \rho_0^*$, the equilibrium strategies are $\hat{\sigma}_D = \{t_1^*, 1\}$, $\hat{\sigma}_{A_1} = \{1\}$, and $\hat{\sigma}_T = \{1\}$. T has incentives to enforce and can effectively retaliate against predation. The dictator chooses to honor his commitments, and A_1 invests.

2. Otherwise, the equilibrium is $\hat{\sigma}_D = \{t_1^*, 0\}$, $\hat{\sigma}_{A_1} = \{0\}$, and $\hat{\sigma}_T = \{0\}$. D can act as a predator with impunity, because either T will not

enforce or ρ does not inflict major damage. Player A_1 anticipates predation and chooses not to invest in the first place, despite a favorable tax rate.

Alternatively, when $t_D^*(C_D) > t_1^*$ there are two possible SPNEs in which the dictator offers protection at a higher tax rate than what A_1 is willing to accept. If $R \geq R_0^*$ and $\rho_T \geq \rho_0^*$, the equilibrium strategies are $\hat{\sigma}_D = \{t_D^*(C_D), 1\}$, $\hat{\sigma}_{A_1} = \{0\}$, and $\hat{\sigma}_T = \{1\}$. Otherwise, the equilibrium profile is $\hat{\sigma}_D = \{t_D^*(C_D), 0\}$, $\hat{\sigma}_{A_1} = \{0\}$, and $\hat{\sigma}_T = \{0\}$.

Proposition 1 is illustrated in Figure 2.3A. The implications are better understood in comparison with the case of related firms, and are discussed in more detail at the end of the following section. At this point, it suffices to say that selective credible commitments are possible, but are restricted to a small region of high rents, which make private protection attractive. But rents alone do not guarantee credibility, because it is also necessary to have powerful third-party enforcers. Thus, although regions C and D both include sufficiently high rents, commitments are only credible within region C in Figure 2.3, where penalties are high enough to deter predation.

3.4 OVERLAPPING PROTECTION AND PREDATION RISK

I now examine the impact of overlapping protection by analyzing the case in which a private enforcer has vested interests in two firms (Fig. 2.4, page 42). As with the previous game, I seek to derive conditions for policy credibility in the context of an individual agreement between D and some firm A_1.

This second game extends the previous one by incorporating the risk of predation and the resulting changes in payoffs. First, the dictator, while protecting a second firm, receives a share of the associated rents, and thus this firm's cost of government is lower than before. Given a tax rate t_2 and rents R_2 associated with A_2, the new cost as it interacts with A_1 is now equal to $\tilde{C}_D = C_D - t_2 R_2$. Second, the payoffs following a decision not to enforce are different because of the risk of predation. If D preys with impunity on A_1, he proceeds to prey on A_2 as well, and thus obtains additional payoffs of $(1 - t_2)R_2$. When D preys on the second firm, T loses the protection fees bR_2 that he received from the second firm.[38]

The SPNE for this game is defined exactly as before. We want to find the optimal responses for σ_D, σ_{A_1}, and σ_T. From the previous section, it is clear that the relevant strategic situations have to do with the behavior of D and T in the last two stages. To be sure, D must initially announce a tax policy that induces A_1 to participate, but this value is entirely determined

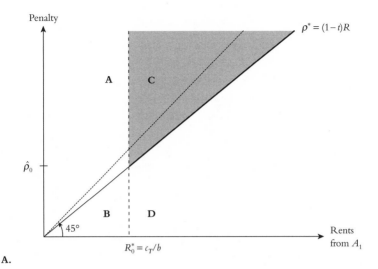

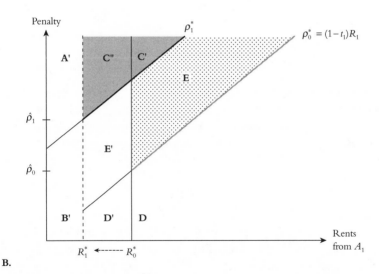

Figure 2.3   Credible Commitments with Private Protection
(A) Implications from proposition 1. (B) Implications from proposition 2.

by exogenous parameters involving the dictator's cost and the asset holder's reservation value. The investment decision hinges on whether D can make a credible commitment. Hence, the rest of this section will focus on the conditions that induce credibility.

For T to enforce, the gains from enforcing are the same as before—namely, $bR_1 - c_T$—but the cost of not enforcing is no longer zero. Player T

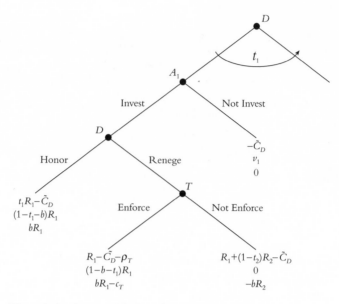

Figure 2.4   Game with Overlapping Protection

now stands to lose not just the rents from A_1, but also the rents from A_2, so the new enforcement condition is $bR_1 - c_T \geq -bR_2$. Rewriting this condition in terms of R_1, we can find a critical value that would make T indifferent: $R_1^* = c_T / b - R_2$. Thus, when T has vested interests in other protected firms, an attack on A_1 will induce T to enforce when

$$R_1 \geq R_1^* \qquad (2.5)$$

Note that $R_1^* < R_0^*$ for all positive R_2, so overlapping protection increases the willingness of T to enforce. This is an intuitive result because even if R_1 is relatively low, what matters to T are the total protection fees, $b(R_1 + R_2)$. Player T reasons that an attack on A_1 is effectively also an attack on A_2, and so T is moved to defend both sources of protection fees.

If the shared enforcement condition does not hold, then D can prey with impunity and confiscate the rents from both firms (which is clearly more desirable than preying on just one firm). Thus, when condition (2.5) fails, A_1 can anticipate predation and can withhold from investment, regardless of whatever promise was initially made.

If T is willing to enforce, it remains to be seen whether he can deter the dictator. Before, in the isolated case, the dictator only had to incur a penalty at least as large as the gains from preying on A_1 alone, or $(1 - t_1)R_1$. But now D stands to gain more from predation—an additional predation gain of $(1 - t_2)R_2$. For D to honor his commitment, it must be the case that $t_1 R_1 - \tilde{C}_D \geq R_1 + (1-t_2)R_2 - \tilde{C}_D - \rho_T$. We can find the value of ρ_T that makes T indifferent and define it as $\rho_1^* = (1-t_1)R_1 + (1-t_2)R_2$. We can then establish a new commitment condition that requires T to retaliate with a harsher punishment:

$$\rho_T \geq \rho_1^* \tag{2.6}$$

If D is able to make a credible commitment, then A_1 will want to invest. Whether D is able to offer a favorable tax rate, however, will depend on his own participation constraint. If $\tilde{C}_D$ is still very high, despite the rents produced by A_2, then the tax rate offered to A_1 would be too high to induce participation.

The following proposition summarizes the equilibrium analysis for this second, expanded game.

Proposition 2 on Overlapping Private Protection. If $t_D^*(\tilde{C}_D) \leq t_1^*$, private protection is mutually beneficial for D and A_1, and there is a unique SPNE determined as follows:

1. If $R_1 \geq R_1^*$ and $\rho_T \geq \rho_1^*$, the equilibrium strategies are $\hat{\sigma}_D = \{t_1^*, 1\}$, $\hat{\sigma}_A = \{1\}$, and $\hat{\sigma}_T = \{1\}$. Player T has incentives to enforce, D chooses to honor his commitments, and A_1 invests.

2. If $R_1 \geq R_1^*$, but $\rho_T < \rho_1^*$, the dictator is not credible, and hence the equilibrium strategies are $\hat{\sigma}_D = \{t_1^*, 0\}$, $\hat{\sigma}_A = \{0\}$, and $\hat{\sigma}_T = \{0\}$.

3. If $R_1 < R_1^*$, T does not have incentives to enforce, in which case D acts as a predator, and A_1 chooses not to invest: $\hat{\sigma}_D = \{t_1^*, 0\}$, $\hat{\sigma}_{A_1} = \{0\}$, and $\hat{\sigma}_T = \{0\}$.

Alternatively, when $t_D^*(\tilde{C}_D) > t_1^*$ there is no equilibrium with investment because A_1 does not participate. If $R_1 \geq R_1^*$ and $\rho_T \geq \rho_1^*$, the equilibrium strategies are $\hat{\sigma}_D = \{t_D^*(\tilde{C}_D), 1\}$, $\hat{\sigma}_A = \{0\}$, and $\hat{\sigma}_D = \{1\}$. Otherwise, the equilibrium is $\hat{\sigma}_D = \{t_D^*(\tilde{C}_D), 0\}$, $\hat{\sigma}_{A_1} = \{0\}$, and $\hat{\sigma}_T = \{1\}$.

Figure 2.3B illustrates the implications of proposition 2, and has the same horizontal and vertical axes as Figure 2.3A to enable comparisons with the previous case of an isolated firm. The fact that T now protects two firms has two countervailing effects. First, T has greater incentives to enforce because he stands to lose more. This change in incentives is reflected in a shift of the minimum rent line from R_0^* to R_1^*. All things being equal, this change would have enlarged the previous credible commitment region C (the same as regions C′ and E) to also include regions C″ and E′. In other words, private enforcers in regions C″ and E′ would now be willing to protect.

However, all things are *not* equal because D is now tempted to attack both A_1 and A_2. This additional predation incentive is represented with an upward shift of the minimum penalty line from ρ_0^* to ρ_1^*, which disqualifies enforcers in E′ who are willing to protect, but who are not powerful enough to punish D.[39]

The new credible commitment region therefore encompasses regions C′ and C″, a smaller region than C.[40] Region C′ is a subset of C. That is, already powerful enforcers will be just as effective with shared protection as if they were protecting just one firm. From the perspective of a new firm seeking private protection, sharing a private enforcer is unequivocally beneficial if the private enforcer is already in region C′. This situation means that the enforcer is already powerful enough, and the added protection fees from A_1 will only increase T's incentives to enforce. In addition, enforcers in C″ who were previously powerful enough but unwilling to enforce can now become willing and reliable enforcers. Region C″ also enables firms with relatively lower rents to be protected. In contrast, previously capable enforcers, those found in region E, will be equally incapable of inducing credibility under this new scenario because they cannot inflict a harsh enough penalty.

This second model demonstrates that overlapping protection increases the incentives to enforce and lowers rent requirements for some firms, but the required punishment to deter D from acting as a predator increases as well. The set of enforcers that can effectively induce credibility is thus *reduced* with respect to the case of isolated firms. With related firms, only powerful enforcers can offer private protection successfully. Again, the reason is that selective predation becomes more tempting for the dictator, thus requiring a stronger deterrent.

3.5 NETWORK RESPONSE TO SELECTIVE PREDATION

Having one common protector for multiple firms represents just one type of overlapping protection. To investigate more general patterns of overlapping protection, we can conceptualize the previous model in terms of the supply of private enforcers. When the supply is limited, as would be the case when firms can only hire one protector, the enforcer must be very powerful. Otherwise, firms with none or weak enforcers should expect predation.

When the supply of private enforcers increases, however, firms do not have to rely on one single actor. Firms could hire multiple enforcers to pool their individual punishment capacities. Moreover, each of the enforcers could have distinct vested interests in other firms. In this more general setting, firms seeking private protection from particular enforcers would then be embedded in various patterns of overlapping protection, defined by the connections of a firm's enforcers with other enforcers.[41]

To examine this new context, I extend the previous model to include the possibility of overlapping protection between two enforcers protecting two firms: A_1 and A_2. From now on, I will denote an enforcer k by G_k to connote the likelihood that powerful enforcers are public officials or political actors with ample resources to punish D. The number of players in this new game will increase from three to four: D, A_1, G_1 (previously T), and G_2. In particular, I assume that G_1 protects both A_1 and A_2, whereas G_2 protects only A_2. The interests of G_1 and G_2 thus overlap because of their common protection of A_2.

The question of interest is whether D can make a credible commitment to the first firm. As before, I assume that there is an existing separate agreement between D and some actor A_2 that produces positive rents R_2, and that this agreement already satisfies the conditions for successful private protection—namely, that A_2's enforcers are willing and able to deter predation. Therefore, A_2's behavior does not need to be modeled for my purposes.

I make a few auxiliary assumptions that simplify notation, but will not affect the conclusions I reach. First, I assume that both firms are subject to a common tax rate, denoted as $t_1 = t_2 = t$. Second, I assume that both firms pay the same percentage of rents for private protection, or $b_1 = b_2 = b$. Third, I assume that the second firm is more profitable, $R_2 > R_1$, to justify the fact that A_2 hires two protectors.[42]

Finally, I assume that the two enforcers incur the same private enforcement cost $c > 0$, but have different capacities to punish, ρ_1 and ρ_2, respectively. To justify the assumption that A_2 is being protected, it must be the case that G_1 and G_2 have the collective capacity to punish the dictator. Because the enforcement capacity of G_1 to protect A_1 is under examination, it is reasonable to assume that G_2 must be the more effective enforcer such that $\rho_2 > \rho_1$.

The sequence of this third game, as illustrated in Figure 2.5, is the same as before for the first two stages, but the implementation and enforcement stages have been modified to accommodate overlapping protection and the propagation of predation risk. In particular, there are two instances when overlapping protection increases predation risk. First, if G_1 decides not to protect A_1, the second firm is immediately put at risk, as explained in the previous section. But this time, there is a second actor that can compensate for G_1's inaction, so G_2 gets to move afterward.

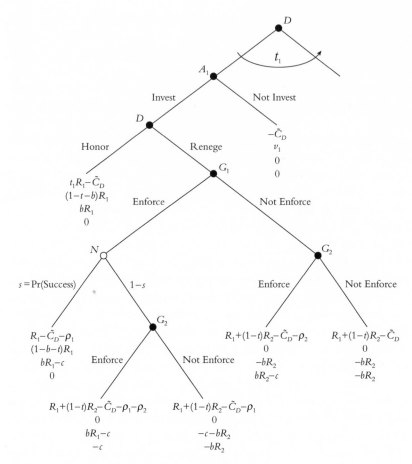

Figure 2.5   Networked Game with Two Enforcers

Second, G_1 could choose to enforce, but be ineffective, thus inducing risk on A_2. I model the effectiveness of the first enforcer with a chance node following G_1's decision to enforce. With a positive probability $0 < s \leq 1$, G_1 successfully punishes D for predation, thus ending the game. A_2 is unaffected. With probability $1 - s$, however, G_1 fails—a situation that requires G_2 to retaliate against D to protect the second firm.[43]

Player G_1's enforcement choice affects not only the risk of predation, but also the distribution of protection fees. Protection fees are only accrued if the source of rents is effectively protected. Moreover, protection fees are selective benefits. Enforcers who forgo their responsibility to fight off predation do not receive a protection fee. As before, the specified payoffs specify changes in utility with respect to the status quo of a protected A_2.

If G_1 enforces, it obtains a protection fee bR_1 either when his retaliation is successful, or when he gets assistance from G_2. Otherwise, he simply incurs a private cost c without compensation. If G_1 chooses not to enforce, he forgoes both sources of rents, reflected in a payoff of $0 - bR_2$. In this case, G_2 can appropriate the first enforcer's fee if he chooses to enforce.[44] The corresponding payoffs for G_2 would be $bR_2 - c$ if he enforces. If G_2 does not enforce, he does not incur the private cost, but then he loses his protection fee. This situation is reflected in a negative payoff of $0 - bR_2$.

The dictator's payoffs are similar, except that the cost of government is reduced by the rents he receives from A_2. Given receipts of tR_2, the relevant cost when facing A_1 is now denoted by $\tilde{C}_D = C_D - tR_2$. In addition, predation gains are different. Not only can D try to appropriate all of A_1's rents, but he can also capture A_2's after-tax rents: $(1 - t_2)R_2$.

Players D and A_1 have the same strategies as in previous games—namely, $\sigma_D = \{t, H\}$ and $\sigma_{A_1} = \{I\}$, with $t \in [0,1]$ and $H, I \in \{0,1\}$. G_1's strategy is denoted as $\sigma_{G_1} = \{E_1\}$, with $E_1 = 1$ if it chooses to enforce and $E_1 = 0$ otherwise. G_2's decision following $E_1 = 0$ will be denoted by E_2. The second enforcement opportunity for G_2, following G_1's failed protection attempt, will be denoted by E_2^N. G_2's enforcement choices E_2 and E_2^N are defined similarly to E_1. G_2's strategy can therefore be written as $\sigma_{G_2} = \{E_2, E_2^N\}$. In equilibrium, each of these strategies must be a best response to the optimal strategies of other players.

I derive the corresponding SPNE through backward induction, starting with G_2's optimal choice for E_2. Let R_2^* denote the level of rents at which G_2 would be indifferent between enforcing or not. Then, G_2 will enforce if the second firm produces sufficiently high rents, or

$$R_2 \geq R_2^* \equiv \frac{c}{2b} \qquad (2.7)$$

Similarly, we can define R_2^N to define the level of rents at which G_2 would be indifferent after G_1's failed protection attempt. In this case, $E_2^N = 1$ when the following condition holds:

$$R_2 \geq R_2^N \equiv \frac{c}{b} \qquad (2.8)$$

Clearly, $R_2^N > R_2^*$, reflecting the selective nature of protection fees. Player G_2 is more motivated to enforce when he acts unilaterally. In other words, he can tolerate lower values of R_2 when individual protection fees bR_2 do not cover his enforcement cost, *provided* that G_1 remains inactive, in which case G_2 gets all protection fees.

Player G_1's choices are affected by the relative value of R_2 with respect to R_2^* and R_2^N, so we need to consider three cases: (1) high rents, with $R_2^* < R_2^N \leq R_2$; (2) intermediate rents, $R_2^* \leq R_2 < R_2^N$; and (3) low rents, $R_2 \leq R_2^* < R_2^N$. I consider each of these cases separately.

In the case of high rents, G_2 always enforces. Hence, G_1 knows that the expected payoffs from enforcing would be equal to $s[bR_1 - c] + (1-s)[bR_1 - c]$. If G_1 does not enforce, he incurs no cost, but loses the protection fees from A_2, bR_2. Thus, G_1 will choose to enforce when the following condition holds:

$$R_1 + R_2 \geq \frac{c}{b} \tag{2.9}$$

We know that condition (2.9) is satisfied because $R_2 \geq R_2^N = c/b$, so both G_1 and G_2 choose to enforce. If D then reneges, he gets $R_1 - \tilde{C}_D - \rho_1$ with probability s, and $R_1 + (1-t)R_2 - \tilde{C}_D - \rho_1 - \rho_2$ with probability $1 - s$. Otherwise, D gets $tR_1 - \tilde{C}_D$ for honoring his commitment. D will be indifferent with a critical penalty ρ_N^* equal to the collective punishment that erodes predation gains. In this case, D will choose $H = 1$ when the following *network commitment condition* holds:

$$\rho_1 + (1-s)\rho_2 \geq \rho_N^* \equiv (1-t)\Big[R_1 + (1-s)R_2\Big] \tag{2.10}$$

The network commitment condition demonstrates how overlapping protection can serve to deter predation. When $s < 1$, there is a need for assistance from the second enforcer, but the added enforcement need not exploit G_2's full capacity, because $(1-s)\rho_2 < \rho_2$. If $s = 1$, the second term on the left-hand side drops out, and the condition simplifies to $\rho_1 \geq \rho_0^*$, with a basic requirement that G_1 be strong enough on his own.

From A_1's perspective, recruiting a networked enforcer would therefore be more desirable than an isolated one. As long as both enforcers are willing to enforce, the network of overlapping protection acts as a backup system in case the first enforcer is ineffective. This is the case despite the fact that A_1 has no vested interest in A_2's rents being protected by G_2.

In the case of intermediate rents, G_2 will offer conditional enforcement. Because $R_2 \geq R_2^*$, G_2 will enforce if G_1 does not enforce. But because $R_2 < R_2^N$, G_2 will not have incentives to provide assistance after G_1's failed protection attempt. The expected payoffs for G_1 if he enforces are then equal to $s(bR_1 - c) + (1 - s)(-c)$. If G_1 does not enforce, he loses bR_2. Rearranging terms, we get that G_1 will enforce if the following condition holds:

$$sR_1 + R_2 \geq \frac{c}{b} \qquad (2.11)$$

This enforcement condition for G_1 is never satisfied because $sR_1 + R_2$ is no greater than $((1 + s)c)/(2b)$, which implies that $sR_1 + R_2 < (c/b)$ for any value of s.[45] But despite G_1's lack of incentives, predation can still be deterred if G_2 is powerful enough. The payoffs for D are $tR_1 - \tilde{C}_D$ from honoring, and $R_1 + (1-t)R_2 - \tilde{C}_D - \rho_2$ from reneging. We can find a penalty value that would make D indifferent, and define it as $\rho_2^* = (1-t)(R_1 + R_2)$. Hence, D will commit as long as

$$\rho_2 \geq \rho_2^* \qquad (2.12)$$

Note that $\rho_2^* \geq \rho_N^*$. Condition (2.12) is therefore analogous to the case $s = 1$, where G_1 successfully retaliates against D by himself. Again, the overlapping protection enables network enforcers to substitute for one another when one either lacks the incentives or the capacity for unilateral retaliation. When both enforcers do have incentives to protect, then the network is even more effective at deterring predation.

In the case of low rents, G_2 will never enforce. From the perspective of G_1, the expected payoffs for this case are similar to those under intermediate rents. If G_1 chooses to enforce, G_2 will not enforce. If G_1 chooses not to enforce, he forgoes a protection fee of bR_2, regardless of what G_2 does. Hence, G_1 has the same enforcement condition as in condition (2.11). In this case, however, D will act as a predator because the expected gains from reneging, $R_1 + (1-t) - \tilde{C}_D$, exceed those from honoring, $tR_1 - \tilde{C}_D$. Anticipating this predation, A_1 will withhold from investing, irrespective of the initial tax proposal.

Even if A_1 finds D's proposed policy to be credible, the tax rate may be too high. The participation constraint for A_1 is the same as in the case of an isolated firm: $t_1^* = (1-b) - v_1/R_1$. The participation constraint for D depends on how many firms participate. With the assumption that A_2 was already a participant, it follows that he was also willing to accept a tax rate that met D's requirements—namely, $t_2 \geq C_D/R_2$.

With two participants, the constraint becomes $t_D^*(\tilde{C}_D) = \tilde{C}_D/R_1$ or $t_D^* = (C_D - tR_2)/R_1$, because D is now able to cover his operating expenses with two sources of rents. Using the government's budget constraint, and setting $t_D^* = t$, we can solve for the common tax rate, which will be denoted as $t^* = C_D / (R_1 + R_2)$.[46] Note that A_2 benefits from A_1's protection because the cost of government is spread out between the two firms, despite the lack of direct connections between them. We now have all the information we need to make predictions about possible equilibrium outcomes.

Proposition 3 on Networked Protection. If $t^* > t_1^*$ the dictator and first asset holder benefit from private protection, and there is a unique SPNE determined as follows:

1. If A_2's rents are high enough such that $R_2^* < R_2^N \leq R_2$, both players G_1 and G_2 have incentives to enforce. If $\rho_1 + (1-s)\rho_2 > \rho_N^*$, the dictator refrains from predation, and A_1 invests. The corresponding optimal strategies are $\hat{\sigma}_D = \{t^*, 1\}$, $\hat{\sigma}_{A_1} = \{1\}$, $\hat{\sigma}_{G_1} = \{1\}$, and $\hat{\sigma}_{G_2} = \{1,1\}$. When rents do not fulfill that condition, D acts as a predator: $\hat{\sigma}_D = \{t^*, 0\}$, $\hat{\sigma}_{A_1} = \{0\}$, $\hat{\sigma}_{G_1} = \{1\}$, and $\hat{\sigma}_{G_2} = \{1,1\}$.

2. If $R_2^* < R_2 \leq R_2^N$, the case of intermediate rents for A_2, G_1 has no incentives to enforce, and G_2 offers conditional enforcement, enforcing only when G_1 does not enforce. If the second enforcer is powerful enough such that $\rho_2 > \rho_2^*$, predation can be deterred and the equilibrium is $\hat{\sigma}_D = \{t^*, 1\}$, $\hat{\sigma}_{A_1} = \{1\}$, $\hat{\sigma}_{G_1} = \{0\}$, and $\hat{\sigma}_{G_2} = \{1,0\}$. If the second enforcer is not strong enough such that $\rho_2 \leq \rho_2^*$, then D is undeterred and the equilibrium is $\hat{\sigma}_D = \{t^*, 0\}$, $\hat{\sigma}_{A_1} = \{0\}$, $\hat{\sigma}_{G_1} = \{0\}$, and $\hat{\sigma}_{G_2} = \{1,0\}$.

3. If $R_2 \leq R_2^* < R_2^N$, A_2 produces low rents, and neither G_1 nor G_2 have incentives to enforce, in which case D acts as a predator and A_1 chooses not to invest: $\hat{\sigma}_D = \{t^*, 0\}$, $\hat{\sigma}_{A_1} = \{0\}$, $\hat{\sigma}_{G_1} = \{0\}$, and $\hat{\sigma}_{G_2} = \{0,0\}$.

If, instead, $t^* > t_1^*$, the tax rate offered by D is too high to induce A_1's participation, leading to various equilibria with no investment. For instance, if $R_2 \geq R_2^N$ and $\rho_1 + (1-s)\rho_2 > \rho_N^*$, the equilibrium strategies are $\hat{\sigma}_D = \{t_D^*(\tilde{C}_D), 1\}$, $\hat{\sigma}_A = \{0\}$, $\hat{\sigma}_{G_1} = \{1\}$, and $\hat{\sigma}_{G_2} = \{1,1\}$. Otherwise, the equilibrium is $\hat{\sigma}_D = \{t_D^*(\tilde{C}_D), 0\}$, $\hat{\sigma}_{A_1} = \{0\}$, $\hat{\sigma}_{G_1} = \{0\}$, and $\hat{\sigma}_{G_2} = \{0,0\}$.

The main implication from proposition 3 is that overlapping protection effectively merges the rents from the two separate private agreements. That is, for predation to be deterred, the network must be able to impose a collective penalty that exceeds predation gains: $(1 - t)(R_1 + R_2)$. This penalty can be imposed unilaterally by either player if he is powerful enough, or it can be imposed in combination. Either way, the network provides a backup system to protect the property rights of A_1 and A_2 even when their own enforcers may be unwilling or unable to punish D.

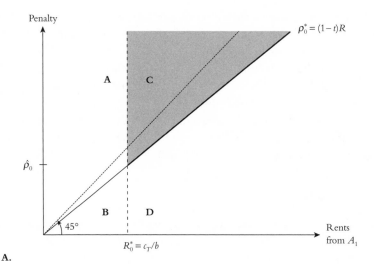

A.

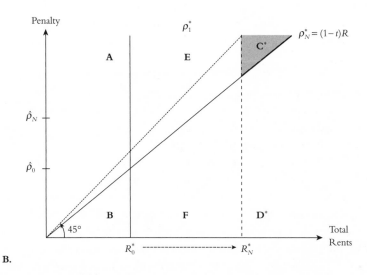

B.

Figure 2.6 Credible Commitments with Networked Protection
(A) Implications from proposition 1. (B) Implications from proposition 3.

Figure 2.6 illustrates these implications with two changes to the original parameter space with an isolated A_1. From the perspective of D, facing two smaller but networked firms is analogous to facing a larger firm with rents $R_1 + R_2$. For $s = 0$, the minimum penalty line ρ_N^* has the same slope, $(1 - t)$, as for the case of an isolated firm, except that the relevant rents are now equal to $R = R_1 + R_2$ instead of simply $R = R_1$.[47]

However, the penalty requirements will be much higher than for an isolated firm. This result is induced by a shift in the minimum rent line from R_0^* to R_N^*. This shift reduces the size of the commitment region from C to C^*. Note, however, that this region does not preclude participation of enforcers with capacities less than $\hat{\rho}_N$, defined by the intersection of lines R_N^* and ρ_N^*. Again, because the network operates as a backup protection system, what matters for commitment is that there be at least one enforcer with high capacity. A low ρ_1 does not automatically mean predation if ρ_2 is high enough, or vice versa.[48] Moreover, the region C^* increases with s.

4   Conclusion

This chapter has established conditions under which dictators can make credible commitments to protect property rights. I noted that although it is possible to pass credible policies, the nature of commitments under dictatorships is different with respect to democratic settings. First, dictators will make more selective rather than global commitments. But in order for these selective commitments to be credible, asset holders must find private protection.

Private protection is a type of third-party enforcement, but it is not generated through formal institutions of limited government, which are unavailable in dictatorships. In principle, private protection can be done in a decentralized fashion in which each asset holder pays for private protection.

In this chapter I argue, however, that the structure of private protection is an important determinant of policy credibility. Networks provide an informal enforcement mechanism that can punish a government's attempt to prey against individual network members. The logic behind this claim is as follows. During the process of offering private protection, and when economic actors are searching for private enforcers in a decentralized fashion, there is an emerging network structure that ties the interests of otherwise disconnected actors. This network structure manifests itself in terms of overlapping private protection, which under certain conditions can have a positive effect on credibility. With overlapping protection, the scope of private protection can increase from the narrow focus of protecting one firm's assets to protecting the whole network.

For the most part, the analysis in this chapter revolves around the enforcement of policy commitments. In terms of incentives, the underlying concern was to characterize the encompassing interests of the dictator and influential political actors in economic activity. However, Olson (2000) notes that a stationary bandit also requires a long-term horizon. As it turns out, networks can also elongate a dictator's tenure. An underlying assumption in this chapter was that social structure was durable. That is, the network provided a stable governance structure to ensure the long-term stability of selective credible commitments. On the political side, the network ensured support and resources for the dictators. On the economic side, the network imposed barriers to entry. When combined, networks of private protection—to the extent that they persist—provide the institutional foundation for the requirements of stationary banditry.

Chapter 3

Political Institutions and Consolidated Dictatorship

This chapter provides a historical overview of political institutions in Mexico during the Porfiriato. The Porfiriato is generally characterized as a dictatorship.[1] The evidence for this classification lies in the evident concentration of political power, the ability and willingness to repress, and the lack of political competition manifested in Díaz's various reelections. These general features of the Porfiriato are well known and undisputed. Less is known, however, about the actual process that enabled Díaz to exercise dictatorial powers.

How did Díaz become a dictator? This chapter presents evidence that indicates that the acquisition of dictatorial powers was a gradual process. Moreover, I argue that Díaz's eventual dictatorship was not solely the result of repression and personal ambition, but rather the outcome of a strategic choice of deference by other influential political actors. In other words, Díaz was allowed to become a dictator. Moreover, we can use the available evidence to time the establishment of the Díaz dictatorship midway through his tenure circa 1890 rather than 1876 when he first came to power.

I present various types of evidence to ascertain the extent to which other political actors opposed the executive. I evaluate roll calls to examine whether legislators favored or opposed executive proposals. I also examine the determination of the federal budget to check whether Congress infringed on the ability of the federal government to pursue its goals.

Analyzing congressional–executive relations is also relevant to assess the relative importance of formal and informal institutions. More specifically, if there was a network in which public officials and economic actors came together to negotiate and craft policies as claimed by my theory, we would expect the Díaz government and other influential actors to work out their differences within the network, and not through open political conflicts. In other words, as Díaz consolidates his dictatorship, and he develops a private network for the exercise of his government, we would expect to see less conflict over time, both within policy-making processes but also in terms of the need to fight and repress opponents. In addition to legislators, I also examine political conflict with a review of federal military expenditures during the Porfiriato. The implication is that we should see less resources being devoted to keeping potential opponents (or regional opposition) in check as Díaz consolidates his dictatorship.[2] (See Figure 3.1.)

Figure 3.1   Map of Mexico
Courtesy of the General Libraries, the University of Texas at Austin. Enhanced with the author's legend to denote territorial status of Baja California Sur and Quintana Roo.

The rest of this chapter is organized as follows. The next section describes major political developments in nineteenth century Mexico to understand the political context faced by Díaz when he first came to power. The section also provides a brief description of the Constitution of 1857, which defined the formal rules of the political system. The following section, "Restoring Stability," examines military expenditures to assess the evolution of political conflict. "Institutions and the Emergence of Limited Dictatorship" examines general patterns of congressional–executive relations to ascertain whether the legislature was transformative, in the sense that it revised executive proposals dramatically (Polsby, 1975). The last section concludes my discussion.

1   Political Conditions Before Díaz

Mexico achieved independence from the Spanish Empire in 1821. For most of the nineteenth century, however, political development took place against the backdrop of political instability (Benjamin and Marcial, 1984, p. 325). The first half century after independence was characterized by political instability as a result of continuous fighting and fragile political institutions. The inability to reach consensus on national goals and the identity of governments was further exacerbated by a federal system that gave way to diffused political power and authority among local governments and political bosses. Territorial integrity was another problem. As late as 1867, for example, Mexico was still trying to defend its sovereignty against a French invasion.

One major reason behind political instability relates to the way independence was attained. The War of Independence (1810–1821) was fought and won by a coalition of political factions with very different views about the type of government that should be established thereafter. The definition of the new postindependence governance structure was therefore subject to major disagreements about political organization and national goals (Lynch, 1984).

On one side were the royalists (later known as *conservatives*) who had aligned themselves with the Spanish crown against the insurgents led by Miguel Hidalgo. When the Spanish government in Europe was overthrown in 1821, these conservatives opted for independence from Spain. They nonetheless preferred a centralized government modeled along colonial hierarchies, a national army, and the official religion of Catholicism (Anna, 1984, pp. 81–82; Bazant, 1984, p. 430).

On the other side were insurgent republicans (later known as *federalists*) who also wanted independence from Spain but preferred more drastic po-

litical reforms. These reforms included the establishment of a federal republic to decentralize power and a more secular national government to reduce
the influence of the Catholic Church.

Conservatives dominated initially and were able to impose their preferences upon independence in 1821. To govern the newly independent country,
they created a council of regents led by Agustín Iturbide. Interestingly, Iturbide had previously fought on Spain's side and had practically extinguished
the independence movement. When the royalists defected and decided to
switch their support to the independence movement, Iturbide became their
leader and was influential in securing independence from Spain.

Concurrently, a congress was created to give voice to the various political entities known as *intendancies* that had been established during the colonial period. In fact, those entities located in Central America decided to
secede and became independent nations.[3] In May 1822, the new Congress
formally proclaimed Iturbide as Emperor Agustín I and recommended that
his monarchy be hereditary. Five months later, the emperor would dismiss
Congress and appoint a military junta.

A republic was established in 1823 after military opposition to the arbitrary rule of Agustín I forced him to go into exile. Under the leadership
of General Antonio López de Santa Anna, Congress was restored and a republican constitution adopted in 1824. The new constitution provided for
a federal republic of nineteen states, four territories, and a federal district.
Despite the new constitution, the ideological conflict between conservatives and federalists remained. This led to a very unstable period, resulting
in seventy-five executive governments from 1821 to 1876, during which
time these two factions would fight and alternate each other in government
(Haber et al., 2003, p. 42; Meyer and Sherman, 1995, pp. 313–372).

Santa Anna played an influential political role after the end of the first
Mexican Empire of 1821 to 1823. Not only did he help secure independence, he also gained much prestige from protecting the country against an
attempted Spanish invasion in 1829. In addition, he was elected president
on a few occasions.

In latter years, however, Santa Anna presided over several events that
made him lose his political prestige. During the late 1830s, he replaced the
constitution and got rid of state rights. These actions created political opposition, some of which led to the Texan revolt of 1836, which included
the infamous battle of El Alamo. Later, he also presided over the Mexican
American War of 1846 to 1848 against the United States. The outcome of
the war led to Santa Anna's exile in late 1847 and a major concession of
national territory north of the Rio Grande River in 1848.

Santa Anna was invited back to govern as a dictator when the conservatives reassumed power in 1853. He became more unpopular, however, when
he decreed that his dictatorship be continued indefinitely and when he sold
additional national territory to the United States (in modern-day Arizona
and New Mexico) through the infamous Gadsden Purchase of 1853. He
was finally sent into exile in 1855 and was allowed to return briefly before
his death in 1876 (Bazant, 1984, pp. 441–444).

The temporary defeat of conservative forces in 1855 marked the beginning of the Reform period. Led by a group of formerly exiled political
opponents to Santa Anna, the liberal movement, successor to the federalists,
emerged as the leading political force. This movement embodied its ideals in
a new constitution and in reforms to limit ecclesiastical and military privileges, separate Church and State, secularize education and civil registries,
reduce the property holdings of the Church, and redistribute communal
lands (Bazant, 1984, pp. 457–460).

I.I CONSTITUTIONAL FRAMEWORK

The Constitution of 1857, following the postindependence constitutional
guidelines of 1824, set the basis for a federal republic. Its two basic tenets
were the supremacy of states versus the federation, and the separation of
Church and State (Guerra, 1988, pp. 31–58).[4] The basic political organization was that of a federalist republic in which the states had supreme rights
over the federal government. The federal government was to be divided
in three branches: executive, judicial, and legislative.

The Constitution intended not just to set up a new political structure,
but also to deal with political impediments to the adoption of its embedded
liberal ideals. There were, for instance, strong anticlerical elements aimed
at limiting the political participation of religious interests and diminishing
the influence of the Church in domestic politics. These measures were aug-
mented with reforms embodied in the famous *Ley Lerdo* legislation of 1856
that confiscated property and limited the ownership rights of the Church
(Bazant, 1984, pp. 457–459).

A significant part of the constitution was devoted to preserving the rights
of private citizens and the powers of the legislature. Individual citizens, who
had been previously subjected to the abuses of political and ecclesiastical
authorities, were to be equal under the law and have the right to freedom,
to be safe from judicial arbitrariness, to hold private property, and to vote.[5]
Furthermore, because the Constitution stipulated a federalist government
by the people, almost all offices (including the presidency, state governorships, county governments, and legislative deputies) were up for election,

giving private citizens a greater opportunity in determining political outcomes. Consistent with the stated objectives of limiting the power of the
federal government, the strengthening of the legislature was to be a built-in
mechanism to restrain the actions of the executive branch and prevent the
resurgence of dictatorial and centralist governments.[6]

The Reform period launched by the new constitutional framework and
related reforms was brought to a halt in 1862 by a French invasion encouraged by exiled Mexican conservatives. A huge foreign debt had forced the
government of Benito Juárez to declare a moratorium in 1861. This led Mexico's creditors, including Great Britain, Spain, and France, to engage in a combined expedition to invade Mexico in late 1861. At the end, Great Britain
and Spain withdrew. The French army, however, continued its march toward
Mexico City, which they occupied on June 10, 1863. Napoleon III appointed
a puppet emperor, Maximilian of the House of Habsburg, along with his wife
Charlotte, daughter of the King of Belgium, to govern the new Mexican
Empire as a satellite of the French Empire (Bazant, 1984, pp. 466–469).

1.2 RESTORED (LIBERAL) REPUBLIC

Maximilian was ultimately unable to restore stability and meet the political demands that allowed him to come to power. Domestic political
conditions were not favorable to the emperor. Having failed to convince
Juárez (the deposed president) to join the new government, Maximilian
had to devote his attention to containing republican forces that wanted to
overthrow his government. Because of military conflict, he was unable
to reverse institutional changes from the Reform period. The clergy and
other conservative elements in society readily withdrew their support.

Maximilian was also affected by international considerations. The United
States was pressing France to retire its troops from Mexican territory. Finally,
in 1867, Napoleon III agreed to withdraw his financial and military support
of Maximilian when it became evident that political instability prevented
Mexico from being strategically important to the French Empire.

Republican forces were then able to defeat the weak imperial forces to
restore the republic. Juárez returned to power and was subsequently elected
for a third presidential term, but there remained major political and economic challenges. On the political side, the restored republic did not eliminate the recurrent problems of political dissension and military conflict that
had plagued the country since its independence. Although the conservatives
had been disbanded and did not appear to present major threats in the short
run, there remained much conflict within the liberal movement as many
prominent actors attempted to promote their own interests.

Juárez was certainly the leading figure of the liberal movement that had restored a republican government in the 1860s. While he maintained his desire to be president, it was virtually impossible for other actors to reach the presidency.[7] Although there were challengers, including Porfirio Díaz himself, Juárez was easily reelected a few times. The key question would be who would succeed the popular president. As it turned out, Juárez favored Sebastian Lerdo de Tejada over other prominent actors. When Juárez died, Lerdo de Tejada became president, further straining internal divisions among the liberals.

Lerdo de Tejada ran quickly into political problems as a result of his efforts to centralize power and reelect himself. Díaz, a celebrated military hero with a direct role in ending the French occupation, seized the opportunity in 1876 to revolt in the name of democracy against a government with evident dictatorial aspirations. Lerdo de Tejada would subsequently go into exile the following year.

2   Restoring Stability

Díaz was formally elected president for his first term in 1877 (Guerra, 1988, p. 9; Haber et al., 2003, p. 43). Faithful to his democratic pronouncements, Díaz immediately set to include a no reelection clause in the Constitution to prevent presidents from assuming too much power. As it turns out, within a decade he would have reversed his initial position and managed to enact constitutional changes that allowed him to be continuously reelected.[8] Before he could consolidate his power, however, he had to deal with two major problems: political instability and economic stagnation. This situation placed several constraints on the instruments that he could use to stay in power.

On the political front, the nominal federal republic was not based on a stable set of rules that everyone respected. Despite a liberal constitution that mimicked that of the United States, Díaz could not rely on formal political institutions to manage conflict for two main reasons. First, the instability that characterized Mexico during the nineteenth century had left a legacy of fragmentation, with various regional polities governed by strongmen with political and military influence. Second, the conservative and liberal ideological movements of the nineteenth century had not led to the creation of political parties that could have served as venues for political organization.[9]

Díaz's ability to dispense privileges and economic benefits as a means to attract supporters or deter opponents was severely limited at the beginning of his tenure (Haber et al., 2003, pp. 41–123; Maurer, 2002). The political instability of the period had had detrimental effects on the Mexican economy. The nineteenth century was a period of economic stagnation, caused by political instability, the economic contraction of the mining sector, and the lack of institutional innovations that would have made markets work more efficiently (Coatsworth, 1978). The need to pacify the country only added to the financial burden on the new government, which also faced a severe debt problem inherited from previous governments.

Political order would eventually be restored by centralizing power through a combination of outright repression, rigged elections, and co-optation, but the process took time. In the short run, Díaz mostly relied on repression to suppress open opposition to his government. Later, as opponents were weeded out, and his ability to generate rents increased, he also relied on buying loyalty as a complementary instrument.[10]

Opposition to the Díaz government came from two sources. First, there was new opposition emerging from Díaz's unconstitutional rise to power. Two presidential contenders had an important role in leading political opposition against Díaz. There was the former president Lerdo de Tejada, who had returned from exile and intended to regain the presidency by force. There was also the influential liberal leader José María Iglesias who had a history of opposition to Juárez and Lerdo de Tejada.

In the end, Díaz defeated both Lerdo de Tejada and Iglesias through the use of military force and strategic concessions to their respective supporters. Soon after Díaz came to power, for instance, there was a presumed nationwide conspiracy led from the port city of Veracruz by several generals and supporters of Lerdo de Tejada. Díaz instructed the governor of the namesake state of Veracruz to assassinate the key suspects promptly (Roeder, 1981, pp. 131–137).

Second, there were the local political bosses who reigned in the geographically dispersed entities of the Mexican Republic. Conventional accounts of the early years of the Porfiriato prominently describe Díaz's efforts to restore political stability and to get rid of opposition by powerful local political bosses (Meyer and Sherman, 1995, pp. 433–436, 453–457). These powerful enclaves had emerged throughout the country as a result of the ineffectiveness of national governments to stay in power, let alone govern the vast national territory. For instance, in the Pacific Coast state of Nayarit, the local *cacique* (political boss) reigned supreme. Various army expeditions to assassinate him and dissolve his power had been unsuccessful. The gulf state of Yucatán, on the other hand, was temporarily successful in seceding from the republic. Díaz was able to subjugate regional strongholds through a skillful use of military force.

Reyes (1903) notes that Díaz faced major regional challenges, especially in the northern and southeastern parts of the country. According to Reyes (1903), a general and close associate of Díaz, the early years of the Porfiriato included several conflicts with influential generals in the states of Sinaloa, Chihuahua, and Baja, California. In some cases, not only did these actors interfere with Díaz's directives, as was the case of General Treviño, who was in charge of the army's northern forces, they also conspired against the government, as was the case of General Miguel Negrete, who pledged his support to the previous president, Lerdo de Tejada. Governors or generals who did not comply with Díaz's orders were routinely removed (Reyes, 1903, pp. 275–295).

A concomitant problem to local political bosses was the emergence of bandits throughout the country, especially in areas away from the capital city. Díaz recognized that public security and the capricious behavior of local political bosses needed to be controlled for the continuity of his own national government. Regional pockets of violence and lawlessness were met with the use of the federal army. This included not only the direct use of military force to subjugate opponents, but also the incorporation of bandit groups and the local militia into the corps of the federal army (Roeder, 1981, pp. 61–63).

Whatever open opposition surfaced during his regime, it was met with military force, sending strong signals that the Díaz government was in control. Meyer and Sherman (1995) succinctly describe Díaz's control maneuvers as follows:

> ... Díaz was faced with a number of insurrections.... But Díaz was not hesitant in meeting force with force. Rebel leaders who were not shot down on the field of battle were disposed of shortly after their capture.... Such lessons were not lost on potential revolutionaries elsewhere. (p. 434)

Díaz made great efforts to suppress political opposition before consolidating his dictatorship. Even after suppressing open rebellions, the dictator had to worry about latent opposition, especially from the threat of rebellion by state governments.[11] Meyer and Sherman (1995, p. 456) claim that Díaz spent a quarter of the budget on the military establishment, so there was a recurring concern during Díaz's tenure regarding the relationship between the central government (located in Mexico City) and the states.

There are theoretical reasons to analyze explicit or latent political opposition to assess the relative strength of a dictatorship. Wintrobe (1998) argues that the behavior of dictators can be largely explained by how they deal with the dictatorial dilemma of not knowing their true base of political support. Because dictators generally have enough authority to punish with impunity, individuals or groups are unwilling to reveal their true preferences or political support for fear of retaliation. In actuality, most people will appear to be loyal when, in reality, they are opposed to the regime. Apparent loyalty may be concealing latent opposition or a revolution in the making.

Despite the uncertainty behind apparent loyalty, Wintrobe (2001) argues that the dictator can estimate the amount of loyalty in society, and adjust its behavior accordingly: "Dictatorships with any permanence are those that discover and institutionalize mechanisms that 'automatically' both reward their supporters and monitor their support . . . [including] systematic repression of the opposition" (p. 38). In other words, successful dictatorships learn to manage the dictator's dilemma (of insecurity) more effectively by relying on institutional, rather than simply violent, mechanisms. The implications for Mexico's Porfiriato were straightforward: If Díaz was unsure about the loyalty of states, then it would have been expected of him to buy loyalty from some while repressing political opponents, with both actions resulting in higher military expenditures. These expenditures should therefore decrease as the dictatorship consolidated.

To get a better sense of perceived political opposition, I looked at the evolution of federal spending related to military and police forces. The existence of a latent political threat by states would be reflected in increases in military spending to keep state governments and other independently minded political actors under control. Simply put, high levels of policing (or military repression) would be expected to respond to perceived threats to diminish the power of the central government.[12]

Figure 3.2 shows the evolution of military expenditures as a proportion of federal expenditures, which included subsidies and public debt in addition to civil expenditures. If states were seen as a threat by the federal government, we would expect to see significant resources devoted to military or police purposes by the federal government. The evolution of military expenditures for this period appears to support the view of a recurrent threat by states starting in 1879, shortly after Díaz came to power.[13]

We see that the importance of military expenditures actually diminished over time. As is common in coups, there was an initial spike in military expenditures shortly after Díaz arrived to power, reaching a peak during the Porfiriato in 1885. By 1890, however, the ratio stabilized around 0.20, indicating that states were no longer seen as a threat to the federal government. This year also coincides with Díaz's consolidation of dictatorial powers, as explained in the following section. With these powers, the dictator could appoint friendly governors and otherwise manipulate the political system to

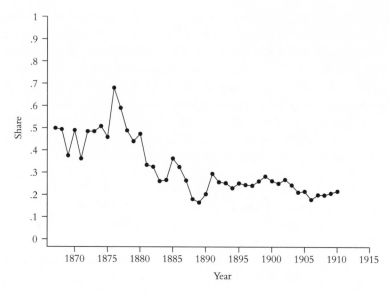

Figure 3.2   Relative Importance of Military Expenditures, 1867–1911

mitigate potential threats by state governors and other political actors. The data clearly indicate that his political tactics were successful.

The data do not permit us to assess whether the major components of the military budget were related to materials or forces that could only be used to respond to regional conflict. Nonetheless, the evidence is consistent with the fact that pacifying Mexico required some time before Díaz was able to consolidate his dictatorship (Duclós Salinas, 1904).

In addition to military action, Díaz had a calculated political strategy to end uncertainty about the selection mechanism for new governments, an inherent problem in political instability. At the executive level, the mechanism was well defined and common knowledge to all: Although he continued to hold presidential elections, Díaz remained the effective head of state in all instances.[14] At the state level, he appointed as governors those generals who had supported him in his rebellion against Lerdo de Tejada and other generals. In cases when he could not remove existing governors, as was the case in Chihuahua and Yucatán, he gained their support through strategic concessions.

In the end, political authority was centralized around the dictator and close associates in Mexico City. Aided by a shrewd combination of rigged elections and outright repression, Díaz was able to dilute the power of factions opposed to the government through additional measures, including strategic concessions to provincial political bosses and the monopolization of political power (Ballard, 1978; Katz, 1986, pp. 3–78). For instance, in 1890, the governor of Nuevo León, General Bernardo Reyes, conspired with Díaz to manipulate deputy and senator elections to please local elites.

An episode from deputy elections in the state of Puebla, held shortly after Díaz's arrival to the presidency, provides another typical story of Díaz's political tactics. Prior to election day, Díaz himself sent a letter to governor Rosendo Márquez listing the president's favorite candidates. The state governor, in turn, forwarded the instructions to district political bosses to ensure that the desired candidates won. When the candidates actually won, local political bosses sent correspondence back to Díaz stating that their mission had been completed. Eventual publication in official congressional diaries completed the round by making public the "official" results of the elections. In another extreme case of manipulation, there were allegations that prisoners in the northern state of Nuevo León were instructed to fill out election ballots to increase the number of votes for candidates favored by Díaz (Guerra, 1988, pp. 40–41).

In simple terms, Díaz restored political order by becoming a dictator, thus reducing any uncertainty about future federal governments. By manipulating the outcomes of lower level elections, he further ensured that that the policies of those selected by him would be consistent with his executive goals. Second, by centralizing power in one office and one location, he reduced political competition, ensuring that all political conflict would be mediated with his participation.

Díaz's tactics proved rather successful, because he managed to stay in power thirty-five years—until 1911. At the turn of the twentieth century, however, the concentration of political power within the dictator's cadre of supporters led to the development of political opposition to the dictator in search of more political freedoms. Among these reformers, Francisco I. Madero of the northern state of Coahuila played a leading role in pushing for democratic reforms. When Madero's efforts were met with repression in 1910, his war cry of "effective suffrage and no reelection" would mark the beginning of the Mexican Revolution. Porfirio Díaz went into exile to Paris in 1911, marking the end of one of the longest dictatorships in modern Latin American history.

3 Institutions and the Emergence of Limited Dictatorship

Against the backdrop of repression and rigged elections, formal political institutions continued to operate throughout Díaz's tenure. What was the nature of these institutions, and why did they apparently fail to prevent Díaz from becoming a dictator? I will argue that Díaz faced real challenges to his authority, and his ability to establish himself as a dictator was contingent on the cooperation of other political actors.

By constitutional design, Díaz faced two sets of institutional constraints: Congress and federalism. A reader familiar with Mexican history could question the relevance of a section that examines institutional constraints within a period that has long been classified as a dictatorship. There are several reasons why this section is important.

First, Díaz faced a larger number of veto players than his predecessors. The main change that took place was the reestablishment of an upper level chamber in Congress, the Senate, which had been disbanded during the Reform period to get rid of the conservatives who had previously dominated the Senate. As it turns out, the Reform period did not eliminate all conservative interests—only those that openly threatened liberal governments. The reestablishment of a bicameral Congress was promoted by the previous president, Lerdo de Tejada, so we can dismiss the possibility that Díaz himself might have created a veto player to counteract the authority of the Chamber of Deputies. When Díaz came to power, Congress would not only include the victorious liberals, but would also be populated by enclaves of economic and political elites.

The Constitution of 1857 empowered Congress with legislative powers as follows. First, Article 65 conferred on both chambers of Congress the right to propose legislation.[15] Second, the passage of laws required the approval of both chambers of Congress.[16] In other words, Congress had a say in which policies were proposed and ultimately enacted into law.

Díaz came to power with promises of democratization, which placed some limits on any presidential attempts to usurp legislative power, at least in the short run. Not only did he replace a former president who had concentrated economic and political power, but the country's political development was moving in the direction of increased political representation to constrain the central government.[17] Given the executive government's weak administrative capacity, severe financial problems, and an unclear base of political support, the now-bicameral Congress in the 1870s was therefore in a stronger position to dominate policy making.

Although both chambers had these general legislative powers, there were some differences in the policies in which they were involved. The evidence shows that, of the two chambers, the Senate became, upon its reinstatement, relatively more important because of the political and economic prominence of its members. Policy-making processes were dominated by senators.

That is, if one wants to study the ability of Congress to constrain the executive government, an examination of the Mexican Senate should provide a fairly accurate depiction of congressional–executive relations.

Although less prominent, the Chamber of Deputies had a critical role in one key area: the federal budget. The Constitution of 1857 did not impose substantive barriers to restrict the decisions that each chamber could make. In fact, Articles 65 to 72 delineated a legislative process similar to that of the U.S. Congress in which both chambers had to reach a consensus in the legislative proposals that were forwarded to the executive government for its approval. The evidence shows that neither deputies nor senators exercised their proposal powers; instead, much of the legislative activity was in response to executive proposals. Despite this somewhat passive role for legislators, the federal budget proposed by the executive government to Congress was one exception in which the Chamber of Deputies retained final approval. In other words, the Chamber of Deputies was the key veto player in the passage of federal budgets.[18]

States, on the other hand, had enjoyed varying levels of autonomy for most of the nineteenth century. The precarious situation in which Díaz arrived to power required that the dictator be able to strike strategic alliances with powerful political actors. State governors and regional political bosses could use this situation to place various demands on the federal government. Given the fragmented nature of Mexican politics, it would have been reasonable to assume that the preferences of members of Congress would be dominated by parochial interests.

The two institutional constraints of Congress and federalism included three major groups of players: the (lower) Chamber of Deputies, the Senate within Congress, and the states.[19] Note that because states were represented in Congress, we should not expect the relative influences of Congress and the states to operate independently of each other. States could be very active in affecting policies through their congressional representations. Even if congressional representations appeared to be weak, the states could have found alternate ways to express their preferences directly to the dictator. As mentioned earlier, Díaz also needed to make regional concessions to ensure that state governments, along with other influential regional actors, did not rebel against the regime.

A second reason for evaluating institutional constraints is that Díaz did not consolidate his dictatorship until halfway through his tenure in 1890. This fact invites further examination of the role of institutions in determining executive behavior. First of all, dictators (or dictators-to-be) do not come to power amid an institutional vacuum. Generally, they will inherit some set of existing political institutions with varying types of constraints, even when they assume power as a result of political instability. Moreover, whether the institutional environment that new dictators face actually constrains their behavior is an empirical issue. But, if there are some binding formal constraints, these constraints must be taken into account to measure accurately the contribution of alternate, informal institutions such as the social networks proposed by my theory of private protection.

Institutional constraints were indeed binding, at least during the early years. Not only did Díaz originally come to power for only one four-year term, but it took at least a decade before constitutional changes enabled him to be continuously reelected. Díaz served seven complete terms between 1876 and 1911, not including a four-year hiatus in which one of his closest generals, Manuel González, assumed the presidency.[20] This interim four-year period had been the subject of considerable debate regarding Díaz's influence. Because he had promised to uphold democratic principles, he abided by the Constitution and stepped down in 1880.

During González's tenure, Díaz remained in public office, working at times as a member of Congress and a cabinet member, and building up a political coalition to amend the Constitution to allow him to be reelected for a second term. Reyes (1903) notes that González was handpicked by Díaz to ensure that other actors did not take control of the state. Reyes (1903, p. 281) claims that during this time, Díaz retained his influence during this period, and was even able to depose the governor of Jalisco in 1882. It was clear even then that he stepped down as part of a long-term strategy to consolidate power, and also that he depended on Congress. After he regained the presidency, he worked again with members of Congress to change the Constitution as needed to allow him to be reelected.

It took several years to convince Congress to allow reelection (ironically, as mentioned, it was Díaz himself who had proposed a no reelection constitutional amendment back in 1878). Article 78, which describes the prerogatives of the executive branch, was amended on October 21, 1887, to allow reelection for the next period and a subsequent reelection after at least one term out of office. The same article was later changed on December 20, 1890, to delete any previous reelection clauses.[21] Finally, the current six-year term was introduced in 1904.

We can thus divide the Porfiriato into two distinct subperiods: an earlier period lasting from 1876 to 1890, during which Díaz did not have dictatorial powers; and a subsequent period lasting until 1911, during which Díaz was firmly in control as a dictator. In other words, not only was Díaz weaker than Congress during his first term, but it was also unclear at that time that Díaz would stay in power as long as he did. Moreover, even if he was expected to last beyond his original four-year term, it was unknown that he would eventually become a dictator.

3.1 SENATORS AND POLICY-MAKING CONSTRAINTS

The consolidation of Díaz's dictatorship involved a combination of both formal and informal arrangements. The evidence shows that both state governors and legislators worked closely in tandem with the executive government. State governments and legislators had incentives to support the Díaz government because they had a prominent participation in a network of private protection, which provided rents to network members. Díaz needed their political support and economic resources, but he also needed them to alter the Constitution, a process that required working within the confines of formal political institutions.

A testable implication of my network theory is that the legislature would not be the main forum in which political actors managed their political differences. This is not to say that the legislature is at all unimportant, but that legislative processes are complemented by a network that mediates political conflict and provides a policy agreement that is then formalized by normal legislative processes. In the case of the Senate, the implication is that senators, just like the deputies not opposing the executive branch or themselves within the chamber, would not be expected to define policy within the legislature.

Could it be that the ability of Díaz to make credible commitments was based on cooperation with senators? Did the Senate attempt to influence policy through normal legislative processes? Is there evidence of opposition to the executive branch by the Mexican Senate at any time during the Porfiriato? The evidence indicates that there was indeed some opposition during the early years of the Porfiriato (which runs against the conventional wisdom that Díaz was in complete control of political processes for the whole period); but after 1890, senators behaved in accordance with my theory.

An analysis of executive–legislative relations during Díaz's dictatorship shows four interesting patterns that are consistent with my theory of networks as a complementary governance structure to formal political institutions.[22] First, the executive government was active in proposing policies to the legislative branch through cabinet proposals or a congressional permanent commission with close ties to the Díaz government. Second, congressional opposition to executive proposals decreased steadily over time. Third, the Congress transferred legislative authority over to Díaz, who was also awarded extensive executive decree authority. Finally, the executive government, in turn, eventually delegated policy making to affected economic groups outside the legislative arena.

Available roll call data from the Mexican Senate for the period 1876 to 1910 illustrates the process in which the legislature deferred policy making to the executive branch.[23] During the first years of the Díaz dictatorship, a higher fraction of senators voted against the majority than was the case by the late 1890s. For example, the number of nonunanimous votes in the early 1880s was about 30 percent of the total votes. By the late 1890s onward, virtually all rolls calls were unanimous votes, with only an average of 4 percent of all roll calls in a given two-year Congress being nonunanimous votes.

Table 3.1 shows the percentage of nonunanimous votes, mostly proposed by the executive government or a congressional permanent commission with close ties to Díaz. The data clearly show a trend in which Congress effectively deferred policy making to the executive branch. Indeed, throughout the whole period, senators invariably deferred to the executive branch in economic matters, particularly in private arrangements between the executive government and economic actors regarding concessions and other exclusive benefits.

One may argue that Congress may have been impeded to act unilaterally against the dictator, but that it would still be possible for some groups within Congress to oppose the dictator systematically. Was there any other type of organized opposition to the executive branch within the senate? Because there were no political parties, we know that congressional opposition could only manifest itself individually or perhaps on a regional basis. In Razo (2003), I have analyzed roll calls for the period 1876 to 1888, before

TABLE 3.1
Roll Calls and Legislative Dissent, 1876–1892

		Number of Roll Calls			Percentage against majority
Congress	Years	Unanimous	Non-unanimous	Total	
8	1876–1878	162	46	208	22.1%
9	1878–1880	79	176	255	69.0%
10	1880–1882	292	121	413	29.3%
11	1882–1884	126	34	160	21.3%
12	1884–1886	187	46	233	19.7%
13	1886–1888	201	32	233	13.7%
14	1888–1890	253	17	270	6.3%
15	1890–1892	238	11	249	4.4%

SOURCE: Compiled from Mexico Congreso Cámara de Senadores (1876–1911).

Díaz's consolidated dictatorship, to get a better picture of how senators related to the executive government. This roll call analysis corroborates the evidence shown in Table 3.1. That is, we do not observe legislative dissension after 1890.[24]

The ability of senators to be more or less compliant with executive proposals depended on regional affiliations and personal influence. There is evidence of regional and seniority effects before Díaz consolidates his dictatorship, meaning that politicians who had been in power for a long time or who came from certain regions were more likely to voice their opposition to the executive government.

Notwithstanding the problems of comparing different congresses, the evidence also reveals interesting dynamics. First, regional preferences evolve consistently with historical accounts of this period. Roll calls indicate that senators from border or northern states remained invariably distrustful of the federal government, but they were less extreme in their preferences at the beginning of Díaz's tenure than other states outside the federal district (Mexico City). Over time, however, the preferences of northern states evolved to reflect greater differences between them and the rest of the country. By the 13th Congress (1886–1888), right before Díaz consolidated his dictatorship, it was senators from northern states who were most dissatisfied with executive proposals. This finding is consistent with the historical evidence of northern elites, who, disenchanted by the political system, led the military revolt that would eventually overthrow the dictator, although we are left with a puzzle. In the 1890s and thereafter, senators invariably threw their support behind the dictator. If there was sustained opposition to executive proposals well up to the time when Díaz established his dictatorship, why the sudden change in preferences? I will argue that despite the mistrust of the federal government, the incentives of senators became aligned with those of the executive government when they realized that deference to the executive branch could create lucrative opportunities for their mutual benefit.

3.2 DEPUTY CONSTRAINTS AND THE FEDERAL BUDGET

As noted earlier, there was a clear division of labor in terms of policy jurisdictions between the two congressional chambers. The lower Chamber of Deputies had exclusive rights over the federal budget by constitutional design, whereas the Senate dominated the rest of the policies in practice. Díaz-Cayeros (1998) notes that deputies' exclusive rights over the budget effectively prevented the executive from exercising veto power in budgetary policy.[25] The purpose of this section is thus to assess whether the Chamber of Deputies attempted to influence fiscal policy of the Díaz government after 1890, when Díaz assumed dictatorial powers—that is, whether Congress wanted to be a transformative legislature with active participation in defining policy, independent from executive preferences.

An analysis of budget policy processes complements the previous analysis of senators in assessing congressional–executive relations. To what extent did deputies attempt to influence fiscal policy? If, indeed, there was a network operating as a complementary governance structure to the Mexican Congress, we should see no conflict in congressional–executive relations between the deputies and the president.

First, the Constitution of 1857 did not give both chambers in Congress authority over the federal budget. Exclusive legislative rights over the federal budget were deposited with the lower Chamber of Deputies.[26] In this context, an analysis of budget politics can give us a sense of the interaction between deputies and the executive government. The implication of my theory is that deputies (and Congress, for that matter) should have gone along with executive budget proposals because their differences in budget preferences would have been resolved within the network prior to their ratification through official legislative processes.

For my analysis, I also take advantage of the fact that Porfirio Díaz was not a dictator when he first came to power in 1876. Although the Porfiriato period in its entirety tends to be characterized as a dictatorship (because Díaz did become a dictator), historians have not really specified at which point Díaz consolidates his dictatorship.[27] The evidence suggests that we can pinpoint the transition to a consolidated dictatorship circa 1890. Thus, we actually have two different types of regimes during the Porfiriato period. Between 1876 and 1890 there is a subperiod with a somewhat democratic political system. This democratic period is followed by a consolidated dictatorship that lasts until 1911.

From a historical perspective, the Porfiriato then provides a natural experiment to examine the evidence from two angles. Not only do I look for evidence of more compliance from deputies and less political conflict (with respect to states), but I also check for differences over time to check whether my predictions hold for the dictatorial period after 1890 and not before.

As a first step for this analysis, I collected time series data on the evolution of the federal budget proposals for the period 1867 to 1911 (Carmagnani, 1994, pp. 373–381). These data include three types of budget figures regarding congressional–executive relations: (1) executive proposals, (2) counterproposals by a budget commission within the Chamber of Deputies, and (3) a final budget approved by Congress as whole.[28] The availability of data prior to 1876 is also useful to assess whether the interaction between Congress and the executive branch was subject to structural changes after the regime change in 1876 (involving Díaz's arrival to power and the reinstatement of the Senate).

Before proceeding with the analysis, I classified my budget data set into three subperiods. First, there is the period 1867 to 1875, before Díaz comes to power. The usefulness of this first period is to assess whether deputy constraints change after Díaz comes to power or whether these constraints are similar to those existing under previous administrations. Second, there is the initial period of Díaz's dictatorship before he changed the Constitution to be continuously reelected. During this subperiod, it is plausible that deputy constraints might be operating because Díaz had not yet assumed dictatorial powers. Finally, there is the period 1890 to 1911 of Díaz's consolidated dictatorship, during which we would expect relatively fewer deputy constraints than during the previous subperiod. Note that the use of these subperiods serves only to check for variations in executive power that may have affected the relative strength of the Chamber of Deputies.

The first test I conducted was to check for constraints that the Chamber of Deputies might have imposed on executive budget proposals. I operationalized these constraints by calculating the difference (in 1900 pesos) between the deputies' final budget and the executive government's budget proposal. Henceforth, I refer to this difference as *deputy constraints*. By *constraints*, I refer to the congressional chamber's ability to revise executive proposals. Greater deviations from an original budget proposal would indicate a greater ability of Congress to reject executive proposals.

The next step in the analysis required the formulation of a null hypothesis: What pattern would we expect to see in the budget series if the Chamber of Deputies actually imposed constraints on the executive government? To answer this question, we need to inquire further about the relative preferences of the Chamber of Deputies and the executive government with respect to fiscal policy. Unfortunately, with the exception of a few congresses during the early years of the Porfiriato, there are no roll call data available to estimate deputies' preferences. In an extensive study of fiscal and political development in Mexico from 1850 to 1911, Carmagnani (1994) argues that deputy preferences over the budget varied over time during the Porfiriato. Prior to the period of consolidated dictatorship, there is historical evidence that the executive government wanted to maximize the total amount of the budget, preferring a larger budget than the Chamber of Deputies. After 1890, Carmagnani (1994) notes that the relationship between the executive branch and Congress became more conciliatory, so that deputies routinely concurred with the executive government in approving a highly expansionary fiscal policy (p. 147).

We can use the budget data to further assess Carmagnani's two claims. First, assuming that the dictator preferred a larger budget than the Chamber of Deputies before 1890, then the difference between final and original budget proposals would be negative for the period prior to 1890. Second, we would expect this difference to decrease over time, as deputies imposed fewer constraints on the dictator.

From 1867 to 1911, I identified forty-three different budget proposals. The time series for this measurement are shown in Figure 3.3. Of these, eight proposals occurred before Díaz came to power, fourteen occurred during the first half of his tenure, and twenty-one proposals occurred after he had consolidated his dictatorship. The evidence indicates that, to the extent that there were any deputy constraints, these constraints operated before Díaz came to power, but were no longer binding after he was in power. Before 1876, the average congressional revision was about −6.6 million pesos or −4.7 percent less than the initial executive branch request. Between 1876 and 1990, the average revised budget was about 0.6 million higher, or 1.4 percent. After 1890, Congress would revise the budget upward, on average of 1.8 million pesos, or 3 percent higher than the executive budget proposal.[29]

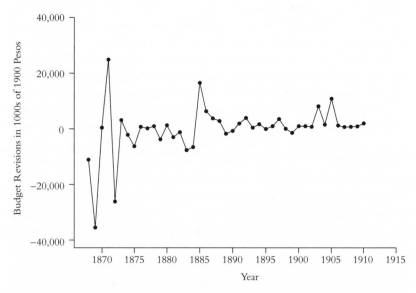

Figure 3.3   Deputy Constraints on the Executive Branch, 1867–1911

Of course, the classification of the data into three subperiods is a very rough instrument to check for the evolution of deputy constraints over time. My purpose is simply to check for structural changes across well-defined subperiods with different regimes. Admittedly, the use of aggregate budget figures obscures many important decision-making processes within Congress. The major reason behind the use of these aggregate data is that congressional documents for the Chamber of Deputies did not include roll calls or other personal information to gauge better the preferences of different deputies.[30]

It is also plausible that the final budget may have been higher for reasons other than a concerted effort by the deputies to cooperate with the executive government. For example, upon receiving an executive proposal, different legislators could have disagreed on the distributional implications of such a proposal, withholding support accordingly unless they obtained some compensation. Compensation to buy votes from affected parties may have, in the end, led to an inflated budget. In such a case, inflated final budgets would not be a reflection of a collective congressional response to the executive branch.[31]

Although the absence of more detailed data prevents me from identifying the actual mechanism producing the final budget outcomes, this limitation does not affect the implications of my analysis. The empirical question at hand is whether the Chamber of Deputies' ultimate budget-related decisions indicated the existence of a concerted effort to modify executive proposals or advance their own budget policy preferences. The results clearly show that the Chamber of Deputies did not constrain the executive government within this policy realm. Whether this lack of constraint was the result of collective action problems is an important consideration, but it does not affect the final conclusion that, for whatever reason, the Chamber of Deputies was very receptive to executive budget proposals.

The lack of a concerted effort does beg, however, the question of the underlying causes preventing deputies from exercising more control over the budget. To address this issue, I conducted a cohesion test within the Chamber of Deputies. Admittedly, I do not have data on individual preferences by each deputy, which would present a more accurate measurement of factions within the Chamber of Deputies.[32] Nonetheless, the available data permit a basic test that speaks to the same question by focusing on two groups: the Budget Commission, which provided a counterproposal to the executive government's proposed budget; and the floor of the Chamber of Deputies, which ultimately approved the final budget.

The sequence that defined the budget started with an executive proposal, which was forwarded to a commission, which in turn forwarded a revised budget for Chamber approval. By checking for differences between the final budget and the intermediate proposal of the influential Budget Commission, we can get a sense of the difference in the preferences of regular deputies versus members of the Budget Commission. I calculated this difference similar to the first test: I measured the difference in 1900 pesos between the final budget and intermediate budget proposal. This measurement can be used as an instrument for lack of cohesion among deputies.

My proposed cohesion measure is important to uncover some of the underlying processes governing the determination of the federal budget. The relevant question in this respect is whether the Chamber of Deputies deferred to executive proposals despite being a more or less divided Chamber.[33] If there is evidence of cohesion, for instance, the implications would be that deputies were willingly deferring to the executive government as a collective body. Alternatively, if we find lack of cohesion, we can infer that the executive government was able to obtain favorable responses to its budget proposals simply because the Chamber of Deputies was so internally divided, that deputies could not have been expected to act as a group to oppose the executive branch.[34]

Figure 3.4 graphs this cohesion measure for the period 1867 to 1911. There are two important features in this figure. First, we see no evidence of a trend, because the graph is fairly flat. The figure indicates that, on average, the Chamber of Deputies agreed with the proposals of the Budget Commission in a similar way throughout the whole period. Second, we

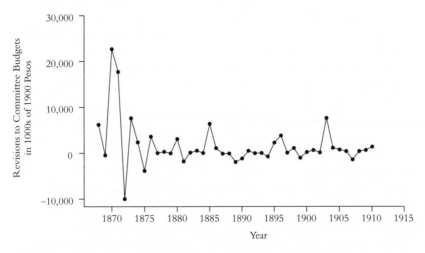

Figure 3.4 Cohesion in the Chamber of Deputies, 1867–1911

do see a lot more variation during the early years, prior to Díaz's arrival to power. The implications of these temporal differences in variation are that the Chamber of Deputies had a more homogeneous group (in terms of budget preferences) after Díaz came to power.

Overall, proposals from the Budget Commission were invariably met with increases in the final, approved budget. In this context, I have no information regarding the relative preferences of members of the Budget Commission vis-à-vis those of floor members, so I cannot make the same assumption that I made previously about executive preferences. It could have been that floor members preferred a higher budget than the Budget Commission, or vice versa.[35] Despite not knowing their relative preferences, the gap in their respective proposals does indicate a difference in underlying preferences, which is useful information for my current purposes. What matters in this analysis is whether there was a systematic difference between the intermediate proposals of the Budget Commission versus the final budget approved by the whole Chamber.

The evidence suggests that there were some differences between these two groups of deputies, but these differences diminished slowly during the Porfiriato. Further analysis in Razo (2003, pp. 99–119) corroborates this statement. There I conducted a nonparametric analysis to check for changes across the three periods defined above. The null hypothesis of equality of means for all subperiods cannot be rejected at conventional significance levels. Similar tests comparing the Porfiriato with the period 1867 to 1874 and comparing the early years of the Porfiriato with the consolidated dictatorship period also failed to reject the null hypothesis of equality.[36] Supplementary regression analysis also clearly indicated that there was no particular trend in how Budget Commission members related to the rest of the Chamber of Deputies. Overall, the substantive implication from this evidence is that the Chamber of Deputies deferred budget authority to the executive government, and this process of deference began before that of the Senate.

4   Conclusion

I set out to examine the political environment in which Díaz operated. I argued that it was not evident that Díaz would become a dictator when he first came to power. In fact, a review of institutions and the political situation of the time suggests that Díaz's tenure could have been just another one of the many weak and short-lived executive governments that had come to power since independence.

As it turns out, Díaz was able to stay in power for a long time, but the establishment of his dictatorship was not an immediate event. This chapter identified three potential sets of veto players that could have constrained executive behavior. Within Congress, there was a Chamber of Deputies and a Senate, with constitutional rights to propose and pass policies in coordination with the executive government. Moreover, the Constitution of 1857 established a federal republic, which empowered state governors with various prerogatives. These provisions, along with a history of powerful regional interests, also placed severe constraints during the early years of the Porfiriato, as the new government sought to remedy one of the main problems in the nineteenth century: political instability.

The available evidence also shows that military conflict became increasingly less of an issue for the dictator, because the share of military expenditures decreased drastically after Díaz had consolidated power (as well as with respect to the period before the Porfiriato). The implication is that former mechanisms for the resolution of political conflict (i.e., military action) were no longer needed given the governance structure set up by the dictator. Both the analysis of military expenditures and the analysis of the determination of the federal budget are consistent with the claim that an informal network acted as the relevant governance structure to conduct business in Porfirian Mexico as will be demonstrated in subsequent chapters.

An analysis of policy-making processes reveals that Díaz did face congressional constraints initially, but the constraints diminished over time. After 1890, Congress apparently became a rubber stamp institution. Both the Senate and the Chamber of Deputies exhibited a tendency to become more complacent with executive proposals, reflecting an underlying process that aligned legislative and executive preferences.

The results from this and the previous chapter raise an interesting puzzle: If legislators consistently deferred to the executive government on economic matters (which dominated the legislative agenda), what incentives did they have to be in Congress? Apparently, being in Congress did not offer any ability to constrain the executive branch even when we know that policies had distributional implications. It is interesting that many of the policies that Díaz passed were private in nature, offering narrow benefits, while sharing costs across all states. Yet, legislators invariably voted in favor of these arrangements. Over time, the Mexican Congress granted more powers to the federal government for the latter to govern by decree and enter into agreements without legislative approval.

To explain the political developments that gave rise to Díaz's dictatorship, we need to answer a series of questions, which are explored in the following three empirical chapters. First, what made the system work? I will argue in Chapter 4 that the main incentive was the generation of rents, or formulation of private policies. In other words, the political establishment worked because its participants benefited while excluding the rest of the population. Second, although the dictator could promise privileges in exchange for support and deference, there remains the question of enforcement. What made Díaz's promises credible? Chapter 5 provides evidence that there was a reliable pool of third-party enforcers who could punish the president even if allowed to attain dictatorial powers. Finally, what was the informal governance structure that aligned the interests of major political actors (and the political and economic elites that they represented)? Chapter 6 shows that the political economy of the Porfiriato was based on a loose coalition of economic and political interests with an encompassing interest in preserving an exclusive network of private protection. The SNA of this last empirical chapter thus reveals in more detail the informal social foundations of Díaz's limited dictatorship.

Chapter 4

Private Policies

What types of policies did Díaz use to promote economic investment? What was the nature of policy making during the Porfiriato? How relevant were private policies? What incentives were there for political and economic actors to support the dictator?

The conventional view in studies of economic history of the Porfiriato suggests that the dictator stimulated economic growth through public policies to attract investment.[1] Among other policies, for example, Díaz is credited with revising commercial codes, enacting banking policies, and redefining property rights (Carmagnani, 1994, pp. 29–33, 49; Katz, 1984, pp. 23–25). All these institutional changes were formally codified in either constitutional changes or enabling legislation. For that reason, it is plausible to think that Díaz resorted to public policies as a generic way to encourage all potential investors.

In contrast to the conventional view, I argue in this chapter that the public appearance of Díaz's institutional changes was merely the formalization of private policy making occurring within a network of protected interests, ratified but not constrained by formal politics. It is an undisputed fact that the policies underlying Díaz's success existed in codified form and were at least nominally sanctioned by formal institutions. In the end, the institutional changes and policies that became law merely formalized what were, in essence, private favors to specific interests. Indeed, it is not surprising that the institutional changes did not take place until after Díaz had consolidated his dictatorship in the 1890s. It was only at that point that he had enough authority to enter into private, lucrative agreements with individual economic actors.

To evaluate the private or public nature of Díaz's policies, I gathered three types of evidence regarding the question of policy definition at different levels of aggregation.[2] First, I examined the general nature of authoritarian government by analyzing *all* known policies and decrees that were passed at the national level after Díaz's dictatorship had been consolidated. Although the central question of my book involves the protection of property rights, this evidence is useful to assess the conduct of government business under Díaz's authoritarian government more generally.

A second type of evidence includes the policies that supported development in Mexico's major industries. In Haber et al. (2003), my co-authors and I established that economic growth during the Porfiriato was based on the protection of big business.[3] These protected interests constituted the network of private protection that enabled Díaz to stay in power while providing incentives for investment and growth. I review these policies to ascertain the terms defining the institutional environment under which Mexico's major firms and economic groups operated. The review of major economic policies is complemented by examining the secondary evidence and previous work on the economic policies of the Porfiriato.

A third type of evidence evaluates the types of policies that particular asset holders obtained during the period 1886 to 1907. Based on primary sources, I evaluated whether particular firms that developed during the Porfiriato received different treatment from the government based on identifiable characteristics. In particular, I assessed whether there was a systematic connection between the generation of rents and the protection that firms received. My analysis shows that different firms obtained different types of benefits even while belonging to the same industry.

Taken together, the historical record provides overwhelming evidence that policy-making processes in Porfirian Mexico were dominated by private agreements between the executive government (sometimes in coordination with state governments) and affected economic actors. It is true that many of the most important policies were devised by and negotiated with industry groups. The purpose of these industry arrangements, however, was not to implement industry agreements indiscriminately with respect to industry members; rather, industry policies set forth the institutional foundations under which economic actors would operate within the network.

In most cases, industry agreements created monopoly rights that benefited only a few. Industry agreements also erected barriers to entry to future entrants. In practice, firms—even those within protected industries such as banking—had to negotiate their property rights on an individual basis in direct proceedings with the government. In sum, the Díaz dictatorship promoted economic growth with a systematic reliance on private policies, in accordance with my theoretical predictions.

To develop my argument, I proceed as follows. In the next section I will assess whether the exercise of government under Díaz was based on public or private policies. To make this assessment, I will analyze an exhaustive listing of policies and decrees for the period 1890 to 1898, when most major economic reforms took place. The following section, "Selective Protection of Big Business," will show that policies were targeted to benefit specific economic groups. This section will also include an analysis of concessions from a comprehensive census of industrial and commercial activity during the Porfiriato. The next major section, "Unprotected Interests," will discuss groups that were not protected under the Díaz dictatorship, and will also include a survival analysis of economic firms to show that small-propertied enterprises were at a disadvantage with respect to the big enterprises that dominated the period. The last section presents my conclusions.

1   Institutional Changes and Policy Specificity

What was the general nature of Díaz's policies? Can we assess the extent to which he relied on public or private policies during the normal course of his authoritarian government? What was the modal type of policy: public or private? Were private policies relegated to economic issues or were they also found in other policy realms?

The Porfiriato is also known for various institutional changes aimed at promoting foreign and domestic investment (Beatty, 2001; Bortz and Haber, 2002; Haber, 1989). Beginning in the 1880s, Beatty (2001) notes that "Porfirian officials undertook a wide range of institutional initiatives in order to facilitate commercial business activity throughout the national economy . . ." (p. 5). A summary of these reforms is shown in Table 4.1.

These reforms have been credited for the success of the Díaz government in encouraging massive foreign investment in infrastructure and capital-intensive industries, promoting domestic investment in various other industries and transforming a predominantly agrarian society with the creation of relatively modern manufacturing and banking sectors (Beatty, 2001; Benjamin and Marcial, 1984, pp. 325–326; Haber, 1989). Conservative estimates of growth in gross domestic product (GDP) during the Porfiriato lie

TABLE 4.1
Major Institutional Changes During the Porfiriato

Year	Policy Domain
1884	New commercial code
	Restructured property rights for subsoils and minerals
1887	Property rights for mineral exploitation and water use
	Changes to commercial code
1888	Introduction of limited liability laws for public corporations
1890	Patent law
1892	Subsoil and minerals
1893	New industries development program
1894	Reforms for mineral exploitation and water use
	Public lands reform
1896	Abolished internal customs
1897	New banking law
1899	Railroad law
1903	Restructured property rights for subsoils and minerals
1905	Modifications to banking law
1908	Modifications to banking law

SOURCE: Compiled from Beatty (2001, pp. 5–6) and the *Mexican Year Book* (1908, pp. 261, 626–645, 653–685).

between 2.1 and 3.3 percent, with a growth rate of 3.3 percent in GDP per capita between 1900 and 1910 (Reynolds, 1970, p. 21).[4]

Despite an apparent laissez-faire approach to economic policy, recent scholarship has also shown that the government exercised much discretion in the implementation of these reforms. Indeed, one major characteristic of economic policy during this period was the high rate of protectionism. Several authors have found very high rates of tariff protection across various sectors of the Porfirian economy (Beatty, 2001, 2002; Kuntz Ficker, 2002; Márquez, 2001). As a cooperative effort between key legislators and the finance minister, José Yves Limantour, broad economic reforms, including the establishment of new tariffs, were passed with the purpose of protecting new industries (Beatty, 2001, p. 7). Not only were tariff rates high, but they were explicitly aimed at increasing the profits of protected industries by lowering the costs of imported factors of production while shielding them from foreign competition (Haber et al., 2003, pp. 128–129).

The fact that there was much protection should not be surprising in light of the fact that dictators cannot make credible commitments to universal protection. Díaz had some dictatorial powers from the beginning of his administration, and these powers gradually increased during the second half of his tenure. I argued in Chapter 2 that under certain conditions dictators can pass credible policies that are amenable to economic development.

Although the intended goal of these policies may be similar to democracies in their attempt to stimulate investment, there is a systematic difference in the types of policies that dictatorships can credibly pass. My theory is not meant to be a general theory of authoritarian government, but, despite its narrow scope about policy credibility, it does generate some useful insights regarding the prevalence of private policies in the exercise of authoritarian government. The main prediction from my theory is that dictators rely largely on private policies or selective protection.

I will proceed to evaluate the hypothesis that dictators can credibly commit only to private rather than public policies. Clearly, an exhaustive analysis of every decision taken by the dictator is beyond the scope of this book. I will focus instead on the narrower question of whether government policies were generally of a private or public nature.

By constitutional design, policies became laws when published in the government's official gazette. Thus, to get a sense of what policies were enacted during the Porfiriato, I collected information on over five thousand decrees published in the official gazette for the period 1890 to 1898.[5] I focused on this period because it was then that Mexico's sweeping economic reforms took place. Also, as I established before, Díaz's dictatorship did not actually begin until circa 1890.[6]

I analyzed my decree data as follows. First, I coded each law or decree in this period by its purported application, as shown in Table 4.2. Second, for each decree, I also recorded the names of private individuals or groups of individuals affected by that policy. When the type of law or decree was difficult to classify, having identified a name determined whether a given policy was targeted to a specific individual or to the general population.

One simple way to estimate the relevance of private policies is to look at the percentage of individualized laws or decrees during the period. In Table 4.2, all but the last category of "Other" are decrees involving private parties. If we take this "Other" category as accounting for public policies, then we can look at the relative share of the remaining categories. This relative share is shown in bold as "Percentage Private."[7]

The percentage of private policies is very high during this period, with an average of 77.2 percent of private policies during 1890 to 1898.[8] One striking feature of Table 4.2 is that all identifiable categories involve very specialized transactions between individuals (or individual firms) and the government. This finding appears to contradict the list of reforms in Table 4.1, which appears to have more of a public, universal character. The evidence from this section does not imply that these reforms were never implemented. However, the specific terms that individuals obtained from appar-

TABLE 4.2
Laws and Decrees, 1890–1898

	Number of Decrees by Year									
Type	1890	1891	1892	1893	1894	1895	1896	1897	1898	1890–1898
Mining concessions	10	46	17	8	6	2	3	3	0	95
Privatization of public land tracts	7	9	1	4	22	27	42	68	36	216
Railroad concessions	14	13	19	39	47	46	31	28	5	242
Public works concessions	1	3	20	52	49	49	29	23	4	230
Naturalizations	1	0	1	1	1	14	9	11	6	44
Patents	20	142	167	126	128	150	165	179	57	1134
Copyrights	10	90	67	53	31	53	54	92	2	452
Receipt of ambassador credentials	8	21	39	36	49	31	21	46	28	279
Small mining concessions	0	0	0	0	1	1	0	0	0	2
Loss of small mines	0	0	0	0	91	376	430	621	122	1640
Other	39	74	56	93	197	184	257	264	115	1279
All decrees	110	398	387	412	622	933	1041	1335	375	5613
Percentage private	**64.5**	**81.4**	**85.5**	**77.4**	**68.3**	**80.3**	**75.3**	**80.2**	**69.3**	**77.2**

SOURCE: Compiled from Azpiroz (1890–1898).

ent public policies were negotiated directly with the government, and thus the terms effectively defined private rather than public policies.

2   Selective Protection of Big Business

This section gives an overview of the policies that stimulated investment in Mexico's major industries. It is based on a detailed study of economic policy during this period from a related project (Haber et al., 2003). A summary is included for the following leading industries in this period: banking, manufacturing, oil, and railways. Agriculture, not discussed here, received variable types of private protection. A larger segment, composed of small landholding and subsistence farming, was not well organized and therefore did not receive much protection. A smaller but more organized segment was oriented toward exportation and operated on a larger scale. This second group obtained protection from local politicians and state governors.[9]

2.1   DOMESTIC INVESTORS

Before the Porfiriato, Mexican governments had a reputation for reneging on their debt obligations. Unsurprisingly, although there was a small group of influential financiers in Mexico, there was no financial system in place that could support the economic development that Díaz wanted to promote.

In addition to his economic goals, Díaz had pressing needs to finance his stay in power during the early years of his tenure, while he sought to restore political stability and get rid of military opposition. For these reasons, the Díaz government engaged in a series of institutional changes that were very favorable to contemporary bankers and financiers.

The basic features of the Mexican financial system were twofold. First, the Mexican government limited the number of national banks to award monopoly rights to well-connected financiers and public officials (Haber et al., 2003, pp. 80–123; Maurer, 2002). In the early 1880s, the government merged two banks to create the dominant bank: the Banco Nacional de México or Banamex (Haber et al., 2003, p. 85). Banamex received various forms of market power and the ability to act as a financial agent for the government. Maurer (2002) notes, however, that Banamex did not operate as a central bank (pp. 52–61).

Banamex was also exempted from fees that applied to other banks. Finally, the 1884 law that created Banamex effectively prevented other competitors from entering the market (Haber et al., 2003, p. 85). Enabling legislation also imposed barriers to entry, and new bank charters had to be approved by the secretary of the treasury. The problem with this requirement for potential entrants was that the secretary of the treasury, José Yves Limantour, happened to be the brother of Julio Limantour, director of Banamex.

Eventually, Banamex's market power had to be shared with another bank, the Banco de Londres y México (BLM), where the minister of finance's brother was a key shareholder. The General Banking Act of 1897 formalized this exclusive arrangement—a duopoly that enabled Banamex and BLM to dominate finance at the national level (Haber et al., 2003, p. 87). The features of this banking law were not surprising, given the close connection between public officials and affected parties. In fact, throughout the period, bankers themselves had a key part in drafting the laws that applied to their industry. Banamex and BLM were then the only two national banks in operation, having crafted a law that prevented future competitors from entering the market (Haber, 2005, pp. 10–14; Haber et al., 2003, pp. 86–87).

A second major feature of the General Banking Act of 1897 was its provision for state-level banks. Although some existing banks were grandfathered under this law, the basic provision of the new banking laws was to allow for only one bank within each state. The selection of this one state bank required the approval of the secretary of the treasury and the Mexican Congress. In practice, the national government, along with state governors, ultimately decided who obtained the bank charter in a given state. The law did not formally exclude other banks from entering state markets, but the

law did impose high capital requirements and other administrative procedures that made it practically impossible for other banks to enter. Hence,
state bank charters had to be obtained in direct negotiations between local
financiers and state and federal officials.

Unsurprisingly, as Read and Musacchio (2001) have shown, the banking
sector was dominated by prominent businessmen and politicians. State governors and other key public officials sat on the boards of state banks, providing protection in exchange for the rents that stemmed from state bank
monopoly positions.

The manufacturing sector was composed of various industries, including
cotton textiles, steel, dynamite, glass, paper, basic chemicals, beer, tobacco,
and cement.[10] One striking feature of their market structure was their high
degree of concentration. Market power in manufacturing also proved to
be rather durable, as evidenced by Mexico's industrial giants whose origins
go back to the lucrative policies they obtained from the Díaz government
(Haber, 1989, p. 27; Haber et al., 2003, p. 125).

Although some of these industries were capital intensive (such as steel
and cement), and thus we would not expect to see a large number of firms,
the fact of the matter is that the allocation of property rights in these industries was not based solely on economic considerations. There is overwhelming evidence that the key players in each of these industries received
market power in response to their political influence and direct economic
benefits that they could provide to the Díaz government.[11] In other words,
the definition of property rights for the influential firms that dominated
these industries was the outcome of direct negotiations between the Díaz
government and private economic actors, despite the public nature of the
institutional changes and economic reforms of the period.

In addition to market power, manufacturing in Porfirian Mexico was
characterized by high levels of protection. Porfirian Mexico had, in fact,
among the highest levels of tariff protection in the world during this period (Beatty, 2002; Kuntz Ficker, 2002). Tariff protection, like all policies,
was crafted in coordination with affected economic groups. Legislative deference to the executive government allowed finance minister José Y. Limantour to offer trade protection on a selective basis to well-connected
industrialists (Haber et al., 2003, p. 129; Márquez, 2001).

2.2 FOREIGN INVESTORS

To attract foreign investment in Mexican oil exploration and exploitation,
the Díaz government resorted to institutional changes to redefine property rights. Prior to the Porfiriato, the Mexican government had retained

exclusive subsoil rights.[12] A series of reforms starting in 1884 through 1909 allowed investors to obtain ownership of subsoil minerals and water.

A critical feature of oil legislation that reflected its private nature involved the procedures to obtain exploration and exploitation concessions. In 1901, a law was passed that gave Díaz special authority to offer concessions without congressional constraints. In addition, the Díaz government offered favorable tax breaks to lower the cost of exploration and exploitation of oil fields (Haber et al., 2003, p. 194). In other words, although there was enabling legislation that had a more public nature (i.e., allowing private individuals to own subsoil property), the implementation of these institutional changes was done at the discretion of the dictator. Both the actual concessions and the tax exemptions were negotiated directly with the executive branch.

The outcome of institutional changes affecting property rights in the oil industry was the rise of two dominant firms, both headed by foreign investors. The largest company, the Mexican Eagle Oil Company, was headed by a British oil magnate, Sir Weetman Pearson. Pearson had previously worked as a public works contractor for the Díaz government, obtaining many of the most important public works concessions of the period (Connolly, 1997). Through his previous work, Pearson, who was a civil engineer by training, was able to establish close relationships with influential businessmen and public officials, including Guillermo de Landa y Escandón, a close associate of Díaz's and mayor of Mexico City. Pearson used his connections to obtain a large concession, accompanied with a generous tax exemption of fifty years (Connolly, 1997, p. 194).

The second largest firm, Mexican Petroleum, was headed by Edward L. Doheny, an oil businessman from California. Doheny had close connections with influential lawyers, like Joaquín Casasús, who was also part of a prominent political family (Haber et al., 2003, pp. 197–198).[13] Doheny was thus able to obtain the first major oil concession, including a ten-year tax exemption. Ultimately, Doheny's company would control about 1.5 million acres of land (p. 194). These two firms (Pearson's as well as Doheny's) also obtained tariff protection against imported and refined oil (Brown, 1993, as cited in Haber et al., 2003, p. 194, fn. 12).

Oil was not the only industry in which foreign investors obtained lucrative concessions. The Díaz government was also particularly interested in railroad construction. Coatsworth (1981) notes that the government initially tried to stimulate this industry through state concessions. During Díaz's first term, for example, twenty states were encouraged to build railroads, but the extent of construction was fairly limited. Díaz realized then that domestic actors were not a reliable source of investment, and proceeded to encourage foreign investment (pp. 37–38).

Foreign investors would deliver the required construction of a national network of railroad lines, which had a positive impact on the economy, but also entailed huge costs. First, to attract foreign investors, the government had to award concessions on very favorable terms, which included monopoly rights, subsidies, and restrictions on the construction of parallel lines. Second, railroad companies would eventually become insolvent toward the end of the Porfiriato, at which point the Mexican government intervened to nationalize most of the railroad industry (Coatsworth, 1981, pp. 38–46).

2.3 HIGHER RENTS AND BETTER CONCESSIONS

The previous section demonstrated that Mexico's leading industries were established on the basis of lucrative concessions that provided market power and rents to beneficiaries. Industry arrangements provided various types of protection to specific interests. One implication of these industry policies is that they could potentially benefit a large set of asset holders at a time. In other words, such private policies at the industry level could have constituted a sort of social or public contract among the government and members of a given industry.

As I have previously noted, these industry arrangements had very restrictive features. Although initiated by groups of asset holders, neither the government nor the asset holders expected these arrangements to provide blanket protection for all asset holders who could potentially benefit from protection in their industry. In fact, one distinguishing feature of all these agreements was the provision of market powers along with provisions to enact barriers to entry to future competitors. The scope of the agreements encompassed whole industries, not because the dictator wanted to provide a universal policy contract to all asset holders in that industry, but rather because the dictator wanted to specify property rights to benefit a few protected firms in that industry.

It is clear that the dominant firms of each industry obtained very lucrative private policies, but there were smaller firms in those industries. Were private policies restricted to the largest firms or the better organized economic groups? Did the provision of private policies stop at the industry level?

To investigate further the customization of economic policies, I collected data on concessions given during the Porfiriato (México, Dirección General de Estadística and Peñafiel, 1908). The data for this section are based on a company registry of 5071 enterprises in Mexico during the period 1886 to

TABLE 4·3

Company Registry Information, 1886–1907

Industry	Average Capital Stock	Average Concession	Corporate Type					
			Public	Collective	*Comandita* Simple	*Comandita* Stock	Cooperative	Total
Arts	56,994	13.8	10	27	6		3	46
Mining	617,808	78.3	599	54	10			663
Manufacturing	123,372	11.5	110	395	81	1	1	588
Agriculture	213,569	24	97	99	28			225
Oil	5,163,769	51.4	15		1			16
Services	128,478	11.1	396	1584	332	3	20	2335
Banking	1,091,527	28.2	34	19	7	1	3	64
Textiles	65,144	13	3	18	5			26
Commercial	32,701	9.8	16	90	17		3	126
Undetermined	883,869	44.7	236	583	141	16	6	982
All Industries	265,875	21.9	1516	2869	628	21	37	5071

SOURCE: Compiled from Mexico, Dirección General de Estadística and Peñafiel (1908).

1907. This information is fortuitously available because the Mexican government was interested in enhancing its tax base, and thus required economic enterprises to register with the government and provide various types of information. The existence of these data is doubly suitable for my purposes. First, it covers the whole period of Díaz's dictatorship, starting in the late 1880s and extending until right before the Mexican Revolution.[14] Second, to the best of my knowledge, this company registry provides a fairly comprehensive listing of all significant economic activity during this period.[15]

For purposes of this project, I collected the following registry variables for each observation: industry, corporate type, domestic or foreign ownership, capital stock (in 1900 pesos), and length of concession.[16] Table 4.3 summarizes this information by industry. Categories in bold type denote industries that were more likely to be concerned about the security of their property rights.

Table 4.3 indicates that the longest concessions were found in the mining and oil industries, both dominated by foreign investors. The more capital-intensive enterprises were located in the banking, oil, and mining industries. These results are not surprising, given the capital-intensive nature of these industries. Especially in mining and oil, the data are consistent with the view that mining and oil companies required fairly long periods for exploration purposes.

The distribution of capital stocks and concessions also varied by corporate type. Public corporations had an average capital stock of 785,132 pesos. Stock companies organized as *comanditas* had corresponding values of 236,749 pesos. The average capital stock for remaining firms was between 36,000 and 42,000 pesos. Interestingly, concession terms did not always correspond to capital stocks. To be sure, public corporations did enjoy better terms, with average concessions of about sixty years. Cooperatives came second, with average concessions of about forty-three years. *Comandita* stock companies had average concessions of about eleven years. The rest had average concessions of about five years.

Overall, we see that public corporations were among those enterprises getting the best concession terms. An intriguing result, however, is that cooperatives obtained fairly long concessions as well. The reason for this finding was that a significant number of cooperatives were in the services industries, dominated by insurance and financial service companies. Although not publicly traded, these enterprises nonetheless required fairly good concession terms to engage in long-term financial contracts.

Another noteworthy fact is that there were significant discrepancies in the capital stocks of domestic and foreign enterprises. I classified enterprises as foreign if they were subsidiaries of foreign corporations.[17] On average, all companies had a capital stock of about 265,000 pesos. Foreign companies, however, had average capital stocks that were orders of magnitude higher, with about 1.8 million pesos as opposed to the average domestic capital stock of 123,000 pesos. In addition, foreign investors got the best concession terms, which were roughly five times longer than for more domestic investors (91.9 years and 18 years respectively).

One testable implication of my theory is that private protection must be associated with higher rents. In terms of the data at hand, the implication is that the length of a concession that an enterprise gets must have been positively related either to its capital stock or the availability of shared profits, as would be the case with companies that issued stock.[18]

I tested this hypothesis by estimating a regression equation of the length of concessions on capital stocks and other company traits. The data on concessions analyzed here should be seen prospectively, as an indication of expectations about future rents. Clearly, as seen here, not all firms survived, but at least at the time that concessions were awarded, there was an expectation that the firm would be around for some predetermined time. The results are shown in Table 4.4.

The results of this regression analysis strongly support the view that companies got better terms when they were expected to produce more rents.[19] The first model inquired about the relative attractiveness of large companies (in terms of their capital stock) and corporations that issued stock (including public corporations and stock *comanditas*). The results are striking. The capital stock provided a modest effect that added about four months to a concession for each additional million pesos in the value of the capital stock. Overall, the independent effect of capital stocks was limited, adding between 0.25 and 0.37 years in the first two specifications for which it is statistically significant, but having a null effect in the third model.

Stock companies, however, were clearly the main beneficiaries. In the first model, being a stock company added almost thirty-one years to a concession. The second and third models add variables to control for differences across industries. Even with the addition of other variables, the effect of corporate type remains both quantitative and statistically significant, with a lower bound estimate of nineteen years.

The second and third models add a dummy variable for foreign ownership. The results, which are corroborated in the third model, show that foreign companies received longer concessions than domestic ones, all things being equal. This advantage ranged from about 7 to 8.5 additional years in concessions.

TABLE 4.4
Determinants of Company Concessions, 1886–1907

Dependent Variable:

Concession in Years

Independent Variables	Model 1	Model 2	Model 3
Capital	0.374**	0.253*	0.00719
	(0.15)	(0.15)	(0.13)
Corporation (stocks)	30.73***	29.98***	19.03***
	(0.81)	(0.82)	(0.80)
Foreign company		8.466***	6.800***
		(1.85)	(1.64)
Mining			37.61***
			(1.33)
Manufacturing			3.090**
			(1.28)
Agriculture			11.28***
			(1.75)
Oil			31.49***
			(5.92)
Services			1.757*
			(0.97)
Banking			13.75***
			(3.39)
Commercial			2.428
			(2.01)
Transportation			30.06***
			(5.26)
Construction and development			18.10***
			(4.00)
Fishing			−6.862
			(21.30)
Communications			15.41**
			(6.20)
Intercept	5.826***	5.734***	2.832***
	(0.53)	(0.53)	(0.83)
Observations	3686	3686	3686
R^2	0.29	0.29	0.45

Standard errors are in parentheses.
***$p < 0.01$, **$p < 0.05$, *$p < 0.1$.

Among industries, the results of the third model also show results consistent with the previous two models. Those industries that required huge investments had, on average, longer concessions. This was particularly the case in the mining, oil, transportation (including railroads and steamships), and communication industries. Coupled with the fact that these industries had major foreign participation, the overall advantage of foreign investors is amplified with a concurrent decrease in the independent effect of capital. For instance, in the expanded third model, foreign companies were estimated to have concessions with about seven more years than domestic ones. In the mining industry, the larger companies actually enjoyed an advantage of about forty-four additional years in comparison to smaller mining enterprises.

Domestic industries that received long concessions also included banking, construction and development, and large-scale agricultural enterprises. The only exception was a relatively small number of fishing companies. Commercial enterprises did not appear to receive preferential treatment as their coefficient is not statistically significant.

3   Unprotected Interests

Not everyone benefited from Díaz's policies. Generally speaking, two groups of people did not receive protection during the Porfiriato. The first, and perhaps the most affected group, included rural populations. A second vulnerable group included smaller enterprises that did not have the resources to hire enforcers or the ability to generate rents that would draw private protection.

Rural populations suffered greatly from industrialization. Underlying Mexico's economic success were major redistributional changes that greatly altered Mexico's land tenure system. Although the distribution of land had been a major issue for the liberals, who dominated politics in the latter half of the nineteenth century, very little redistribution had actually taken place before Díaz came to power (Coatsworth, 1981, p. 187). The Reform laws had called for the abolition of communal lands, as found in Indian villages, in an attempt to promote free enterprise by individuals (see "Political Conditions Before Díaz" in Chapter 3). With the exception of some corporate church property and that of a few conservatives, properties—especially communal ones—had been left intact prior to the Porfiriato.[20] An ongoing process of land concentration throughout the Díaz dictatorship, however, radically altered the rural landscape, leading to masses of dispossessed peasants and Indian villages (Coatsworth, 1981, pp. 5–7; Gómez-Quiñones, 1981, pp. 213–214). Indeed, concerns about land distribution and calls for agrarian reform would provide the major impetus behind the eventual revolution that would bring Díaz down.

Coatsworth (1981) discusses various reasons behind increasing land concentration. Obvious culprits included the dictator's preference for elites and their interests, along with liberals who saw communal property as antithetical to free enterprise. Coatsworth argues forcefully that there were additional incentives for the redistribution of land. One major incentive was speculation in anticipation of higher values for land in close proximity to railways. A second incentive, which was present under Juárez when the Reform laws were promulgated, but intensified during the Porfiriato, was the government's own need to sell public lands for revenue (pp. 149–174).

For purposes of speculation, the main instrument to appropriate property was widespread usurpation of lands, especially among Indian villages. Usurpation occurred either through outright confiscation or legal maneuvering that facilitated the purchase of communal property that, once divided into individual parcels, as prescribed by law, would lose their value.

Coatsworth argues that usurpation of lands was not a novel policy during the Porfiriato. In fact, although there were redistributive effects, there was no official policy to usurp or transfer land from one group to another. Usurpation had become widespread since the somewhat anarchical and unstable situation prior to the Porfiriato, in the absence of a state that could enforce property rights.

Nonetheless, given the Díaz government in promoting the construction of railroads and maintaining peace throughout the country, usurpation was tolerated and perhaps even encouraged locally for the direct benefits that it provided to various political actors. Two prominent examples included the suppression of Indian rebellions, the members of which protested confiscation of their lands in the states of Sonora and Yucatán for purposes of railroad construction projects (Coatsworth, 1981, pp. 5–7).

Usurpations required the complicity of both local officials and rural police forces to suppress property owners who resisted these efforts, so the gains from usurpation would have to be shared with various actors (Coatsworth, 1981, pp. 166–172; Lewis, 2006, pp. 56–59). In addition, usurpation was valuable when lands were acquired at low prices to be later sold at higher ones to railroad companies. Obtaining prior knowledge about future railroad construction was crucial, and could be obtained from published sources, but would have also required tips from better informed public officials.[21]

The second mechanism that facilitated the concentration of land involved the sale of vacant lands (*terrenos baldíos*) in the public domain. Given the government's interests in stimulating foreign investments and export-oriented agricultural activities, these lands were bought by foreigners or large landowners, further concentrating land in fewer hands. Some of the lands were given to foreign concessionaires, especially for railroad concessions and mining enterprises (Coatsworth, 1981, pp. 169–170).

Rural populations that were unable to defend their property rights were historically easy targets. Indian villages, which had never attained political power, had recurrently been subject to the usurpation of their lands dating back to colonial times (sixteenth to eighteenth centuries). The *encomienda* (royal land grants) system under Spanish rule had provided free Indian labor to recipients of land grants. Despite laws aimed at protecting Indian communities (which retained title to their property despite their forced free labor), local governments routinely expanded their property to include the properties of their laborers.[22]

However, Indian villages and peasants were not the only targets. Small-propertied groups suffered similar fates. The sale of public lands was not initiated solely by public officials. In fact, public lands were often sold in response to claims made by private actors. One predictable outcome of private claims entailed disputes made by powerful interests that disputed the property rights of less privileged actors. The use of eminent domain served not just to sell public lands, but to adjudicate property to powerful landowners. In the end, predation against rural interests involved not just the appropriation of Indian lands, but also the properties of small farmers or *rancheros* (Lewis, 2006, pp. 56–59).

Rural populations were not the only disadvantaged groups. The rest of this section explores the systematic inability of small-propertied enterprises to flourish under the Porfiriato. The population under study here is the same sample used for the study of concessions, but the focus here is on survival. The reason behind this analysis is to understand which types of firms were more likely to succeed, independent from their concessions. But concessions alone do not determine profits. Neither do concessions guarantee that firms will continue to operate until the end of their concessions.[23]

3.1 COMPANY DISSOLUTIONS

About 16 percent of the firms included in the official 1886 to 1907 company registry were dissolved before the end of the Porfiriato. The availability of these data enables us to check for the determinants of survival. What determined the ability of firms to survive during this period?

One implication of my theory is that higher rents are needed to pay for private protection. Hence, companies with prospects for higher rents would be more likely to survive than others.[24] To test this hypothesis I conducted a survival analysis using capital (in millions of pesos) as a proxy for rents. I included additional covariates such as industry and corporate type to determine whether survival differed by type of company. The results of this statistical analysis are shown in Table 4.5. [25]

TABLE 4.5
Survival Analysis, 1886–1907

	Model 1	Model 2	Model 3
Capital	0.0661***	0.445*	0.463
	(0.03)	(0.22)	(0.26)
Foreign company		0.107***	0.111***
		(0.06)	(0.06)
Corporation		0.389***	0.477***
		(0.04)	(0.05)
Company × foreign		2.023	1.549
		(1.14)	(0.99)
Capital × corporation		0.763	1.014
		(0.42)	(0.68)
Mining			0.222***
			(0.06)
Manufacturing			1.327***
			(0.13)
Banking			1.619
			(0.49)
Oil			1.102
			(1.11)
Agriculture			0.8
			(0.17)
Observations	5019	5019	5019
Failures	795	795	795
Log likelihood	−6472	−6385	−6355
χ^2	125.5	299.5	359.8

Standard errors are in parentheses.
***$p < 0.01$, **$p < 0.05$, *$p < 0.1$.

The hypothesis that high rents increased the likelihood of survival is borne out by the data. In a baseline model with capital as the only covariate, I obtained a statistically significant coefficient at the 5 percent level, which indicated that an increase of one million pesos in capital made it 93 percent less likely that a firm would be dissolved. The relative risk increases after we control for other variables, but the effect of capital remains qualitatively the same: A one million peso increase in capital makes dissolution about 55 percent less likely.[26]

The type of firm also had a systematic effect on survival. Being foreign, for example, lowered the risk of dissolution by about 90 percent. In addition, being a corporation, as opposed to a partnership or cooperative, lowered the risk to between 41 percent and 52 percent. I included two interaction terms to capture the fact that foreign firms and corporations were likely to have large capital stocks. The two interaction terms were statistically nonsignificant.

These results indicate that the effect of capital was more general and was not restricted solely to foreign firms or corporations. All things being equal, having more capital, and the concomitant increase in potential rents, increased the prospects of survival.

These results on the importance of capital are robust to further differentiation of firms. Using the third model, I introduced selected dummy variables to identify key industries in the sample. First, we see that the effect of foreign firms and corporations remains basically the same. Second, we see that not all industries were equally vulnerable. The only two statistically significant coefficients corresponded to the mining and manufacturing industries. Mining firms were about 78 percent less likely to dissolve. There is evidence that smaller mining operations faced huge risks and had to dissolve, but the large, foreign mining firms that dominated the market were relatively secure. Manufacturing firms in contrast were 33 percent *more* likely to be dissolved.

Further examination of the historical record on federal decrees and policies discussed in the first section, indicates that property rights were in flux and generated many disputes—so much so that of 5613 laws and decrees, 1640 (29 percent) involved the loss of property rights to small mines. Clearly, prospecting was a risky enterprise for which more capital would have been more useful. But these statistics show that it was not just a question of capital.

The distribution of mining concessions was heavily centralized, as was the case for the oil industry (Haber et al., 2003, pp. 234–284). "The 1884 mining code ... made the awarding and regulation of mining concessions a federal, not a state, affair" (pp. 241–242). Hence, property rights in the mining industry had to be negotiated directly with the executive government.

As with previous industries, the discretionary powers of the executive branch led it to award big concessions to selected economic groups. Unlike the oil industry, which had relatively greater capital requirements, mining activity could be performed on various scales. Thus, there was a significant number of small mining concessions, although the industry was very concentrated. In terms of economic significance, the small concessions were dwarfed by "a small number of foreign-owned mining companies ... [which] dominated the production of Mexico's most important products—silver, lead, and copper" (Haber et al., 2003, p. 247).

Property rights were important, and small mines were unable to secure those rights. The documents do not allow an examination of systematic causes for the loss of property, but we do know that the ability to protect property rights was contingent on political connections, and the government systematically favored its allies and powerful interests. Note that laws and decrees showed very few mining concessions. The implication being that the smaller mines belonged to actors with prior property rights, not new concessionaires.

4 Concluding Remarks

This chapter checked whether the policies of the Porfiriato were private or public in nature. To assess the nature of policies, I analyzed three bodies of evidence. The first body of evidence looked at all laws and decrees for the period when most major institutional changes took place, and found that the modal policy was one of a private nature.

The second body of evidence showed that industry policies provided very specific benefits that gave monopoly rights to select economic groups, while enacting barriers to entry to future competitors. In other words, although agreements were at the industry level, the benefits were targeted at specific individuals or firms.

Additional evidence of private policy making was obtained by evaluating the terms that specific firms obtained. By evaluating an exhaustive listing of economic enterprises during the period 1886 to 1907, I established that there was a systematic variation in the specific terms that enterprises obtained, and in survival rates, even when located in the same industry. In summary, the results of this section provide strong support for my hypothesis that firms with higher expected rents (as proxied by their capital stocks) were more likely to obtain better concession terms and last a longer time.

During the Porfiriato, investors faced a comfortable and predictable institutional environment that encouraged long-term investment and economic growth. More generally, dictators who want to make (selective) credible commitments must provide incentives for other influential political actors to support their regime. The main instrument will be the provision of rents as opposed to repression. The source of rents will be an important variable in determining the possibility of sustaining limited dictatorships. If the source of rents, as was the case under Díaz, is future growth, dictators will have to make greater concessions and be willing to tolerate other influential actors. To the extent that these rents come from the investments that the dictator wants to promote, however, the enforcers will be bought with resources that they themselves helped to create. Having to share private rents puts a dictator in a more vulnerable position than if he possessed independent resources to support himself.

The success and persistence of the alliance between government and investors was the result of two mutually reinforcing mechanisms. First, the
political support obtained by directly involving private economic groups in
drafting laws for their own self-interest had multiple purposes. It was indeed
necessary to legitimize Díaz's continuous reelections with the distribution
of rents, but it was also important for political purposes. The added benefit
of selective economic concessions was that they neutralized the opposition
of less privileged groups, such as peasants, who had previously relied on
middle-class and elite groups for guidance and mobilization.

Concentration of political power was essential in framing the expectations of the investment community about the continuity of their government allies. A disorganized peasantry ensured that no other groups with
opposite interests would gain the exclusive favor of government. In addition, Díaz's political maneuvering ensured a careful selection of government officials who supported the dictator and the new policies that were
favorable to investors. Investors could thus rely on a stable government with
views that would not change in the foreseeable future.

Chapter 5

Stable Pool of Private Enforcers

1 Dictators and Long-Term Commitments

By the 1890s, the Mexican government believed that the country had been pacified and was ready to embark on a national development program (Reyes, 1903, pp. 291–295). Both domestic and foreign investors stood to gain from lucrative investment opportunities to jump-start the economy and create new industries. Along with stability, however, formal institutions appeared to have given way to a dictatorship.

The authoritarian nature of the political system created two problems for economic and political actors. For investors, there remained uncertainty about the security of their property rights, especially because they were lucrative, and with Díaz's proven capacity to suppress political competition, the threat of predation was indeed very real. But even if investors trusted Díaz, there remained a political question regarding his stay in power. Given Mexico's tumultuous nineteenth century history, how long would this new dictatorship last?

In the long run, the security of investors' property rights depended not just on persistent incentives to forgo predation, but also on the longevity of the dictatorship. Indeed, the longevity of the dictatorship has been identified as a crucial requirement for dictators to promote growth. Although Olson (2000) did not directly address the issue of policy credibility, his theory of stationary banditry nonetheless identifies long-term horizons as one of two requirements that induce dictators to promote economic growth.

The reasoning behind Olson's (2000) condition is clear. With short-term horizons, dictators have an incentive to confiscate as much property as possible before they leave office. Even long, finite horizons fail to provide the right incentives because governments are prone to an end-of-game effect after which there is no future. Dictators can promise to protect property rights in earlier time periods, but investors will eventually realize that the dictator's tenure is about to end, and hence they will not deem any promises to be credible.

The network theory of private protection provides another rationale for Olson's time horizon requirement. Because selective protection entails selective exclusion, the protection of private policies is inherently a dynamic problem. Property rights can be diminished either by direct predation or through indirect means if privileges are later dispensed to new actors. If dictators are to make a difference in economic performance, they must continually commit to forgo predation *and* to protect long-term investments against current and future competition. Dictators thus need a long-time horizon, not just to restrain themselves from predation, but because they are also the source of special privileges for investors.

Although dictators themselves can incorporate new actors—a form of reneging—the main threat of future competition arises when dictators are overthrown. All things being equal, investors would therefore prefer a long (and credible) dictatorship, but Olson notes that elongating a dictator's time horizon is difficult. Indeed, all dictatorships face a critical problem affecting their time horizon: the problem of succession. What happens after the dictator dies? There may be replacement mechanisms in place, generally involving the designation of an heir or close associate to take over, but there is no guarantee that the mechanism will select a dictator with the same incentives and capabilities. Therefore, as a basic requirement to promote growth under dictatorship, dictators must assure investors that the dictatorship is long-lived.

For sustained growth to occur, it is thus required that there be a governance structure that allows the dictator to manage multiple commitments that arise from offering private policies to various actors. The more commitments there are, the greater the scope of economic activity that the dictator can sustain. Specifically, for this governance structure to encourage long-term, selective credible commitments, it must ensure not only that the dictator stays in power for a long time, but it must also ensure the existence of a long-lived pool (or critical mass) of private enforcers.

Although the continued existence of private enforcers is desirable to make credible commitments, the dictator must now be wary of the political ambitions of these actors. By definition, private enforcers are identified by their ability to punish the dictator. The dictator would prefer a large pool to increase the scope of economic activity that can be sustained with private policies. But if private enforcers are able to organize or otherwise enable collective action, they could bring down the dictatorship.

Dictators thus face a dilemma between ensuring that there is a pool of private enforcers that guarantees the generation of rents, and at the same time preventing these enforcers from turning against them. This dilemma is slightly different from Wintrobe's (1998) dictator's dilemma, which is about managing insecurity to stay in power. The problem I address here is a corollary of Weingast's (1995) *credibility dilemma,* because the source of rents that can be used to buy loyalty of others is contingent on the existence of actors who make the dictator more insecure. In other words, for the sake of credibility rather than safety, the dictator may have to deliberately *increase* insecurity rather than decrease it. Political tolerance must itself be credible, however, so the dictator must devise rules that guarantee access to and endurance of others' political power. Formal institutions can serve this purpose by populating them with influential actors. Put another way, the dictator will share power with influential actors because the latter can serve as guarantors of private policies.[1]

Was there evidence of a persistent governance structure? Was there a reliable pool of private enforcers? One way to assess both the existence of a pool of enforcers and their durability is to analyze political career and mobility prospects. The historical evidence clearly shows that Díaz allowed other actors to become active participants in the political system. Historians have long noted that Díaz maintained himself in power with the use of strategic concessions to officials at all levels of government. There was therefore room for public officials at state and local levels to provide protection in exchange for rents from local economic activity. Katz (1984) aptly summarizes the incentives behind opportunities for private gain by state and local government officials, as follows:

> ...Díaz encouraged or at least allowed...the *caciques* in power...to enrich themselves by acting as intermediaries for foreign investors who wished to settle in these regions or to acquire property there. In this way, Díaz gave the members of the local oligarchy...a powerful stake in the stability of the region. (p. 37)

This quote does not specify the role of formal institutions. The evidence presented in the rest of this chapter will make it clear that political concessions were indeed formalized by enabling influential political actors to become public officials. The next section, "General Profile of Public Officials," gives an overview of public officials to understand their selection. Although public officials were formally elected, and the system was nominally a democracy, public officials were not representative of the general population. Moreover, public officials were not chosen randomly, and had considerable influence and connections, which would have enabled them to assist in both the formulation and enforcement of private policies. The major section titled "Long-Lived Pool of Private Enforcers" of this chapter analyzes political careers within the system to argue that there were ample opportunities for long careers and upward mobility. The last section concludes this chapter with an assessment of the role of formal institutions in enabling the longevity of the dictatorships and associated elites, both of which benefited from sharing rents and power.

2   General Profile of Public Officials

2.1   SOCIOECONOMIC BACKGROUND

This section will examine broader patterns regarding the social background of public officials during the Porfiriato. It will sketch a profile of the public officials that Díaz appointed during this tenure based on Roderic Ai Camp's extensive work on political recruitment and politicians in Mexico.[2]

This section will show that the political system was dominated by elite networks. Indeed, many private enforcers came from prominent families. How did socioeconomic factors affect who attained public office during the Porfiriato? What were the socioeconomic characteristics of the pool of potential private enforcers?

Table 5.1 indicates that a significant number of public officials came from well-to-do families. The middle column, which combines officials from the middle class and upper class of the period, indicates that Díaz relied heavily on the political participation of wealthier citizens.[3]

To the best of my knowledge, there are no systematic data on income inequality during this period, but there are a couple reasons to believe that the middle and upper classes in Porfirian Mexico were relatively small. First, from a historical perspective, Mexico has a long history of income inequality, with a high concentration of economic and political power in a small elite (Anna, 1984; Katz, 1984). Whatever the amount of inequality was there at the beginning of the Porfiriato, this inequality was only exacerbated by Díaz's exclusive policies. Indeed, economic inequality is prominently advanced as a major cause of the eventual revolution of 1910 that would overthrow the Díaz regime (Katz, 1984, pp. 65–78).

TABLE 5.1
Socioeconomic Background of First-Time Officeholders, 1884–1910

Starting Year for Presidential Term	Social Origins (%)	
	Middle and Upper Classes Combined	Upper Class Only
Díaz		
1884	77	29
1889	82	39
1893	82	41
1897	90	53
1901	95	36
1905	90	65
1910	67	17
1884–1910	*83*	*40*

SOURCE: Adapted from Camp (1995b, Table 6.8, p. 174).

A second related reason is that the emergence of a middle class of professionals (lawyers, doctors, and so forth) was a relatively new phenomenon during the Porfiriato (Katz, 1984). In other words, there was a small wealthy elite prior to the Porfiriato, which was joined by a growing—yet limited in size—professional community, located primarily in the Mexico City area.

Along with wealth, public officials had considerable political influence, inherited through family connections. Table 5.2 shows the percentage of politicians with relatives in national offices (in Congress or the executive branch of government). The average share of officials with relatives involved in national politics was 43 percent for the period 1884 to 1910.

This average share is biased downward a bit by the fact that there is a much smaller percentage during Díaz's last administration (which started in late 1910 and lasted less than a year). If we calculate the average share

TABLE 5.2
Family Political Ties, 1884–1910

Starting Year for Presidential Term	Politicians with Relatives in National Politics (%)
Díaz	
1884	39
1889	61
1893	42
1897	57
1901	42
1905	38
1910	25
1884–1910	*43*

SOURCE: Adapted from Camp (1995b, Table 6.11, p. 182).

TABLE 5.3

Family Occupations of Mexican Political Leaders, 1884–1910

Starting Year for Presidential Term	Father's Occupation (%)						
	Professional	Landowner	Manual Laborer	Politician	Military Officer	Businessman	Other
Diaz							
1884	17	21	17	17	17	11	0
1889	5	14	19	33	14	14	0
1893	18	29	18	12	6	12	0
1897	13	37	7	7	20	17	0
1901	15	10	0	40	10	15	10
1905	6	38	0	25	19	13	0
1910	0	0	25	50	0	25	0
1884–1910	*11*	*21*	*12*	*26*	*12*	*15*	*1*

Averages for 1884 to 1910 may not add up to 100 because of rounding errors.
SOURCE: Adapted from Camp (1995b, Table 6.9, p. 178).

without considering Díaz's last few months, then the share increases from 43 percent to 46.5 percent. In other words, the probability that any given public official would have a relative in a high office was almost 0.5, implying very close family connections within the political class.

If we look at a public official's immediate rather than extensive family, we see a similar connection. Table 5.3 summarizes the occupational background of public officials' fathers. During the period 1884 to 1910, the largest share of public officials (26 percent) came from political families. The second largest share of fathers' occupations included landowners (21 percent), who were known to have close connections to their local and state governments (Haber et al., 2003, pp. 285–341).

2.2 OCCUPATIONAL EXPERIENCE

As seen before, the typical socioeconomic background of a public official was that of a relatively well-to-do official with close political connections, likely a father with political experience and relatives in national offices. In this section, I will look more closely at the experience that public officials brought when they assumed public office. In particular, I will look at government experience at the local level, business experience, and military experience. Of the three, military experience played an important role in the selection of public officials (along with the maintenance of the political system by military coercion).

Table 5.4 shows three major types of experience that were sought after during the Porfiriato. First, Díaz recruited a large percentage of public officials with previous experience at the local level. This is not a surprising result given Díaz's well-known strategy of co-opting local leaders to support his regime. What is interesting, however, is that these data suggest that there was upward mobility even for lower level public officials, not just those in higher offices.

Second, although the shares of businessmen are relatively smaller, they nonetheless reflect a very active participation of economic actors in government. On average, one out of five public officials in the Porfiriato had experience in the private sector prior to assuming office. (Indeed, the most influential public officials often had concurrent political and business positions.) Last, but not least, we see a very high percentage of public officials with military experience. As I have noted before, Díaz relied heavily on his military connections to pacify the country, especially during the earlier years of his tenure (thus the relatively higher percentages in the 1880s).

The last type of experience, in military positions, is especially relevant, given the prominence of governors in Díaz's network of private protection. Many state governors were or had been generals in the Mexican army. The role of the military during the Porfiriato period has not received much attention as a subject in its own right.[4] One reason for this omission is the limited, or passive, role that military officials have had with respect to other political actors in modern times.[5] It was certainly the case that the Díaz government was not a military junta, and the role of the army was limited to pacification efforts to restore political stability. Nonetheless, as part of Díaz's

TABLE 5.4
Previous Experience of First-Time Officeholders, 1884–1910

Starting Year of Presidential Term	Local Officeholders (%)	Businessmen (%)	Military Officers (%)
Díaz			
1884	40	21	54
1889	42	18	46
1893	42	20	32
1897	38	27	16
1901	42	17	11
1905	36	17	9
1910	29	18	35
1884–1910	*38*	*20*	*29*

The rows do not add up to 100 for two reasons. First, when the rows exceed 100, it is because of overlapping among the three categories. Second, when the row sum is less than 100 (as for the 1884–1910 average), it is because there are other categories (such as landowners, professional experience, and so on) not included in the original tables.

SOURCE: Adapted from Camp (1995b, Table 5.1, p. 126; Table 5.4, p. 132; and Table 5.5, p. 136).

strategy to pacify the country, he relied on military personnel to assume political positions.

Many governors during this period were, in fact, generals in the Mexican
Army. For that reason, it is important to consider the role of the military to
understand the coercive nature of Díaz's network. Díaz himself was a general
and had risen up through the ranks as a result of his distinguished military
career, fighting for the liberal movement and against the French invasion of
the 1860s. Díaz, therefore, had considerable respect as a military figure, which
would explain why influential network players would not rebel against the
dictator. What the generals offered was additional protection against political
opposition that would disrupt the political equilibrium of the Porfiriato.[6]

Camp (1992) notes that the military has had a long history of participation in public office, but that participation was much higher in the nineteenth than in the twentieth century. Table 5.5 summarizes one of Camp's
(1992) most important findings. A striking feature of this table is the high
percentages of military officers during the Porfiriato. For the first half of
the Porfiriato (until the early 1890s), one in two public officials in the Porfiriato had a military background. This percentage decreases steadily, reaching a low point of 26 percent by 1910. However, this low percentage still
indicates that one of every four public officials had a military background
by the end of the Porfiriato. Overall, it is clear that Díaz had to accommodate not just prominent business elites, but also important members of the
military whose coercive power could help him stay in power.

TABLE 5.5
Military Experience

Years	Percentage	Years	Percentage
1885–1888	55	1924–1928	34
1888–1892	51	1928–1930	29
1892–1896	44	1930–1932	32
1896–1900	34	1932–1934	33
1900–1904	30	1935	24
1904–1910	26	1935–1940	27
1911	25	1940–1946	19
1911	22	1946–1952	8
1911–1913	24	1952–1958	14
1913–1914	50	1958–1964	15
1914–1915	64	1964–1970	7
1914–1920	46	1970–1976	10
1920	35	1976–1982	6
1920–1924	40	1982–1988	5

Shaded years denote Porfiriato years.
SOURCE: Camp (1992, Table 4.1, p. 67).

2.3 CONNECTIONS TO ELITE NETWORKS

The previous section hinted at the close connection between public officials and economic elites. In addition to providing a critical monitoring and enforcement role on behalf of the firms they protected, there were, in many cases, additional connections having to do with previously established personal or business relationships.

Although they are not the focus of this book, elite networks did have a role in the system of exclusive privileges that prevailed during the Porfiriato. Access to public office depended heavily on economic prestige. Hence, we cannot really talk about public officials without also addressing their connections or role as economic elites. In fact, although we lack systematic sources of individual portfolios to examine where public officials invested their own assets, the historical literature does identify several prominent political actors as asset holders themselves (e.g., the Terrazas-Creel clan in the state of Chihuahua).

Given the small number of economic and political elites, it is not surprising that many of them were related, but what was the extent of these connections? As it turns out, there was a great deal of overlap between political and economic elites. Not only did the latter provide a steady supply of public officials, but even while in office, public officials maintained close connections with economic elites (not restricted solely to relatives). The distribution of power that prevailed during the Porfiriato was one in which a fairly cohesive group of political and economic actors shared decision making and awarded themselves special privileges at the expense of the general population, as will be seen in the following chapter.

As noted in the introductory chapter, the mechanism that brought credibility to Díaz's policy pronouncements was a network of private protection. This network was built on the basis of the mutual interests of asset holders who wanted rents, and public officials who used their political power to enforce private deals and share those rents. But public officials and economic actors were not always clearly distinguishable. The rest of this section will give a preview of relevant network relations that were important in formulating and protecting private policies. I emphasize that these connections do not represent the core theoretical relation of overlapping protection presented in Chapter 2, but they do illustrate the social context that enabled private protection.

Generally the term *elite networks* refers to privileged groups in society that interact with one another while excluding the rest of society. The network–analytic approach of this book requires a more specific definition beyond simply a collection of people. The rest of this section will address the connection between elite networks and Díaz's network of private protection with an SNA of personal relations. To analyze personal relations, I collected data from historical sources on various types of personal relationships between two people (e.g., whether they related to each other or were friends) as well as business relationships (whether two people were business partners or co-owners of a given company). When I use the term *elite networks,* I refer specifically to the resulting pattern of social connections or the social structure involving both people and their connections (not just a distinctive group of people).

I was able to identify 352 personal ties from the existing historical literature. I should note that this type of relational data is not widely available, and so it is more difficult to establish a complete picture of how social relations affected the political economy of the Porfiriato. The following results are indicative of the important role that elite networks played during the Porfiriato, but the evidence shown here probably underestimates the existing connections.[7]

One way of examining elite networks is to look at social relations. For that purpose, I reviewed the historical literature and was able to identify 282 ties of a social character. My coding strategy allowed for family and friendship relations. In the following text, I provide an overview of the structural properties of social relations and highlight the presence of public officials.[8]

The density estimate for this network is 0.008, suggesting that there were not many connections spanning large groups of participants. One feature of this network, as shown in Figure 5.1, is the visualization of various family clusters. Many names in this sociogram would be readily recognizable to students of the Porfiriato. For instance, in the lower left quadrant of the diagram, there is a cluster of elites related to the Madero family (which included the governor of Coahuila and the president who succeeded Díaz in 1911). On the opposite side, there is a cluster of elites related to the Quijano-Rivero family group, which was one of the predominant economic groups of central and south–central Mexico, along with other groups like the Díaz Rubin, Mendirichaga, and Hernandez families, also shown in Figure 5.1.[9]

In terms of the number of connections, the most central players included a list of the most important economic and political elites of the time, as seen in Table 5.6. Among the central players, one finds the most prominent public officials of the period. As will be seen in Chapter 6, these public officials are key in the construction of an exclusive network of private protection, given their multiple connections to other influential officials.

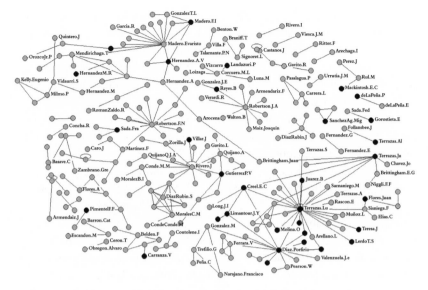

Figure 5.1 Structure of Social Relations
Nodes in black denote federal public officials or governors during the
Porfiriato, in addition to former and future presidents Sebastián Lerdo de
Tejada, Francisco I. Madero, and Venustiano Carranza. Nodes are not indi-
vidually identified when a relative with the same surname is already named
among its immediate neighbors.

TABLE 5.6
Centrality of Social Relations

Representative Node	Degree	Frequency	Frequency (%)
José M. Botello, Jr.	1	150	58.14
Miguel Ahumada	2	53	20.54
Carlos Bracho	3	19	7.36
Felipe Arellano	4	13	5.03
Francisco I. Madero	5	7	2.71
Enrique C. Creel	6	5	1.94
Juan Terrazas	7	3	1.16
Felix Mendirichaga	8	2	0.76
Joseph A. Robertson	9	1	0.39
Felipe N. Robertson	12	1	0.39
Porfirio Díaz	14	1	0.39
Evaristo Madero	16	1	0.39
Jesús Rivero	18	1	0.39
Luis Terrazas	28	1	0.39

"Degree" denotes the number of individual connections.
SOURCE: The author's own compilation of social connections.

A second way of examining elite networks is to look at business relations. In contrast to social relations, evidence of business connections is sparse. I identified seventy business ties between eighty-seven economic and political actors. The condition to establish such a tie between two actors was that they be either business partners or co-owners of some enterprise. Of these seventy ties, twenty involved a public official.[10]

Mapping the structure of this business network, Figure 5.2 shows a relatively dense network with certain node members that bridge various clusters. For example, Enrique Creel (Creel.E.C) serves to connect one group of northern elites with other family members and economic actors from other regions. Other prominent public officials, like Fernando Pimentel y Fagoaga (Pimentel.F.F), are also featured in this elite network. Other than governors, my database does not include information on state-level officials, however, so the diagram does not capture all political influence. For instance, General Gerónimo Treviño, a former governor of the state of Nuevo León, is shown here as a private actor. Along with his family, Treviño remained influential at the state level, but did not hold a governorship or federal office during the Porfiriato.

The structure of this network is similar to that of social relations. First, the low density of 0.019 indicates a fairly local character to most connec-

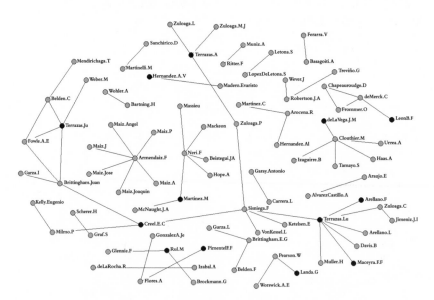

Figure 5.2   Structure of Business Relations
Nodes in black denote public officials or governors during the Porfiriato.

tions. Just like social relations, however, there are a few actors with broader participation. Among the central players, we can find members of the influential Terrazas-Creel clan that dominated Chihuahuan politics, as well as other northern economic elites like the Brittingham family (close friends of the Terrazas).[11]

A rich collection of regional historical studies has recognized the close link between economic and political elites.[12] Gutiérrez Alvarez (2000) has noted, for example, that there was a spatial component that brought political and economic actors together. Political actors with relative autonomy dominated their local economies with support of local elites. Examples of influential political–economic elites include the following family groups: the Terrazas-Creel clan in the state of Chihuahua; the Madero, Garza, and Zambrano families in northern Mexico; and the Molina clan in the southeastern state of Yucatán. Despite their regional character, these elites were connected to one another, either through marriage or political connections or by ethnic networks (Gamboa Ojeda, 2000, pp. 181–189; Gutiérrez Alvarez, 2000, pp. 55–59; Haber, 1989, p. 187).

3   Long-Lived Pool of Private Enforcers

The previous section suggests that public officials were important participants in elite networks. Economic elites in particular could potentially make use of public officials to guarantee selective commitments obtained from the dictator. I argue in this book that, in fact, public officials were key in constraining government opportunism. To establish this claim, one must ensure that public officials were not only temporarily influential, but that they would be long-lasting sources of third-party enforcement. These considerations invite a more detailed analysis of political careers—the subject of this section.

To assess mobility prospects of public officials, I constructed a database of political careers for 1691 public officials during the period 1876 to 1911. For each of these 1691 public officials, I collected information on the various government positions they held at any time within this thirty-five-year period. These government positions included congressional positions (deputy and senator), state-level positions (governors), and executive positions (subcabinet, cabinet, and ambassadors).[13] Each position corresponded to one observation in my sample, and I collected 6153 observations of variable lengths.[14] For each observation, I coded for the position's type, office holder, and length of time in office, along with regional information for congressional and governor positions. I collected all positions held by a given official to construct a "chain" of positions in chronological order. This sequence of positions constitutes a *political career*.

This analysis provides a retrospective view of political careers for the whole period, but does not always give a sense of the incentives that public officials might have had at particular times during the course of the Porfiriato. To look more closely at the evolution of political careers at different times, I focus on political mobility. By looking systematically at the possibilities of career advancement for different types of positions, one obtains a better assessment of the relevance of political incentives during the Porfiriato.

The evidence shows that there was a well-developed and stable system of political careers. For one, there is evidence of influential public officials who held offices for long periods of time, including governors as well legislative and executive officers. Moreover, my political mobility analysis shows that there were opportunities for career advancement that provided incentives for public officials to cooperate with the dictator. In fact, many of the officials with long tenures were also members of a social network that distributed economic rents. Chapter 6 indicates that prominent officials used their long-lived careers to obtain economic, not political, benefits. To the extent that they had political aspirations, it was because political office enabled this select group to enrich itself.

To assess the placement and mobility of public officials, I collected data on the careers of all governors and federal public officials during the Porfiriato. I will first describe some salient features of my data set in terms of the length of positions and careers. The descriptive analysis will be followed by a statistical analysis of political mobility, the primary method to assess the incentives of public officials to work with the dictator rather than overthrowing him.

3.1 OVERVIEW OF POLITICAL POSITIONS

The 1691 public officials in my data set held an average of 3.6 positions during the Porfiriato. My data include a mix of fixed and variable lengths. Deputies and senators served about twenty-month terms encompassing four sessions within a two-year congressional period. The Constitution prescribed that governors had similar terms to that of the president (four-year terms during 1876–1904; a six-year term starting in 1904). In practice, however, the record on the length of gubernatorial positions shows a lot of variability, with some gubernatorial positions lasting much less than four years whereas others lasted for decades.

The average length was 22.3 months (roughly one year ten months), with a standard deviation of 14.2 months (one year two months). In fact, only 2.2 percent (138 of 6153) of the positions lasted less than a year. Most positions other than congressional ones had variable lengths, ranging from a minimum of four days to a maximum of twenty-seven years four months.

To get a sense of which types of public officials had the longest positions, I compiled a list of positions with a length that exceeded fifteen years, roughly about half the dictatorship period. This list is shown in Table 5.7 An interesting feature of this table is that it is dominated by governors.[15] When we consider the governor's state and region (shown in parentheses), however, the list does not appear to be dominated by any particular region.[16]

We can also examine political careers in terms of accumulated seniority, or years in public office. This cumulative measure is calculated by adding the length of all individual positions held by one person. There is huge variability

TABLE 5.7

Public Officials with the Longest Positions

Name	Office Level	First Year	Length of Position in Years
1. Próspero Cahuantzi	Governor (Tlaxcala: Central)	1885	27
2. Francisco González de Cosío	Governor (Querétaro: Bajio)	1887	24
3. Aristeo Mercado	Governor (Michoacán: West)	1891	20
4. Manuel Mercado	Subcabinet	1882	19
5. Teodoro Dehesa	Governor (Veracruz: Central)	1892	19
6. Mucio Martinez	Governor (Puebla: Central)	1892	18
7. José Limantour	Cabinet	1893	18
8. Joaquín González	Governor (Hidalgo: Bajio)	1893	18
9. Francisco Cañedo	Governor (Sinaloa: West)	1892	17
10. Leopoldo Romano	Governor (Nayarit: West)	1880	17
11. Joaquín Baranda	Cabinet	1884	17
12. Abraham Bandala	Governor (Tabasco: East Gulf)	1895	17
13. Miguel Cárdenas	Governor (Coahuila: North Border)	1894	16

SOURCE: The author's own data collection.

in the length of careers. There are some people in the sample whose careers did not last very long. The average career lasted 6.76 years, with a standard deviation of 7.26 years. Most of the people (95 percent) had careers lasting anywhere from 1.71 years (twenty months) to 22.20 years. This is not to say that some people did not enjoy very long careers. Table 5.8, for example, is a list of all people in my database with career lengths of at least thirty-five years.[17] Had this table been extended to include public officials with thirty cumulative years or more in office, it would have included twenty-nine additional entries, including many governors.

The evidence suggests that positions lasted longer at higher levels of government. Position length was also expected to be higher if the office holder had already accumulated experience working in the government. The impact of the hierarchy of government positions on seniority was less clear. On the one hand, seniority is correlated with higher levels of government. On the other hand, there is a negative effect among people who hold of-

TABLE 5.8
Public Officials with Longest Careers

	Name	No. of Positions	First Position	Last Position	Seniority (Cumulative Years)
1.	**Luis Torres***	21	Senator	Senator	61
2.	**Francisco Rincón Gallardo**	28	Senator	Senator	60
3.	**Salvador Dondé**	26	Senator	Senator	53
4.	**Angel Martínez**	23	Senator	Senator	50
5.	**Agustín del Río**	20	Senator	Senator	49
6.	**Manuel González Cosío**	17	Senator	Cabinet	48
7.	**Luis Curiel***	18	Deputy	Governor	48
8.	**Manuel Mercado**	15	Deputy	Senator	47
9.	**Manuel Ortega Reyes**	20	Senator	Senator	42
10.	**Epifanio Reyes**	21	Deputy	Senator	42
11.	**Canuto García**	19	Senator	Senator	42
12.	**Mariano Martínez de Castro***	17	Senator	Senator	42
13.	Guillermo de Landa Escandón	17	Senator	Senator	41
14.	Roberto Núñez	18	Senator	Deputy	39
15.	Genaro Raigosa	19	Senator	Senator	39
16.	Jesús Castañeda	19	Senator	Senator	38
17.	Agustín González	18	Deputy	Senator	36
18.	José Villada*	13	Deputy	Deputy	35
19.	Manuel Fernández Leal	10	Senator	Senator	35
20.	José Limantour	10	Deputy	Senator	35
21.	Luis Rojas	18	Senator	Senator	35

*People who were governors at some point in their careers.
SOURCE: The author's own data collection.

fices within the executive branch. The implication is that attaining higher office increases the prospects of a longer career, except at the very highest levels of government.

3.2 POLITICAL MOBILITY

The previous analysis suggests that governors and senators benefited greatly from available opportunities to assume public office. What about other political actors? Did they also have incentives to work within the system? For a systematic analysis of these questions, I will now analyze political mobility.

Political mobility refers to the ability of an official to move from one type of public office to another from time to time. Two basic types of information are required to measure mobility correctly. First, we need to specify a relevant set of public offices that people could assume. Second, we need an index t to keep track of time. After the positions and time index are specified, we can define political mobility more precisely as a transition from time t to time $t + 1$, during which a public official moves from a lower to a higher office within the specified hierarchy.

I focused on a set of five positions, including two types of legislative positions (deputies and senators), one state position (governors), and two types of executive positions (subcabinet and cabinet members). For obvious reasons, the top level of the hierarchy, the presidency, was off limits to all public officials but the dictator, with the exception of the period 1880 to 1884 when Díaz was temporarily replaced by General Manuel González.

I opted for two-year congressional terms as the defining unit of time. Unlike the other positions with variable terms, congressional terms were fixed throughout the whole period, and thus provided a consistent subdivision of the Porfiriato period. This period included eighteen congresses, starting with the Eighth Congress (1876–1878) and ending halfway through the Twenty-Fifth Congress (1910–1912).

I should note that the choice of the relevant unit of time or time interval is important for accounting purposes, but does not bias my results in any significant way. The unit of time is important to account for transitions of various types over a fixed interval, and must be consistently applied over the whole period. However, the actual length of this time interval (the length of congressional positions) does not significantly affect the transition analysis of other positions.

For the transition analysis to be accurate, it must measure the actual probability that a given position will change states between adjacent periods.[18] My two-year interval meets that requirement. For example, take a position whose length is smaller than this time interval. Suppose that the length is one year, so this position is recorded as having started and ended within the same unit of time *t*. This coding may imply that the position lasted two years, but in actuality the transition analysis only concerns itself with changes over time, and is thus independent of the position length. In this case the probability that the officer holding this position will hold any position in the subsequent period is zero, which accurately measures the transition probability of a one-year position. Suppose instead that the length of a position is, say, three years. This position will be coded as being held at some time *t* as well as *t* + 1. Again, the coding does not have implications for the length of the position. What the coding captures is a transition from a given position at time *t* to the same position at time *t* + 1. The corresponding transition probability is 1.0, which correctly implies that the position will continue beyond time *t* into the subsequent period.[19]

I used three different subperiods for my analysis based on two criteria: data availability and regime changes. As I have noted before, Díaz was not always a dictator. I have identified a regime change circa 1890. The main regime change occurs when Díaz changes the constitution to be reelected continuously. This occurs in 1890, when Article 78 of the Mexican Constitution is amended to delete previous reelection prohibitions. After 1890, the regime was undoubtedly dictatorial (Katz, 1984, p. 30). Not only is Díaz reelected continuously, but my analysis of roll call data also indicates that political power is concentrated on the executive branch.

I analyzed position changes with the use of a transition probability matrix. Rows correspond to the current position of a public official at time *t*, whereas the columns correspond to the official's position in the next period, *t* + 1. In these types of matrices, each cell has a value between zero and one. This value indicates the probability that an official currently occupying the office identified by the entry's row will move to the office identified by the corresponding column. I also add an extra column to capture the possibility that a public official leaves the system. The sum of row entries minus the last column indicates the probability that an official will remain employed in government during the following period.

As a first step, I calculated transition probabilities as the relative frequency of position changes during three periods: (1) between 1876 and 1890, before the dictatorship was consolidated; (2) after 1890, after dictatorship was consolidated; and (3) the whole period, from 1876 to 1911.[20] The purpose of these calculations was to assess the degree of mobility for the whole period, and also to determine whether mobility patterns changed after Díaz had consolidated his dictatorship. To simplify comparisons, I include the transition probabilities of these three periods in Figure 5.3.[21]

Position at Time $t + 1$

		Deputy	Senator	Governor	Subcabinet	Cabinet	Exit
	Deputy	0.70	0.04	0.02	0.01	0.00	0.23
		0.57	0.05	0.02	0.00	0.00	0.35
		0.79	0.03	0.02	0.01	0.00	0.15
	Senator	0.09	0.68	0.04	0.01	0.02	0.16
		0.13	0.59	0.06	0.01	0.03	0.19
		0.05	0.75	0.03	0.01	0.02	0.14
Position at Time t	Governor	0.06	0.12	0.66	0.01	0.02	0.13
		0.08	0.20	0.58	0.01	0.00	0.13
		0.06	0.09	0.69	0.00	0.03	0.13
	Subcabinet	0.24	0.13	0.05	0.44	0.03	0.10
		0.24	0.24	0.18	0.12	0.00	0.24
		0.25	0.10	0.01	0.52	0.04	0.07
	Cabinet	0.09	0.25	0.04	0.02	0.53	0.06
		0.08	0.42	0.00	0.04	0.46	0.00
		0.09	0.22	0.05	0.02	0.55	0.08

Figure 5.3 Relative Frequency of Position Changes During the Porfiriato Each cell presents three relative frequencies for a position change from the corresponding row position. The first entry corresponds to the whole period: 1876 to 1911. The second entry is for the period 1876 to 1890. The third entry denotes probabilities after 1890 under a consolidated dictatorship.

The relative frequencies of position changes indicate three features of a very stable pool of private enforcers. First, if we look along the diagonal cells of Figure 5.3, it is clear that public officials had a high probability of being reelected to the same office, indicating a high degree of continuity. An asset holder recruiting a public official would have known that there was a high probability that the official would be around for a long time. Second, there is significant movement across offices, especially between senators and governors, and senators and subcabinet and cabinet members. In other words, even while not holding onto the same public office, public officials had a high probability of moving into other influential positions. Finally, the probabilities are higher during the consolidated period after 1890, suggesting that Díaz was successful in populating political institutions with officials who would stay in office for a long time.

In summary, the analysis shows that public officials had very stable political careers patterns, especially after Díaz had consolidated his dictatorship. For instance, Figure 5.3 indicates that after 1890, the probability of a deputy becoming a senator in a subsequent period was a mere 0.03, the probability of being reelected was 0.79, and the probability of ending a political career as a deputy was 0.15. Thus, for a given cohort of deputies, fewer than one-fifth were not reelected, thus ending their careers. But almost all other deputies were reelected for a second period, and, what is more, a small minority did move on to higher office.

The mobility prospects of senators were similar for the same period. Senators were reelected for a second term with a probability of 0.75, but there were also opportunities for senators to move on to governorships or to the executive branch, with respective probabilities of 0.03 and 0.03 respectively. The probability of moving down to a deputy position (0.05) was larger than for career advancement, and the probability of not being reelected was just 0.14. Legislators could look forward to being in office for some time, not just one congressional term.

Although we see mobility between the legislature and state governors, Figure 5.3 shows that governors and executive government officials were each in a class by themselves. First, some legislators eventually became governors. Second, we also note that a small number of governors also moved on to higher office, although a few actually became deputies or senators after having had a governorship. Governors had relatively stable careers, perhaps because they also represented independent sources of power that could not be easily controlled by the government. Governors had a 0.69 probability of being "reelected" every two years (or continuing in power for two more years) or move to a cabinet position with probability of 0.02. They could end their careers as a governor with a probability of 0.13, lower than the probability of becoming a legislator (0.15). The evidence on subcabinet and cabinet members is qualitatively similar. There was some movement at that level, but these cabinet members did not come from lower ranks. They started and ended their careers within the same branch of government.

For a more systematic test of the proposition that positions were more stable during the latter half of the Porfiriato, I estimated a series of statistical models to check for the determinants of position changes from one congressional period to the next. Given some position at some congressional period t the dependent variable was a public office in the subsequent period $t + 1$.

Because I was solely concerned with transitions from one position to another, I treated positions at any given time as a categorical variable without imposing a hierarchy of positions. More specifically, I relied on a multinomial logit model that estimated the probability of attaining certain office at time $t + 1$ as a function of two covariates: the relevant subperiod (before or after consolidation) and the experience of public officials (measured in cumulative years in public office).[22]

The idea behind the first independent variable was to check for subperiod differences, to parallel the presentation in the transition probability matrix. The second independent variable captured observable heterogeneity in terms of seniority or years of accumulated public office experience.[23] This specification was run separately for each position at time t, and included individual-level clustering corrections to account for the fact that some individuals occupied various positions for long periods of time.[24]

Table 5.9 shows the results of estimating a multinomial logit regression model of the mobility prospects of five positions during the Porfiriato. Each column corresponds to a given position at time t, starting with deputies and ending with cabinet members. At time $t + 1$, an official could either stay in the same position, move to another one, or leave office. To model the transition, it is necessary to choose one possible state at time $t + 1$ as a baseline against which to compare the other options. These regression results take as a baseline the probability that a given official becomes a deputy during a subsequent period to assess the odds of other positions.

The coefficients shown here are thus relative risk ratios (*rrr*) or the odds of moving to some position over the odds of becoming a deputy. The constant for a given position at time $t + 1$ gives the odds of attaining that position as opposed to becoming a deputy. For instance, the coefficient for Senator in the first column gives odds of 0.06 for a deputy becoming a senator as opposed to continuing in the same position.[25] These odds adjust for two other independent variables that control for the period of analysis and other observed heterogeneity. The term *Consolidated* in Table 5.9 refers to the latter half of the Porfiriato starting in 1890, which I have previously established to be a dictatorship. The term *Experience* is a cumulative measure of years in public office.

Legislative Positions. Deputies were more likely to stay in the same position, with variable odds of moving to other positions. Adjusting for period and experience, the *rrr* was higher (0.68) that they would exit the system, followed by the prospects of becoming senators (0.06), governors (0.02), or subcabinet members (0.01). The odds of becoming cabinet members were nil, however. The odds were slightly better during the consolidated dictatorship period, as the corresponding relative risk ratios are all higher in magnitude than those of the constant. However, even during this period it was more likely that deputies would continue to be deputies. Political experience, however, had a consistently positive impact on the odds of moving to other positions.

TABLE 5.9
Multinomial Logit Analysis of Political Careers

	Deputy$_t$	Senator$_t$	Governor$_t$	Subcabinet$_t$	Cabinet$_t$
Position at time $t + 1$					
(deputy = baseline)					
Senator					
Consolidated	0.19	3.77	0.49	0.32	0.28
	(6.08)	(5.02)	(1.20)	(0.77)	(1.02)
Experience	1.09	0.98	1.02	1.02	1.05
	(3.83)	(1.12)	(0.68)	(0.31)	(1.98)
Constant	0.06	5.32	2.21	0.82	3.34
	(17.56)	(10.24)	(1.71)	(0.15)	(1.06)
Governor					
Consolidated	0.42	0.80	1.74	0.06	ND
	(2.28)	(0.41)	(1.07)	(2.34)	
Experience	1.07	1.01	0.99	1.03	1.01
	(3.35)	(0.25)	(0.55)	(0.67)	(0.31)
Constant	0.02	0.48	8.28	0.58	0.00
	(16.14)	(2.44)	(5.24)	(0.43)	(18.40)
Subcabinet					
Consolidated	0.74	0.84	0.04	10.67	0.47
	(0.28)	(0.12)	(1.72)	(1.55)	(0.49)
Experience	1.09	1.03	1.14	0.82	0.96
	(2.09)	(0.55)	(2.91)	(2.95)	(0.94)
Constant	0.01	0.07	0.07	1.83	0.67
	(9.08)	(4.50)	(2.75)	(0.46)	(0.25)
Cabinet					
Consolidated	0.86	0.94	ND	ND	1.08
	(0.18)	(0.09)			(0.07)
Experience	1.07	1.05	1.03	0.98	1.00
	(1.69)	(2.00)	(0.71)	(0.38)	(0.02)
Constant	0.00	0.14	0.00	0.00	5.47
	(8.98)	(4.69)	(23.99)	(18.43)	(1.58)
Exit					
Consolidated	0.37	3.08	21.01	0.78	ND
	(10.31)	(4.22)	(1.33)	(0.19)	
Experience	0.97	0.95	0.92	0.79	0.98
	(3.43)	(2.83)	(2.48)	(2.82)	(0.53)
Constant	0.68	2.01	2.77	4.31	0.00
	(5.32)	(3.84)	(2.19)	(1.48)	(26.54)
N	3895	1665	497	86	144
df	15	15	14	14	13
Null deviance	6598.57	3426.12	1069.02	251.84	370.02
Residual variance	6274.92	3318.00	1027.68	198.88	352.91
Log likelihood	−3137.46	−1659.00	−513.84	−99.44	−176.45

NOTE: Z scores are in parentheses. *ND* denotes position changes with limited data to estimate coefficients for Consolidated period.

Senators were also likely to continue in their positions, and the odds increased during the consolidated period. During the consolidated period, the *rrr* for becoming a senator was slightly better (0.19), after controlling for experience. Experience improved the odds even more. Each additional year of experience increased the *rrr* to 1.09, or 9 percent higher than other deputies, even after controlling for the consolidated period of dictatorship. Interestingly, political experience had a mixed effect on mobility. More years of accumulated experience increased the odds of moving to a governorship or executive-level position, but made it less likely to stay as a senator. Longtime senators thus had a better chance of moving up to higher offices than less experienced legislators.

Gubernatorial Positions. The odds for governors were in favor of retaining their position, followed by an exit or senatorial position. The consolidated period brought about more stability for governors, with 74 percent better odds of retaining office than governors during the first half of the Porfiriato. Years of experience had a mixed effect, with an added boost for transitions to senatorial or subcabinet positions, but not otherwise. A peculiarity of the data set is apparent here, with the omission of a transition to cabinet positions. As it turns out, some public officials held concurrent positions, and this was particularly the case at the highest level, where one observes some overlap among governors and executive-level positions.

Executive Positions. The pattern for subcabinet and cabinet positions resembles that of the other positions. Executive officials were more likely to continue in the same office, but cross-movement at this level was more limited. Political experience increased the prospects of moving to a governorship, but not to another executive-level position.

Long-Term Mobility. Overall, the multinomial logit analysis corroborates my previous claim about the stability of public positions and the importance of seniority or experience. To assess stability, we can look at the odds of public officials remaining in the same office with respect to the baseline probability of becoming a deputy. For senators the *rrr* of remaining a senator was 3.77; for governors, 1.74; for subcabinet members, 10.67; and for cabinet members, 1.08.

These regression results provide a relative assessment of mobility with respect to the baseline case of becoming a deputy during a subsequent period. The actual probability of becoming a deputy varied from time to time, however, so we lack information on actual transition probabilities. One can

obtain a more complete picture of political mobility during the Porfiriato
with the use of conditional plots to visualize transition probabilities. Figures
5.4 through 5.8 illustrate the transition probabilities for legislative, gubernatorial, and executive-level positions. The transition probabilities are estimated for each congress during the Porfiriato, using current mean values
for cumulative years of experience and by disaggregating time.[26]

Figures 5.4 and 5.5 show the trajectory of transition probabilities for
deputies and senators, respectively. One salient feature of these plots is the
ascending trend of the probability of remaining in the same office. Although
during the early years there was some movement between deputy and senator positions, over time the probability of remaining in the same office
overwhelmed other position changes. For deputies, the transition probability of remaining a deputy during subsequent periods increased from about
0.5 during the early years to almost 0.9 by the end of the Porfiriato. For
senators, the corresponding probabilities increased from about 0.55 in 1875
to almost 0.8 in 1910.

For the most part, there was limited movement between the two positions. During the early years, there was some upward movement from dep-

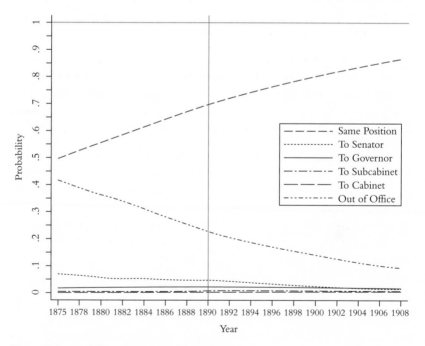

Figure 5.4 Mobility Prospects for Deputies

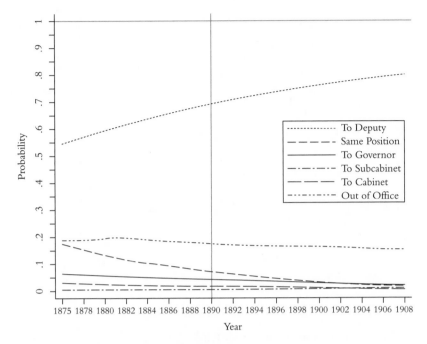

Figure 5.5   Mobility Prospects for Senators

uty to senator, but this transition probability decreased over time. Senators were likely to become deputies during the early years (with probabilities close to 0.20), but over time that movement ceased. From the beginning, senators were more likely than deputies to move to other positions, although the corresponding transition probabilities were relatively low.

The increase in the probability of remaining in the same office was also paralleled by a decline in the probability of exiting the system. This effect was stronger for deputies, whose probability of being out of office was reduced from about 0.45 to 0.10 during the whole period. Senators, unlike deputies, experienced a higher probability of being out of office than deputies throughout the whole period, but this probability decreased from initial rates of 0.2 during the early years to about 0.15.

Governors, like legislators, also experienced much stability. Figure 5.6 shows that probability of governors retaining their position increased from about 0.55 during the early years to about 0.70 toward the end of the Porfiriato. Although governors shared the same terms as the president, their tenures did not follow the same electoral calendar. During the early years, some governors were deposed when they failed to accomplish the dictator's

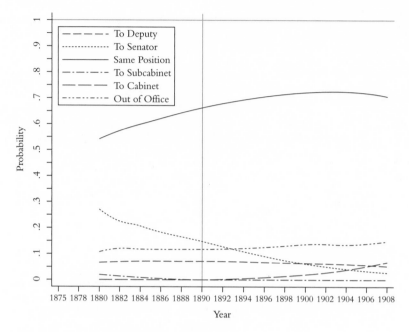

Figure 5.6   Mobility Prospects for Governors

quest for stability; but for the most part, they were instrumental in bringing about stability because of their military experience (Reyes, 1903). It was also the case that governors switched positions and oftentimes became senators. The probability of that change was as almost as high as 0.3 during the early years, although it became less frequent toward the end of the period. The probability of moving to a deputy position was relatively constant for the whole period, but the probability of attaining a cabinet position increased over time. Finally, the probability of being out of office for the whole period was between 0.1 and 0.15.

Public officials in executive positions experienced more movement across offices than either legislators or governors.

For the first half of the Porfiriato, Figure 5.7 shows that mobility prospects for subcabinet members were fairly limited. Either they stayed in the same position or became deputies. Over time, the probability of retaining a subcabinet position reached its highest point at about 0.4, with a concomitant decrease in transitions to deputy or gubernatorial positions. This pattern was accompanied by a parallel increase in transitions to cabinet positions, and an increasingly low probability of being out of office.

The mobility pattern for cabinet members was very different. For cabinet members, Figure 5.8 shows that they initially had a higher probability

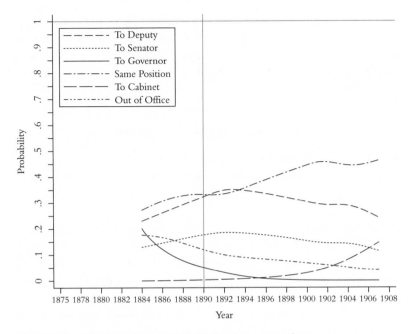

Figure 5.7   Mobility Prospects for Subcabinet Members

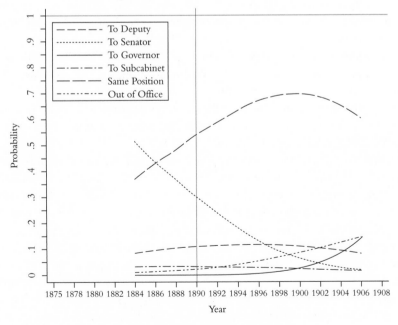

Figure 5.8   Mobility Prospects for Cabinet Members

(0.5) of becoming a senator rather than continuing in the same position (probability ≈ 0.4). Over time, they were more likely to stay in the same position. The probability of becoming a senator fell drastically, coupled with a systematic increase in the probability of attaining gubernatorial positions or exiting the system.

4   Conclusion: Governance Structure and Formal Institutions

The purpose of this chapter was threefold: (1) to assess the role of public officials in elite networks, (2) to evaluate whether public officials had stable careers, and (3) to assess whether there was a permanent governance structure in place.

This chapter set out to examine further the role of public officials (as potential private enforcers) in elite networks. Private enforcers had additional economic and political ties to other important groups in society. The evidence on the profile of public officials indicated that public officials were likely to come from well-to-do families, with already existing political connections to family members in government. In addition, the collected network data corroborate the close connections between public officials and social and economic elites. Overall, the evidence in this chapter is consistent with the view that public officials (as a pool of potential enforcers for private agreements between the dictator and individuals) would have had the incentive to protect the property rights of the firms from which they obtained rents.

In addition, the general profile of public officials indicates that public officials had experience in the local government, business sector, and Mexican army, suggesting political mobility and career advancement. In particular, Díaz relied heavily on military officers to serve in various public offices, especially during the earlier half of the Porfiriato, to help pacify the country and to keep political opposition under control.

The central analysis of this chapter consisted of a detailed examination of political careers to inquire whether public officials could be deemed a durable source of private protection. To that effect, I derived the probabilities of career advancement at different levels of government for the whole Porfiriato period. These data indicate that one of the requirements of a long-lived network (the longevity of influential political actors) was satisfied. Public officials could look forward to long political careers and opportunities for career advancement. In turn, economic actors who entered into private agreements with the dictator could readily tap into an existing pool of long-lived public officials who could provide private enforcement.

Despite the focus on public officials, this chapter further clarified the conditions that enabled Díaz to make credible commitments. To understand how formal and informal institutions relate to one another, it helps to think about the conditions that enable networks of private protection to deter predation. At heart, what the network provides is third-party enforcement brought about by a collective response of self-interested public officials to protect their own interests.

This protection can be effective at particular points in time, but there remains the issue of whether actors perceive this structure to be long-lasting. Indeed, if we expect economic and political actors to extend their time horizons (making decisions based on the existence and effectiveness of an informal network), they must also have reason to believe that the network is neither transitory (a rare event) nor sporadic (sometimes it works; sometimes it does not). In short, the network needs to have a long lifetime.

It is precisely this requirement for persistent governance structures that highlights the relative importance of formal institutions.[27] Formal institutions not only allow some actor to become a long-lasting dictator, but also that there will be a stable pool of private enforcers. Indeed, the reason that potential enforcers are attractive is the fact that they have some measure of permanent political influence. Formal institutions lower the search costs of private protection by facilitating the identification of influential political actors. Favoritism to existing elites is ensured by allowing these groups to populate formal institutions. By design, there are no alternate mechanisms to ratify membership in the network; hence, all future membership expansions are necessarily illegal, thus imposing barriers to entry to excluded groups.

The importance of elites cannot be overstated. Indeed, if we look at the typical profile of public officials, we would not have predicted Díaz to have come to power. This is not to say that he did not possess military prestige and particular advantages at critical junctures, but it is clear that there was no prior reason to believe that he was inevitably the only candidate to have become a dictator. An evaluation of Díaz's career, including his more humble background (which would have excluded him from elite networks), shows various pitfalls. Already an ambitious politician before he became president, he endured failed bids to assume executive power and had been passed over when more privileged actors were selected.

Understanding how political actors become dictators is critical, because it can also inform us about dictators' vulnerability to social pressure. In the case of the Porfiriato, I have advanced the claim that Díaz was deliberately given dictatorial powers by a cadre of influential actors. These actors retained their influence even while delegating policy-making authority to the executive government. Just as they had made him a dictator, they could take away his privileges. As history shows, this outcome indeed occurred with the advent of the Mexican Revolution. Much is made of the important contribution of peasants and, to a lesser extent, workers, but the main reason why Díaz was overthrown is because those elites that supported his dictatorship decided that his dictatorial career had ended.

Formal institutions were particularly important in guaranteeing that there would be a de facto dictator in place. Note that a dictatorship by itself does not guarantee long-term horizons. Olson (2000) notes that societies under dictators must continually address the problem of succession given the finite life of any given dictator. The continuity of Díaz's regime turned out to be a minor problem given the underlying political arrangement. The death or overthrow of Díaz would not translate into a lack of authority and an institutional vacuum, because the same people who had established his dictatorship were still there to set up a new one if needed (if not nominally a dictatorship, they nonetheless had the ability and prerogative to defer to and monitor a new executive with concentrated powers). In other words, the dictator could be replaced at lower cost than in a situation in which formal institutions did not function at all.

Certainly, if a change was necessary, we would not expect an exact replication of the process that made Díaz a dictator. Indeed, the Mexican Revolution placed additional constraints that clearly prevented replicating the exact same dictatorial system as that found under Díaz.[28] But the system that emerged after the Revolution was very much based on the governance structure set up during the Porfiriato (Haber, 2005; Haber et al., 2003).

Chapter 6

Network of Private Protection

Political stability was well received by economic actors who were eager to benefit from new investment opportunities. Along with stability, however, formal institutions appeared to have given way to a consolidated dictatorship. Clearly, the private policies described in Chapter 4 afforded various privileges to economic actors. But the authoritarian nature of the political system nonetheless created uncertainty about the security of these lucrative property rights. Would the dictator renege on his commitments?

To circumvent the threat of predation, these economic actors had an incentive to recruit public officials to obtain and ensure selective protection (what I call *private policies* in Chapters 2 and 4) through direct access to policymakers. What is more, in many cases, economic firms relied on their connections to enable themselves to craft their own regulatory environment. Having public officials on board also enabled firms to monitor the behavior of the executive government or other government actors to prevent undesirable policy changes.

Indeed, the connections between firms and influential public officials is well-known in the literature, although the exact logic behind these connections has not been explored. This chapter fills that gap in the literature with a systematic study of those connections.

The focus of this chapter is on big business, which characterizes the type of protected industries during this period (Haber, 1989; Marichal and Cerutti, 1997). For the analysis, I collected relational data from Mexico's most important companies for the period 1907 to 1910. Analyzing the composition of corporate boards is important for two reasons. First, we would expect a large number of public officials on these boards to mitigate policy conflicts between the government and private actors. That is, the more public officials on corporate boards, the more likely it will be that the government shares the policy preferences of economic actors. The underlying reason for consensus on policies is that government actors have a stake in the welfare of the corporations in which they participate. Second, more public officials on corporate boards reflects a higher degree of integration between political and economic actors. That is, the distinction between political and economic actors gets blurred within the confines of their informal coalition.

My selection of the period 1907 to 1910 was based on the availability of corporate information. Clearly, the available information reflects the state of affairs toward the end of the Porfiriato. Notwithstanding this limitation, there are two reasons why this analysis is appropriate for the question at hand. First, the political economy of the Porfiriato circa 1906 reflects a mature system. That is, the information I analyzed with my 1907 to 1910 sample clearly reflects the rules of the game affecting political and economic behaviors, and it directly addresses the question of how a dictator was able to make credible commitments to investors.

Second, we know from historical analysis that the system in 1907 does not look particularly different from that instituted in the late 1890s, when the major institutional changes that governed economic activity were enacted. Analyzing the latter period starting in 1907 thus gives a rough approximation of how the system worked after Díaz wanted to promote investment.

The structure of protection during the Porfiriato was based on a network of private protection, with participation from a small group of economic and political elites. There were several relations at work here—in effect, various networks—but the key relation for this chapter is the overlapping interests of public officials who were tied to various economic interests.[1]

The network analysis shows that, in fact, the social network that operated in Mexico had, also, a well-defined group of influential network players who could punish the dictator if he were to renege on his commitments.[2] Although driven by self-interest and the pursuit of additional benefits, public officials found themselves offering protection to multiple groups. This decentralized behavior gave rise to an emergent network structure with firms being protected by multiple public officials. This network structure established ties between otherwise disconnected economic groups with their respective private policies. As the number of connections increased, an individual enforcer had an increasingly greater stake in the network. A higher number of connections of overlapping protection thus created a critical mass of enforcers that would be collectively hurt if the government were to prey on any asset holder.

The logic presented here has a direct parallel to Olson's (2000) concept of encompassing interests in his theory of stationary banditry. The Díaz government became a dictatorship because political actors deferred to the executive government to facilitate the passage of lucrative policies to selected economic actors. Economic actors, in turn, returned the favor by sharing the profits of economic growth with public officials. Motivated by potential rents, public officials would be especially eager to protect firms, because profits depended on the performance of protected groups.

Potential collusive behavior between some public officials and the executive government was mitigated because the economic benefits that public officials received were dispersed across various industries and were not concentrated among a few public officials. The networked structure of private protection thus gave a large collection of influential actors an encompassing interest in economic performance.

The rest of this chapter is organized as follows. In the next section, "Related Economic Activity," I provide a preliminary assessment of network connections at the industry and company levels. The following two sections provide a more detailed network analysis of overlapping private protection. In "Structure of Private Enforcement," I examine the presence of public officials on corporate boards to identify the most central enforcers with the highest stakes in preserving a network of private protection. In "Expanding the Scope of Protection," I provide a statistical analysis of the role of public officials in enhancing broader links among corporate directors. The last section contains my concluding remarks.

1 Related Economic Activity

As noted in Chapter 2, predation risk increases with the degree of connectedness to other firms, so more connected firms would also be more vulnerable. The implication for successful networks (when predation is deterred) is that participant firms must be closely linked to one another. This section addresses this implication for the Porfiriato. Were economic actors in Mexico well connected? How did industries relate to one another? To what extent did they perceive to have a shared fate with other protected interests?

To answer these questions, I collected information for a network analysis of the composition of boards of directors for Mexico's 149 large companies toward the end of the Porfiriato.[3] The unit of analysis in SNA is a network, a system, or collection of social relations. More precisely, a network is defined as a collection of nodes and the existing ties among those nodes. The two networks analyzed in this section involve economic entities at two levels of aggregation (industries and companies) that are connected because they share common private enforcers.[4]

I.I PROTECTION BY INDUSTRY

Although a great variety of economic actors were able to negotiate and define their property rights directly with the Díaz government, some were more vulnerable than others in terms of their ability to defend those property rights. Is there evidence that private protection was distributed according to the vulnerability of different asset holders?

One testable implication of my theory is that there should be more private enforcers among domestic enterprises. Recall from Chapter 2 that in the absence of formal political institutions, asset holders must provide their own enforcement mechanisms. In the case of industries such as mining and oil, which were dominated by foreign firms with recourse to third-party enforcement, we should expect to see a lesser need for informal coalitions between corporations and government officials.

In contrast, we should see the largest concentration of government officials in industries without ties to foreign governments. Given the prevalence of domestic investors in banking and manufacturing, there should be more public officials in banking and manufacturing.[5] This is not to say that these sectors lacked any foreign connections. Gamboa Ojeda (2003), among others, has noted that there were networks of immigrant financiers with established ties to international actors, but the function of these external actors was to provide resources rather than protection.

The first network involves connections among industries. In the previous chapter I showed that many policies were negotiated at the industry level. Public officials therefore had not only direct stakes in specific companies, but also cared about the durability of industry-level agreements. As the number of public officials with multiple board positions increases, one would expect a greater common interest in ensuring that larger subsets of the network be protected from government opportunism. These "shared stakes" can be examined by studying relationships among industries. This type of relationship enables us to see the distribution of public officials through the different industries that comprise the network.

To visualize the distribution of protection, Figure 6.1 shows the number of connections and the structure of private protection at the industry level. In this diagram, known as a *sociogram,* each node (circle) in the diagram rep-

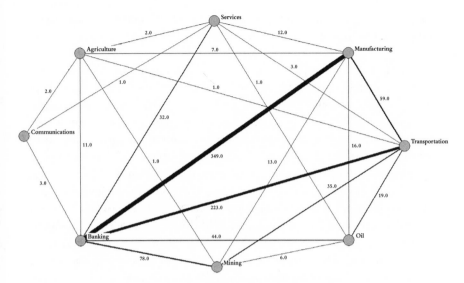

Figure 6.1 Network Distribution of All Directors by Industry

resents a major industry. A line between two industries indicates at least one public official in common with any of their respective corporate boards.[6] The numbers alongside the lines indicate the number of common industry affiliations by public officials. These numbers are indicative of the strength of available protection and shared stakes between any two industries.

When we look at the distribution of public officials across industries, we see the postulated pattern. One salient feature of the network is that banking and manufacturing are the most closely linked industries, as measured by the number of cross-industry links. The connectedness between these sectors was to be expected, because most economic activity was related to manufacturing, which also requires finance.

Governors were very active on the corporate boards of banks. This result was partly driven by the fact that state banks were heavily regulated. In fact, for the most part, states only one had one bank. The governor, as the chief executive in the state, had a prominent role in his state's bank. In this respect, the presence of governors on state bank boards is consistent with my theory that owners of state-level banks would want to get favorable private policies, which required close connections not just with policymakers in Mexico City, but with their respective governors and state-level officials.[7]

Another noteworthy feature is the lower number of connections between agriculture and the rest of the economy. One part of the story is that in facilitating the creation of this network, the federal government excluded agriculture by design. Economic policy during the Porfiriato unambiguously favored industrial development (Haber, 1989; Marichal and Cerutti, 1997).

The fact that industry was favored does not imply, however, that there were no major agricultural enterprises. Another reason why agriculture does not play a prominent role in the network is the result of the nominal absence of directors simply because these enterprises were not always organized to have boards of directors. In fact, the type of agricultural activity that was protected under the Porfiriato was large-scale export-oriented agriculture, dominated by influential regional businessmen. The historical record does indicate that this type of agricultural activity had important political connections, but the connections were at the state level and were not reflected in the sample that I constructed (Haber et al., 2003, pp. 285–341).

The remaining industries also had ties to the rest of the network, although the intensity of those ties varied from one industry to another. In addition to banking and manufacturing, the transportation sector (basically railroads, but also some water transportation) also had a high number of common directors. Of all the industries, the numbers attached to transportation appear to run contrary to our expectation that we would find a high concentration of private enforcers. In particular, railroads had a significant foreign investment. Mining also showed a significant number of ties to other industries.

As it turns out, the large number of connections in industries with foreign investors was not entirely driven by the need for protection. Unlike domestic sectors, federal law required these companies to have at least one government representative on the board of directors as a condition for concessions given to foreign investors. Like the oil and mining industries, railroad construction had an important participation from foreign investors. Railways were thus also required to have government officials on their boards of directors. Although these public officials benefited and did provide private protection, they also had a concomitant role in monitoring the behavior of foreign investors. In fact, in the case of railroads, the government was seriously concerned about the viability of these concessions, and eventually the government took over after these firms proved insolvent, as noted in Chapter 4.

Foreign investors had alternate sources of enforcement, which mitigated their need for informal coalitions with domestic government officials. This is not to say that foreign investors did not have domestic investment partners. Indeed, these firms had various connections with prominent businessmen who were not directly involved in government. The terms of the concessions obtained by foreign firms did, however, benefit from connections to prominent public officials like Enrique C. Creel and Guillermo de Landa y Escandón.

1.2 COMPANY PERCEPTIONS OF SHARED STAKES

Although a focus on aggregate links between industries is consistent with the prediction that there was more private protection in more vulnerable industries, we can further examine the evidence by identifying the highest concentrations of overlapping protection among firms. Overlapping protection is defined by the existence of a common public official on the board of two firms. Checking whether two companies were connected allowed me to minimize the independent effect that size of firms could have on the actual number of connections. The disadvantage is that this binary condition gives companies with few connections equal weight as those companies that had many more connections. In other words, it treats the former companies as if they were just as vulnerable as the latter ones.[8]

The relevance of the links illustrated in Figure 6.2 is that they propagate the risk of predation. That is, if the dictator preys on any given firm, there is a higher likelihood that he will also attack related firms, as explained in Chapter 2. In terms of the sociogram presented in Figure 6.2, it is clear

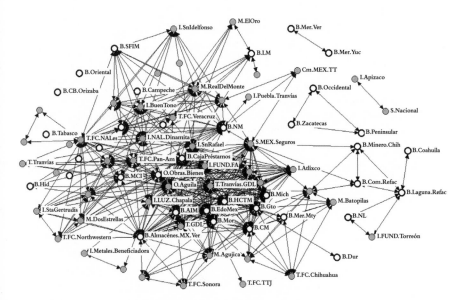

Figure 6.2   Overlapping Protection of Companies
NOTE: Banking companies are distinguished by lighter nodes with thicker outlines.

that most related companies were located in the manufacturing and banking sectors. In fact, the top central companies of this network are primarily in the banking sector, an unsurprising feature given the general need for finance across industries. We would expect these sectors to be more vulnerable because of their dense connections, in addition to the fact that they were mostly domestic industries. Figure 6.2 also shows the connections that the transportation industry (railroads) had with manufacturing and banking, suggesting that even railroad companies were vulnerable, although not to the same extent as manufacturing companies or banks.

We can examine the extent of overlapping protection by calculating the density of company connections. Before showing my results, I illustrate why density matters and how it is calculated.

Figure 6.3 relates network connections to the theory presented in Chapter 2. In this diagram, the relevant nodes are companies denoted by A_i. The relevant connection is the existence of common public officials G_i, who sit on multiple corporate boards.[9]

The density of a network is a measure that ranges between zero and one. If public officials restrict themselves to participating in just one company, the density would be zero because there is no relationship among companies in terms of overlapping private protection. In contrast, if all public

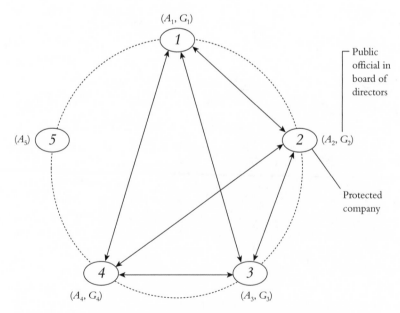

Figure 6.3   Sample Density Diagram of Encompassing Interests

officials sat on all corporate boards, then the density of the network would be one, because all companies would be connected. Intermediate density values thus reflect varying "shared" stakes in the system. The more dense the network, the greater the common interest of associated public officials to resist government predation, as discussed in Chapter 2.

There are ten potential ties among the nodes in Figure 6.3. With six observed ties, the density for this sample network is therefore equal to 6 ÷ 10 or 0.6. We can calculate the density for the network of connected companies presented in Figure 6.2 in a similar fashion. There are 149 company nodes, with a potential maximum number of ties equal to 11,026. The number of actual ties is 805, which implies a density of 0.07.

Roughly speaking, this density can be interpreted as the percentage of companies that would be affected if the dictator preyed on an arbitrary node.[10] Density can also be interpreted in terms of the expected collective response of affected economic actors to potential predatory behavior. Assuming that public officials will gather around the companies in which they participate, there is a 0.07 probability that public officials will react negatively to government predation on any given company.[11]

Thus far, the network has been analyzed from a global perspective. That is, we can readily assess the overall architecture of the network and recognize channels for the propagation of predation risk. An underlying assumption behind the analysis thus far is that participants themselves had knowledge about the global characteristics of the network. This assumption is defensible for private enforcers on the basis of the relatively small number of public officials. Public officials surely had knowledge about the various opportunities to offer private protection throughout network. Selected firms, especially national banks, certainly possessed this type of knowledge as well.

It is plausible, however, that not all companies had knowledge about the whole network. If, indeed, companies had only limited knowledge about the extent of overlapping protection, this lack of information would cast doubt on the mechanism that I propose in this book. From the perspective of economic actors, my theory argues that an *arbitrary* economic actor would agree to a selective policy and deem it credible because the private enforcers he hired would protect relevant property rights. For a few firms, this condition could have been easily satisfied by recruiting highly influential players. For most firms, however, the success of private protection depended not just on the enforcers they hired, but on the enforcers' connections to other enterprises. For example, if a company could pay only for a small number of private enforcers with limited stakes in other firms, the company could infer that the network could not protect its property rights, and hence it would choose not to invest.

How could firms assess the degree of connectedness to other enterprises? SNA provides a natural way to address this question directly through the use of ego network analysis. Ego networks are *local* networks within a larger network. These networks are constructed by identifying a particular node (ego) within a larger (global) network and mapping this node's connections to other nodes (denoted as *alters*). An ego network then directly accounts for any given node's actual connections to other members.

For a given network of size n, we can construct n individual ego networks.[12] Each node has its own ego network with different connections to some alters, but not necessarily to all other nodes. An ego network thus provides an accurate map of a company's relevant social context. We can examine whether this local structure would create incentives to enter into private agreements with the dictator.

There are three network statistics of interest that provide information about how a company perceives its place within the global network. The first is the size of a local network, measured in terms of directly related participants. For example, if firm A is connected to two companies B and C, the size of its network would be equal to two. For this sample, the average size and standard deviation for all firms was ten, indicating a high degree of connectedness among companies.

The second measure is the density of connections among one company's related firms. This measure captures the fact that alters themselves were directly related. The average density for all ego networks was 0.60 with a standard deviation of 0.39. This is an important result because, as a general rule, larger networks tend to have lower densities, simply because it is more difficult to expect all node members to be directly connected. For the average ego network size of ten, there is a maximum number of forty-five ties that can occur among the related nodes. A density of 0.60 therefore indicates the existence of about twenty-seven directly related alters for a typical ego network.

Lastly, a measure related to density is the average distance among all pairs of alters. By definition, an ego node can reach its alters in one step, so this third measure captures the distance among the remaining nodes. The closer this distance gets to one, the denser the network. In an ego network with a density equal to one, all alters are directly connected. In my analysis, the average distance across all ego networks was, in fact, very close to one, with a typical value of 1.02 and a standard deviation of 0.62. An attack on any given node would have thus readily propagated to all other nodes in about one step.

TABLE 6.1

Ego Network Analysis for Selected Companies

Rank	Company	Size	Ties	Pairs	Density	Average density
1.	Cia. Mex. De Petróleo "El Aguila"	42	604	1722	0.35	1.837
2.	Almacenes Generales de Deposito de México y Veracruz	30	492	870	0.57	1.471
3.	Cia. Bancaria de Obras y Bienes Raices	30	506	870	0.58	1.423
4.	Cia. de Papel de San Rafael	29	470	812	0.58	1.51
5.	Banco Central Mexicano	28	438	756	0.58	1.452
6.	Cia. Fundidora de Fierro y Acero de Monterrey	28	444	756	0.59	1.479
7.	Caja de Préstamos	27	452	702	0.64	1.356
8.	Banco de Guanajuato	26	420	650	0.65	1.354
9.	Cia. de Seguros La Mexicana	26	378	650	0.58	1.655
10.	Cia. del Ferrocarril Nacional de México	26	274	650	0.42	2
11.	Cia. Hidroeléctrica e Irrigadora de Chapala	25	376	600	0.63	2
12.	Banco Nacional de México	23	212	506	0.42	2
13.	Banco Agrícola e Hipotecario de México	22	380	462	0.82	1.177
14.	Banco del Estado de México	22	370	462	0.80	2
15.	Banco de Morelos	22	380	462	0.82	1.177
16.	Banco Hipotecario de Crédito Territorial Mexicano	20	362	380	0.95	1.047
17.	Banco de Michoacán	20	362	380	0.95	1.047
18.	Cia. de Tranvias y Fuerza de Guadalajara	20	362	380	0.95	1.047
19.	Cia. Harinera y Manufacturera Nacional	20	342	380	0.90	2
20.	Cia. Industrial de Atlixco	19	342	342	1.00	1

SOURCE: The author's own calculations.

Table 6.1 illustrates these network statistics for the ego networks of selected firms, including above- and below-average sizes. Companies with the greatest number of ties to other companies were typically located in the banking sector, industry, services, and railroads. Alone among other firms in its industry, the top firm (the Mexican Eagle Oil Company), had the largest number of direct connections. Note, however, that in terms of density, the most important ego networks were to be found in the banking and manufacturing sectors. In the latter, the Compañia Industrial de Atlixco, a textiles company, had a local network in which all nineteen companies were directly related to each other!

To summarize, the evidence thus far supports the notion that economic actors would have reason to fear predation given their connections. The high degree of connectedness would have also provided incentives for public officials to retaliate against predation. This result holds under various informational assumptions for private economic actors. On one extreme, if companies possessed global knowledge of network features, then they would be assured that a critical mass of public officials would protect the network. On the other extreme, even if companies had only local knowledge of overlapping protection, the structure of ego networks would have led a given company to realize that there was a (locally) dense collection of public officials with the incentives to protect their own (ego) network.

2   Structure of Private Enforcement

Although companies had a vested interest in preserving a network of private protection, the credibility of private policies ultimately depended on the behavior of public officials. To examine the incentives of public officials, I proceed to examine the structure of private protection. Here, I will look in more detail at the important participation that Read and Musacchio (2001) attribute to Mexican politicians in their comparison of Mexico's and Brazil's business networks. With my theoretical framework, however, I see the participation of government officials not just as a means of private enrichment, but as a crucial mechanism in which they get rents in exchange for private protection. The key question to be explored is whether the architecture or structure of this network had properties that would enable it to act as an enforcement mechanism for selective (private) policies.

The type of relationship between economic and government actors that I explore here involves an exchange of rents for private protection. Data on the composition of corporate boards provide the required relational data by identifying which public officials are "affiliated" with particular companies. I concentrate on this type of connection to examine the incentives of public officials in obtaining director fees, which were directly tied to economic performance.

By coding for the presence of public officials on boards of directors, I check only for one type of stake, or partial payment for private protection. Detailed information on individual investment portfolios is unavailable to calculate the total stake that each public official had in a given enterprise. My analysis thus represents a lower bound of actual protection benefits. It is generally well-known that public officials received director fees and that participation in corporate boards was offered to major shareholders, so the actual incentives to protect were probably much stronger than what I demonstrate with the available relational data (Table 6.2).

TABLE 6.2
Corporate Concessions to Politicians and Director Fees

Industry	Percentage of Initial Concessions to Politicians	Corporate Board Fees as a Percentage of Company Profits
Banking	55.3	7.9
Insurance	100.0	9.0
Manufacturing	22.2	8.5
Mining	32.4	8.0
Railways and transportation	50.0	7.8

SOURCE: The author's own calculations based on companies included in México, Banco Central Mexicano (1908).

The government report of public corporations contains information that enables a preliminary assessment of the economic interests of public officials. Examining the history of these companies, one can figure out whether initial concessions were given directly to a public official or a group of people, including at least one public official. Table 6.2 shows the percentage of concessions to public officials. The lowest percentage occurred in manufacturing, where only 22 percent of concessions involved public officials. All concessions for insurance companies, however, involved a public official. In general, at least in the case of a corporation, there is strong evidence that some public officials had a direct stake in the profits of the firms with which they were associated.

As an additional benefit, one can also calculate the percentage of company profits that were distributed to boards of directors, as shown in the third column. Boards were relatively small in size. My estimates indicate that directors on corporate boards received approximately one percent of the annual corporate profits in compensation for their work. This percentage amounted to significant payments, especially in the case of large banks, but is nonetheless only a *lower boundary* of the participation of public officials in economic activity. In addition, a particular public official could hold seats in multiple firms. The larger the number of different boards on which a public official resided, the greater that official's stake in the protection of those companies.

2.1 CENTRAL PLAYERS AND POLITICAL INFLUENCE

To what extent did private enforcers see themselves as having a shared stake in maintaining a network of private protection? To answer that question, I examined a network restricted to directors who were public officials, which left me with a sample of 103 nodes. The relevant tie is whether any

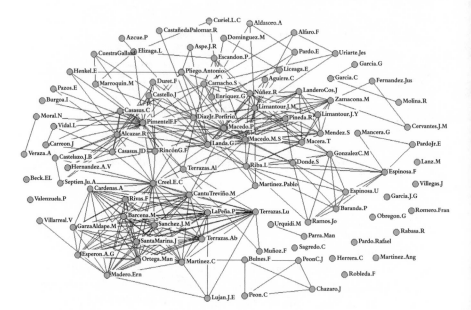

Figure 6.4   Overlapping Protection of Public Officials

two public officials sit on the same corporate board, or whether they protect at least one company in common. We can explore the importance of
overlapping private protection by calculating the distribution and centrality of public officials within this network.

Figure 6.4 illustrates the structure of private protection in Porfirian
Mexico. This network had a density of about 8 percent, which represents a
fairly large number of connections given all the possibilities.[13] Visual exploration of this network also reveals that the ties are not uniformly distributed.
Indeed, many ties are built around a small number of central players, a network feature examined later in more detail.

Despite the lack of uniformity in connections, there was a critical mass
of central players with dense connections who had the ability and incentives to curtail predation. SNA provides different measures of centrality,
which are useful to understand various aspects about the role and influence
of particular network members. If a public official sat on many boards, there
was clearly an individual interest in the well-being of the affected firms. In
principle, a public official with board seats in all the corporations would
have a stake in the whole network.

We can measure centrality more precisely by analyzing the patterns of
connections from any given public official to the rest of the public officials

in the networks. Three common measures of centrality include (1) *degree* (accounting for the number of directly connected neighbors), (2) *betweenness* (the extent to which a player is positioned between other network players), and (3) *Eigenvalue* or *Bonacich centrality* (a recursive measure of centrality that takes into account the centrality of connected neighbors).[14] Although the three measures produce slightly different rankings of the centrality of network players, the set of top central players is virtually the same for all three measures. Thus, the list in Table 6.3 is ranked by betweenness. Regardless of how we measure ties, the evidence clearly indicates that the central players were all prominent public officials.

We can complement the network centrality statistics with visual analysis to assess the role of central players within the larger network. In so doing, SNA provides a striking picture of the participation of public officials on corporate boards. Figure 6.5 illustrates two salient features of the Porfiriato network that have been emphasized by economic historians. First, the

TABLE 6.3
Centrality of Public Officials

Rank	Name	Actual Degrees	Share of Degrees (%)	Normalized Betweenness (%)	Normalized Eigenvalue (%)
1.	Fernando Pimentel y Fagoaga	29	5.60	16.60	41.80
2.	Julio M. Limantour	20	3.90	6.50	32.60
3.	Guillermo de Landa y Escandón	25	4.80	6.50	43.70
4.	Manuel Araoz	19	3.70	4.90	31.90
5.	Enrique C. Creel	14	2.70	4.80	24.30
6.	Porfirio Díaz, Jr.	14	2.70	4.40	21.50
7.	Luis Riba y Cervantes	17	3.30	4.20	32.10
8.	Pablo Macedo	22	4.30	3.90	37.50
9.	Miguel S. Macedo	21	4.10	3.90	36.70
10.	Manuel Zamacona e Inclán	10	1.90	3.50	19.00
11.	Roberto Nuñez	15	2.90	1.50	29.60
12.	Salvador Dondé	13	2.50	1.40	23.00
13.	Ramón Alcázar	16	3.10	1.30	25.70
14.	Rafael Dondé	12	2.30	1.10	22.20
15.	Manuel González Cosío	12	2.30	1.10	22.20
16.	Antonio Pliego	10	1.90	0.60	21.40
17.	Tomás Macera	10	1.90	0.20	22.00
18.	Francisco Rincón Gallardo	10	1.90	0.20	20.80
19.	José de Landero y Cos	8	1.60	0.00	18.70
20.	José Y. Limantour	8	1.60	0.00	18.70
	Minimum	0	0.00	0.00	0.00
	Maximum	29	5.60	16.60	43.70
	Mean	6	1.20	1.10	10.20
	Standard deviation	6.4	1.20	2.60	11.40

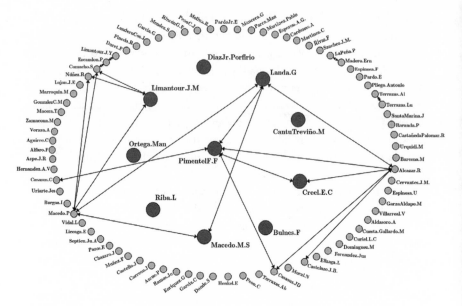

Figure 6.5 Central Network Players
NOTE: This diagram shows major public officials with overlapping seats in boards of
directors. The most central players are placed in the middle and denoted with larger
nodes. Selected links are shown for officials with more than ten mutual company
affiliations.

political economy of the Porfiriato was based on an elite network of bankers and influential public officials. To make the diagram more legible, I show
ties only for the most connected officials. Of the 103 public officials who
served on corporate boards, there was a small group of public officials who
appeared in a large number of corporations.

This figure is a striking example of the prominence of certain individuals
in managing access to finance and political connections. In particular, the
most central player in the network was Fernando Pimentel y Fagoaga, who
in his dual function as a government official and prominent banker had an
important role in monitoring the allocation of financial resources throughout the network. In 1907, for example, Pimentel y Fagoaga served on the
boards of seventeen companies spanning various industries.

Fernando Pimentel y Fagoaga was mayor of Mexico City, a member of
Mexico's monetary commission, and one of the most prominent bankers in
Porfirian Mexico (Read and Musacchio, 2001, Table 3). Unlike most of the
other central players, Pimentel y Fagoaga did not have an extensive political
career prior to his stint as mayor of Mexico City, but he came from a very

prominent family, whose influence in Mexico spanned for centuries prior to Díaz's arrival to power.

Being mayor of Mexico City has historically been an extremely strategic office because for a long time Mexican presidents made that appointment as a cabinet-level position. The importance of this cabinet-level position, along with being at the center of Díaz's government, put Pimentel y Fagoaga in a privileged position to be well informed of, and to be an active participant in, all government policies. Along with proximity to the dictator, this office did not carry any local political accountability. Direct elections for this office did not take place until very recently, in 1997, when Cuauhtémoc Cardenas (former presidential candidate and son of the legendary postrevolutionary president Lázaro Cardenas) got elected as mayor.

The evidence also shows two other important influential connections. First, Pimentel y Fagoaga was also senator for the state of Durango during the last years of the Porfiriato. Second, Pimentel y Fagoaga came from a prominent aristocratic family that had emigrated from Spain's Basque region to Mexico in 1697 (Sanchiz, 2000, p. 130). In Mexico, the Fagoaga family established an economic empire in the northern state of Zacatecas, which included various haciendas, trading centers, and a private bank, which according to historians was the most prominent bank in eighteenth-century Mexico (Sanchiz, 2000, p. 131).

Pimentel y Fagoaga descended from one of the most prominent families of New Spain (colonial Mexico). There were various nobility titles among family members, including the noble houses of the Count of Alcaraz, the Count of La Torre de Cosío, and the Heras Soto Family.[15]

From this last family came Fernando's father, Francisco Pimentel Heras Soto. Pimentel Heras Soto was named ambassador to Mexico in 1865 by Emperor Maximilian, during Napoleon III's short-lived empire in Mexico. Pimentel Heras Soto was also a noted literary scholar, listed as being a member of fourteen literary organizations in Mexico and twelve foreign organizations, including the New York History Academy, the New York Anthropological Society, France's Ethnographic Society, and the Vienna Geographical Society, among others (Sanchiz, 2000, pp. 152–153).

Not surprisingly, Fernando Pimentel y Fagoaga had a major influence in drafting new regulations for financial activity in Mexico. Although he was not named minister of finance, his family, political, and economic connections enabled him to have a hand in every significant economic endeavor during the Porfiriato, especially in the banking industry.

Pimentel y Fagoaga is joined by a list of prominent bankers and public officials who served similar roles at both the federal and state levels. At the

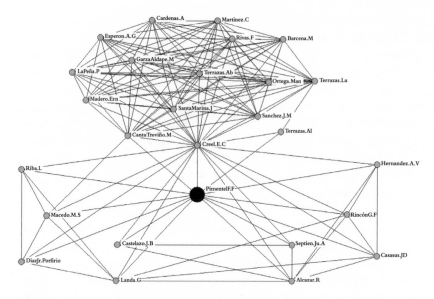

Figure 6.6   Pimentel y Fagoaga's Political Connections

state level, state governors such as Creel and Terrazas were crucial in determining both the rules governing the economic environment of state banks
and the distribution of finance among local enterprises. Another way of
assessing Pimentel y Fagoaga's influence is to examine his ego network or
connections to other network members. As seen in Figure 6.6, Pimentel y
Fagoaga was directly connected to the most influential political actors of
the period.

To examine further the influence of central players, I will provide brief
biographies of a partial list of private enforcers that typify various roles and
backgrounds of key network participants. Biographical information for this
section was taken from secondary sources, including that of Camp (1991),
and other historical studies, and from my own database of political careers.
To put their vested interests in private protection in perspective, Table 6.4
(pp. 150 and 151) summarizes the affiliations these players had with network
companies.

Cronies.   One of Díaz's closest cronies, Guillermo de Landa y Escandón,
came from an aristocratic and wealthy family. de Landa y Escandón "joined
Díaz's inner circle in 1886 when he joined the effort to amend the constitution … to permit Díaz's reelection" (Haber et al., 2003, p. 197).

de Landa y Escandón's early education is unknown, but he received his
high school and professional education in Europe (Camp, 1991, p. 119). He

was also a founding member of the Jockey Club in 1883, a social club that attracted Díaz's closest supporters and the most prominent families of the Porfiriato.[16]

According to Camp (1991), de Landa y Escandón was the nephew of Manuel Escandón, a "capitalist and financier of the Mexico City–Veracruz railroad" (p. 119). This railroad was of much strategic importance because it connected the center of government, Mexico City, with the most important port in Mexico, which was also a gateway for trade with Europe. In addition, de Landa y Escandón, had family members who were involved in national politics. His brother, José, served as a federal deputy for the state of San Luis Potosí from 1896 to 1898 (Camp, 1991, p. 119).

de Landa y Escandón was one of the longest serving public officials during the Porfiriato. My career analysis indicates that he spent thirty-four years in public office.[17] His long political career included various stints in the Mexican Senate, representing various states from all over the country. He was senator from the state of Morelos (just south of Mexico City), for the state of Chihuahua (along the U.S. border), and Oaxaca (in southern Mexico). In addition, he served as governor of the federal district in 1900 and 1903 to 1911, having served as president of the city council in 1900 (Camp, 1991, p. 119).

As was the case with Pimentel y Fagoaga, de Landa y Escandón was part of Díaz's inner circle of supporters and advisers. The historical literature for this period regularly identifies de Landa y Escandón as one of the most important brokers in the various private deals in which the Díaz government was engaged. Connolly (1997), for example, argues that de Landa y Escandón was instrumental in facilitating the awarding of extensive public works contracts to Sir Weetman D. Pearson, whom Connolly (1997) identifies as the dictator's "contractor." Pearson is perhaps better known for his role in the oil industry, as mentioned in an earlier chapter, where he founded the Mexican Eagle Oil Company, one of the two largest oil companies in Mexico during this period.[18] de Landa y Escandón thus played a big role in providing access to the dictator to foreign investors.

A more typical dictator's crony was perhaps the dictator's own son, Porfirio Díaz, Jr. Unlike his father and other relatives, there is no record of Díaz, Jr. holding any public office.[19] There is, however, ample evidence of Díaz, Jr. actively participating in the various industries that were promoted by his father.

The Díaz family was politically influential, although its influence was geographically limited before the dictatorship was consolidated. Porfirio Díaz was born in the southern state of Oaxaca. Díaz did have some national notoriety because of his military role in the liberal movement that drove

TABLE 6.4

Selected Public Officials and Their Company Connections, 1907–1910

Company	Pimentel y Fagoaga	de Landa y Escandón	Limantour	Díaz, Jr.	Alcázar	A. Terrazas	Creel	Camacho	C. and J. Casaús
Almacenes Generales de Deposito de México y Veracruz	1	1			1				1
Banco Agricola e Hipotecario de México	1				1				1
Banco Central Mexicano	1				1		1		1
Banco Comercial Refaccionario						1	1		
Banco de Guanajuato	1				1		1		
Banco de Hidalgo				1					
Banco de Michoacan					1				
Banco de Morelos	1								1
Banco del Estado de México	1				1				
Banco Hipotecario de Crédito Territorial Mexicano	1				1				
Banco Internacional e Hipotecario de México			1	1					
Banco Mercantil de Monterrey							1		
Banco Mexicano de Comercio e Industria		1							
Banco Minero de Chihuahua						1	1		
Banco Nacional de México						1		1	
Batopilas Mining Company							1		
Caja de Prestamos	1								
Cerveceria Moctezuma, Orizaba			1						
Hidroeléctrica é Irrigadora de Chapala	1			1					
Chihuahua and Pacific Railroad							1		
Chihuahua Mineral Railway						1	1		
Compañia Bancaria de Obras y Bienes Raices	1				1	1			
Compañia Carbonifera "Agujita"					1				
Compañia Cigarrera Mexicana	1								1

Company										
Compañía de las Fábricas de Papel de San Rafael								1		1	1
Compañía de Seguros La Mexicana			1							
Compañía Fundidora de Fierro y Acero								1		
Compañía Harinera y Manufacturera Nacional								1		
Compañía Industrial de Atlixco								1		
Compañía Manufacturera Buen Tono								1		
Compañía Mexicana de Petróleo "El Aguila"				1			1	1		
Compañía Minera de Real del Monte y Pachuca							1	1		
Compañía Minera Dos Estrellas									1	
Compañía Nacional Mexicana de Dinamita y Explosivo								1		
Ferrocarril Mexicano México a Veracruz								1		1
Guadalajara Tramways, Light and Power Company						1		1		1
Mexican International Railway Company					1					
Mexican National Packing Company					1			1		
Mexican Telegraph Company					1					
Mexico Northwestern Railroad Company								1		
National Railroad Company of Mexico								1		
Pan–American Railway							1	1		
San Idelfonso Tejidos de Lana								1		
Santa Gertrudis Jute Manufacturing Company, Ltd.									1	
Sociedad Financiera para la Industria en México								1		
Sonora Railway, Cananea, Rio Yaqui, and Pacific Rai	1									
Vera Cruz Terminal Co., Ltd.	1									

Connections are denoted by "1."

NOTE: This table is an example of a (two-mode) affiliation network between two distinct sets of nodes (companies and public officials, respectively). Affiliations have a value of one. A complete relational dataset would also code lack of affiliation as zeroes (not shown here for presentation purposes).

SOURCE: The author's own data collection. See the Appendix for sources.

out the French Empire, but it was in Oaxaca where the Díaz family was politically influential. Felix Díaz, the brother of the dictator, was governor of Oaxaca and a high-ranking military official. Other younger members of the Díaz family held legislative positions representing their home state of Oaxaca (Camp, 1991, pp. 68–69).

Unlike most of the other prominent families, the Díaz family came from modest origins. President Díaz's father was a tinsmith, businessman, and veterinarian. Scholars note that Díaz had to work to support himself while in college, working as a shoemaker and carpenter (Camp, 1991, pp. 68–69). Díaz obtained much prestige from an illustrious military career, which included the famous Battle of Puebla that dealt the French their worst defeat, working his way up to become a general (Benjamin and Marcial, 1984, pp. 332–333; Katz, 1984, p. 15).

Adding to his military prestige, Díaz, Sr. joined an influential family when he married his second wife, "Carmen Romero Castelló, [who] was the daughter of Manuel Romero Rubio, Díaz's secretary of government" (Camp, 1991, p. 68). By marrying into the Romero Rubio family, Díaz established personal ties to one of the most influential cliques in Mexican politics and business, thus extending his realm of influence beyond his military connections. With respect to this family connection, Katz (1984) says,

> ...Romero Rubio was in many ways the architect of the Porfirian State. It was he who transformed the institution of the *jefe político* [local political boss] and who controlled and manipulated the country's governors. His clique consisted mainly of civilians: financiers, landowners, technocrats, bureaucrats, and so on. After his death in 1895, his most successful and intelligent pupil José Yves Limantour, finance minister from 1893, became the acknowledged leader of the clique. (pp. 38–39)

Financiers.   Pimentel y Fagoaga was one of many influential financiers who participated in politics. Two other prominent financiers included Ramón Alcázar and Julio M. Limantour.

Alcázar's importance during the Porfiriato came from two sources: his prominence as a banker and his political career. Like Díaz, there is no historical evidence that he came from an illustrious family. However, Alcázar, along with Pimentel y Fagoaga, was a prominent banker, as evidenced by his participation in the banking sector. In addition, Alcázar had a long political career that spanned a couple of decades. For the period 1888 to 1898, he was deputy for the central state of Guanajuato. Later, he was senator for the western state of Sinaloa for the period 1900 to 1910.

Limantour was a banker and federal deputy for the period 1900 to 1910 (Camp, 1991, p. 121). Limantour had a great deal of economic influence by virtue of his interests in Mexico's two largest banks: the Banco Nacional de México (Banamex) and the Banco de Londres y México (BLM). As noted in Chapter 4, these two banks had the only national charters along with a variety of benefits that effectively made the banking sector a duopoly. Limantour was a director for Banamex as well as a major shareholder in BLM. Given the policy-making ability granted to bankers, Limantour was partly responsible—although not in an official manner—for the direction and maintenance of Mexico's financial system during the Porfiriato.

Although Limantour did not attain higher political office beyond the Chamber of Deputies, he had important political connections. His father had been a close associate of the former liberal president Benito Juárez. The Limantour family had extensive properties in Veracruz. In addition, Julio's brother, José Y. Limantour, was secretary of the treasury from 1893 to 1911, at the time that the major economic reforms of the period took place. José, like de Landa y Escandón, was also a founding member of Mexico City's jockey club (Camp, 1991, p. 121).

As noted previously, the secretary of the treasury had the final say in the awarding of banking privileges and state-level bank charters. Concurrently with this cabinet-level position, José Y. Limantour was head of the Chamber of Deputies in the late 1890s.[20] Taken together, the two Limantour brothers were among the most influential policymakers in the Porfiriato by virtue of their control of finance, as a selective benefit of Díaz's network of private protection.

Unlike other prominent network players, there is contradictory evidence regarding the origin of the Limantour family. On the one hand, Carmagnani (1994, p. 431) provides a biographical profile of José Y. Limantour in which he is said to have been born in Mexico City in 1854. On the other hand, the historical record indicates that José was a former French captain, who arrived in the port of Veracruz in 1858 (presumably for the first time, given Limantour's military position). José's intent was to sell arms to the Mexican government during a brief period of civil war during the late 1850s (Bazant, 1984, pp. 460–461). It is unclear whether the Limantours had any political connections prior to the Porfiriato. In any case, at some point José Y. Limantour joined the influential clique led by Romero Rubio (Díaz's secretary of government and the dictator's future father-in-law). Upon his patron's death, José became the acknowledged leader of the Romero Rubio clique (Katz, 1984, pp. 38–39).

Regional Power Holders.   The main example of officials with independent political power was the Terrazas-Creel clan that dominated the border state of Chihuahua (south of New Mexico and Texas). Alberto Terrazas served as governor of Chihuahua from 1910 to 1911. He was member of a family that had dominated politics in the state of Chihuahua for more than four decades.

Alberto's brother, Juan Terrazas, served as deputy for the state of Chihuahua (Camp, 1991, p. 210). Both Alberto and Juan were brothers of the better known General Luis Terrazas. During the Porfiriato, Luis Terrazas was senator for the state of Chihuahua from 1886 to 1890. He was also governor of the same state from 1879 to 1884 and from 1903 to 1904 (p. 210). Toward the end of the Porfiriato, Luis also became senator for the state of Campeche on the opposite end of the country.

Enrique Creel was the son of an American who had served as the U.S. consul in Chihuahua City (Katz, 1998, p. 47). He had ample local government experience, having served on the city council of Chihuahua City and in the state legislature in the early 1880s. He later served as federal deputy for the state of Chihuahua in the 1890s. From 1900 to 1902 he served as deputy for the neighboring state of Durango.

Creel married into the Terrazas family when he became Luis Terrazas' son-in-law. Later, Enrique succeeded his father-in-law as governor of Chihuahua and was subsequently named by Díaz as secretary of foreign relations (Camp, 1991, pp. 57–58). The alliance of the Terrazas and Creel families created an insurmountable political force in the state of Chihuahua (Wasserman, 1984, pp. 43–70).

> Chihuahua provides another example of the blurring of the lines between governors and the business elite.... [T]he Terrazas-Creel clan ran the state as practically a family business enterprise. Luis Terrazas served as governor from 1860 to 1873, 1879 to 1884, and 1903 to 1904, and his son-in-law Enrique Creel followed in the governorship from 1904 to 1910. Their holdings ran across banking, ranching, agriculture, manufacturing, food processing, mining and smelting, dry goods retailing, railroads, and public utilities. By 1910 they were the single largest employer in the state. (Haber et al., 2003, p. 49)

Legislators.   To represent influential legislators, I will briefly describe the background of Sebastián Camacho and two brothers, Carlos and Joaquín Casasús.

Sebastián Camacho came from a distinguished family. His father was a diplomat, governor, and statesman (Camp, 1991, p. 35). Camacho had a long political career, serving as federal deputy for the state of Jalisco from 1888 to 1898. He also served as mayor of Mexico City in 1894 and federal deputy for the state of Guanajuato from 1894 to 1898.

From 1894 to 1896, Camacho was president of Congress. Later, he served as senator from the Federal District (Mexico City) from 1900 to 1914. He had economic interests in mining and industrial businesses, and also served as president of Banamex (p. 35).[21] Camacho was also a member of the Jockey Club, along with other prominent members of Díaz's inner circle of advisers.

Carlos and Joaquín Casasús were grandsons of José Casasús y Fotosaus, a sailor and merchant from Spain. Their father, Francisco Asis Casasús y Echazaralta, was a boat builder and carpenter in the (Gulf of Mexico) state of Campeche.

Carlos Casasús was a federal deputy for the state of Mexico (around Mexico City) from 1894 to 1912. Carlos was also related by marriage to Olegario Molina, landowner and governor of Yucatán (pp. 41–42).

Joaquín Casasús was a former professor of the National Schools of Engineering and Law, founder and dean of the National School of Business, federal deputy for the state of Tabasco from 1886 to 1902, senator from Veracruz from 1908 to 1910, and ambassador to the United States from 1905 to 1906. He was a close associate of Miguel Macedo, subsecretary of government (1906–1911). Joaquín's niece married into the family of Justo Sierra, Díaz's minister of education (pp. 41–42).

3 Expanding the Scope of Protection

The previous section used SNA to explore the critical relation of private protection. By construction, the composition of this network was restricted to ties between public officials and corporations. Restricting the number of board directors was necessary to isolate the enforcement mechanism underlying the regime of selective property rights.

Public officials were distributed across all industries, and influential network players had a vested interest in individual enforcers protecting the whole network. As it turns out, public officials served an additional role in bridging the interests of otherwise disconnected actors. One way of assessing the importance of public officials is to see how their inclusion affects the structure of interlocking directorates. As noted earlier, public officials had close social connections to economic elites, so restricting ties to public officials may underestimate the incentives to retaliate. For example, if a public official has relatives who are attacked by the dictator, that official would be expected to respond even if he does not sit on the board of the affected company. By looking at private actors as well, we can get a better appreciation of the vested interest of all directors beyond the rent incentives of private protection.

This section analyzes the network with an expanded set of actors. Clearly, public officials had an encompassing interest in the preservation of the system, but it may be argued that other actors benefited as well. Certainly, asset holders themselves benefited greatly from private protection when available. In addition, other investors and private actors also had a stake in the protection of the companies with which they were affiliated. Thus, I analyzed the participation of 684 private actors in addition to the 103 public officials analyzed earlier. The number of corporations remains fixed at 149, but the set of directors has now increased from 103 to 787.[22]

The main result of this analysis is that public officials provided the glue that brought together the interests of various actors, both political and economic, across various industries. The end result was that there was a larger collection of people with an encompassing interest in preserving this system.

To examine the role of public officials more systematically, I will make use of a class of statistical models of networks known as *exponential random graph* or *p** (p-star) *models* (Anderson et al., 1999; Wasserman and Robins, 2005). This approach provides a sound inferential foundation to network analysis beyond descriptive statistics and visualization.[23] Before presenting my results, I will briefly describe how these statistical models enable researchers to model entire networks.

Networks are defined by a set of nodes and their existing ties. Typically, not all pairs of nodes will be connected to one another. The basic approach behind p* models is to model for a given set of nodes the existence of potential ties, each a discrete, binary variable. In this sense, the models resemble the more familiar methodology of logistic regression, where a dependent variable Y is either zero or one, and the quantity of interest is the probability $Pr(Y = 1)$.[24]

Besides that superficial resemblance, however, p* models differ from logistic regressions in two fundamental ways. First, the binary variable in a logistic regression accrues solely to a corresponding observation or individual. In contrast, a tie involves two separate nodes or individuals. Second, unlike logistic regression, the dependent variable for p* models is not just one binary variable, but the collection of all existing and interdependent ties. Understanding the formation of particular ties remains a central task, but the main thrust of p* models is to consider the existing network x as a realization of a random variable X that could have produced several other network configurations. In other words, the dependent variable is the *entire* network.[25]

To understand the utility of p* models, one could posit a baseline model in which ties are created independently, irrespective of social aspects. This process would lead to network configurations that would resemble social networks, but would have been generated by chance alone.[26] A challenge of network theories, such as mine, is to establish that relevant social networks are not trivial in that sense. In other words, networks under consideration do not conform to this baseline model and are, in fact, driven by other proposed theoretical mechanisms.

The main advantage of p* models involves the use of more realistic network models than the baseline case. If ties are not assumed to be independent of one another, the use of p* models enables us to examine how the presence of a network facilitates the creation of ties that would otherwise be devoid of social structure. Moreover, ties can themselves be building blocks of aggregate social structure. By recognizing that nodes considering additional ties are already embedded in some social context, we can further examine how that context plays a role in determining the aggregate network structure. For instance, two nodes may want to establish a tie if they are already part of an existing dense network, but not otherwise. Other network properties, like clustering, or the lack thereof, may increase or decrease the likelihood of establishing additional ties.[27]

For a more systematic examination of structural factors, we can calculate various network statistics that specify different properties of the network and its components. If we collect these network statistics in a list or vector $\mathbf{z}(\mathbf{x})$, an important theoretical result is that the aggregate network configuration can be explained in terms of those structural properties, or[28]

$$Pr(X = x) = \frac{1}{\kappa}\exp(\boldsymbol{\theta}'\mathbf{z}(\mathbf{x})).\tag{6.1}$$

The vector $\boldsymbol{\theta}$ is a collection of parameters associated with corresponding network statistics in $\mathbf{z}(\mathbf{x})$. To illustrate the meaning of this formula, suppose that $\mathbf{z}(\mathbf{x})$ contained just one element, $z_1(x)$, which represented the number of existing ties or so-called *edges*. Then $Pr(X = x) = (1/\kappa)\cdot\exp(\theta_1 z_1(x))$. If the estimate of the corresponding coefficient θ_1 were positive, this result would establish that in the aggregate, the network x exhibits a larger number of ties than one would expect in the baseline case. From the perspective of a potential tie, the positive coefficient would reflect the attractiveness of establishing an additional tie given an already higher than expected number of ties. If the estimate is negative, then one obtains an opposite effect in which the network exhibits fewer ties than expected by chance alone. Finally, if the estimated coefficient is zero, this network would be indistinguishable from the baseline case of independent probabilities for each tie.

By including additional network properties as conditioning variables, one can get a better appreciation of how social context affects the formation of ties. In practice, statistical models will include multiple network statistics, the number of which will vary by application. My application of p* models in this chapter includes four relevant network statistics related to the number of network ties, propensity to have ties with two or three nodes, and triangulation to check for clustering effects. These network properties will be explained in more detail when I discuss my results.

In addition to structural properties, ties may be determined by other separate processes. For instance, ties can be formed solely on the basis of individual attributes that nodes may find attractive. These considerations lie behind social selection models that expand the basic p* model framework to include individual attributes. That is, network structure can then also be conditioned on node, not just network, properties. More precisely, the probability of observing the actual network becomes $Pr(X = x|Y)$, where Y denotes information that characterizes nodes irrespective of their network position or network structure (Robins and Pattison, 2005, pp. 209–210).

All in all, p* models enable a multilevel approach that clarifies the nature of emergent social structures. Ultimately, the quantity of interest is the network in its entirety, but one obtains a better appreciation of the aggregate features of the network by examining how individual ties are formed. Of course, ties are not created in a vacuum. My approach here will examine both social structure as well as individual node traits as determinants of overall network structure.

The twofold approach used in this book will allow us to examine the importance of both (network) structural and (individual) node traits. The added value of an explicitly network-centric approach is to examine whether a network could have existed solely by chance and, if not, whether it was conditioned on node attributes, which could then be analyzed in a well-defined social context. By considering two types of determining factors, one can also examine micro- and macro-level effects concurrently for a more complete network analysis.

My application of p* models involves the analysis of connections between corporate directors during the latter years of the Porfiriato. The set of nodes includes 787 directors, some of whom are public officials, who have affiliations with 149 large companies. I identified 11,607 ties among these 787 directors.

The statistical analysis for the boards network consisted of four p* specifications and was conducted in two steps. First, I constructed a baseline model with four basic structural components to focus on the importance of social structure on network formation:[29]

$$Pr(X = x) = \frac{1}{\kappa} \exp(\theta_1 L + \theta_2 \textit{Two-Star} + \theta_3 \textit{Three-Star} + \theta_4 \textit{Triangle}) \quad (6.2)$$

The first parameter (edges) refers to the effect that adding one link has on the probability of additional links. In other words, how attractive is it to establish a link with another node, all things being equal? The two-star and three-star coefficients reflect the propensity of nodes to have concurrent ties with two or three directors. A fourth component, the existence of triangles, represents clustering, the propensity for nodes to establish direct ties when they already share common ties to other third parties.

Results for this baseline specification are shown under model 1 in Table 6.5. All four coefficients are statistically significant at the 5 percent level and indicate two major features of this network. First, ties are not deemed very attractive when they lead to simple relationships involving one or two potential (but separate) partners. In other words, the network is not as attractive to players with null or few additional connections. Second, more complex relationships involving connections with more people or the creation of clusters are deemed more attractive. The end result is that the network will not be uniformly dense, but instead will be characterized by clusters of multiple connections among a relatively small number of players.

An important fact in the interpretation of these structural results is that higher order structural components depend on lower levels. For example, when considering one additional tie, in order for a node to have three ties to other nodes, it must be the case that the node is already connected to two other nodes. Put another way, for a three-star configuration to arise, there must be a two-star configuration already in place. Likewise, for a triangular structure to arise, it must be the case that two nodes are already connected to a third one. These considerations will be taken into account when evaluating the estimates for θ_2 through θ_4.

The estimate for the edges coefficient is -0.2173, which implies a tie probability of 0.4459.[30] In other words, there is less than a fifty–fifty chance that a tie between any two nodes will be established. The two-stars coefficient is also negative (-0.2062), reflecting a lower than expected number of two-star configurations given the existing number of ties. If the first of two

TABLE 6.5
Corporate Board Network P-Star Analysis

	Dependent Variable: $Pr(X = x)$		Model 1	Model 2	Model 3	Model 4
Structural Determinants	Edges ($\hat{\theta}_1$):		−0.2173 (0.5197)	−2.5954 (0.7405)	−2.6994 (0.9834)	−2.3346 (0.6631)
	Two-stars ($\hat{\theta}_2$):		−0.2062 (0.0085)	−0.2069 (0.0144)	−0.2080 (0.0213)	−0.2115 (0.0130)
	Three-stars ($\hat{\theta}_3$):		0.0020 (0.0002)	0.0019 (0.0003)	0.0020 (0.0004)	0.0020 (0.0003)
	Triangle ($\hat{\theta}_4$):		0.9722 (0.0117)	0.9991 (0.0335)	0.9866 (0.0356)	1.0028 (0.0193)
Role of Influential Political Actors	Current G ($\hat{\theta}_5$)			1.1340 (0.6249)	1.1151 (0.6500)	
	Old G ($\hat{\theta}_6$)				−0.3416 (1.0476)	
	Experience ($\hat{\theta}_7$)					0.0457 (0.0187)
	AIC		11014	10594	10598	10522
	BIC		11057	10647	1062	10575
	Residual deviance		11006	10584	10586	10512
	Log likelihood		−5503	−5292	−5293	−5256
	Number of nodes	787				
	Number of ties	11607				
	Network density	0.038				

NOTE: Standard errors in parentheses. AIC and BIC stand for the Akaike and Bayesian Information Criterion, respectively.

potential partners already has one connection, then the probability of an additional tie depends on whether the second partner has an independent tie. In the case when the second partner has no other ties, the first player will make a connection with a probability of 0.3957. In the case when the second partner does have one tie, then the probability goes down to 0.3476. All things being equal, the first node would prefer to have a greater number of ties than the second node.

The three-star and triangle parameter estimates show a different story, as evidenced by the positive sign of their coefficients. Indeed, the probability of a tie definitely increases if it leads to either a three-star configuration or a triangle (clustering). In the case of three-stars, the estimated coefficient is 0.002, which increases the probability of a tie marginally. If only one of the two players is involved in a two-star configuration, then the probability of a tie is 0.3962. If both players are part of two-stars, then the probability increases to 0.3966.

The coefficient for triangle configurations is 0.9722. The predicted probability for a tie depends on how many other nodes are already connected to the two nodes under consideration. If no triangles are added (which implies that the nodes do not share connections with other players), then the probability of an additional tie is determined by lower level structures, as specified earlier. In contrast, if the two players have a common connection to a third party, then the probability that they will want to establish a tie would be 0.6343, which almost doubles the probability compared with more simple network configurations. A tie will almost certainly take place if the two players have a high number of prior common connections. For instance, if the two directors share a connection with two or three other nodes, then the probability of a tie goes up to 0.8213 or 0.9239 respectively.

Beyond structural determinants, I also examined the importance of public officials, which is the main quantity of interest behind this statistical analysis. I expanded the baseline model with the attribute of whether potential partners were current public officials (denoted by G, as in the model of Chapter 2):[31]

$$Pr(X = x) = \frac{1}{\kappa} \exp(\theta_1 L + \theta_2 \textit{Two-Star} + \theta_3 \textit{Three-Star} + \theta_4 \textit{Triangle} + \theta_5 G) \quad (6.3)$$

The quantity of interest is $\hat{\theta}_5$, which is equal to 1.1340 and is statistically significant at the 10 percent level.[32] Note that this new specification (model 2 in Table 6.5) retains the previous structural variables, which is important to assess the relative influence of social structure and node attributes. For the most part, social structure operates similarly to the baseline model, except in the simplest of structures. The dominant structural components of the baseline model retain their influence, because the estimates for three-stars and triangles are basically the same for all models.

What changes drastically is the probability of a tie when only lower level structures are at work. Without social structure, if we focus solely on the edges parameter, the probability of a tie between private actors is about 0.07—orders of magnitude lower than in the baseline case where ties can be established with a probability of 0.45.

Of course, one major reason for this decrease in tie probability stems from the fact that partners are not selected randomly. In particular, partners who are also public officials are deemed more attractive. If a public official is involved, the probability of a tie more than doubles—to about 0.19.[33] All things being equal, directors want to be associated with public officials rather than private actors.

The previous paragraph considered only the case in which the two nodes are establishing their first tie in the network. In contrast, if they are already embedded in the network, higher level structures can be enabled, with a concomitant increase in the probability of an additional tie. To illustrate, if nodes are already connected to one other player in common, then the probability of an additional tie increases from 0.07 to 0.17. If they share two independent common connections, then they will want to establish an additional tie, with a probability of 0.36. This increase in probability is irrespective of the type of actor. If, in addition to sharing multiple connections, the additional tie also involves a public official, then the probability of a tie would increase from 0.17 to 0.39 (in the first case of one common connection) or from 0.36 to 0.66 with two common connections. The greater the number of common connections, the more certain it will be that the nodes will want to establish a direct connection.

The second model reinforces the previous result that the network exhibits clustering. All things being equal, directors want to relate to other well-connected directors. In addition, we can see that there is a preference for associations with public actors. Hence, we will see much clustering around public officials.

To investigate further the role of political actors, I ran two variations of the second model. In that model, I only considered public officials currently in office, which excludes other board directors with prior experience in the public sector. In fact, because of the nature of data collection, a director who may have held a public office as late as 1904 would be coded as a private actor in 1905 and thereafter. However, it is plausible that such actors could also be viable private enforcers because they retained political influence, or otherwise could provide valuable information to prevent predation. To investigate this possibility, I coded for directors who had previously been in public office at some point during earlier years of the Porfiriato. A third model was therefore constructed as follows:

$$Pr(X = x) = \frac{1}{\kappa} \exp(\theta_1 L + \theta_2 Two\text{-}Star + \theta_3 Three\text{-}Star$$

$$+\, \theta_4 Triangle + \theta_5 NewG + \theta_6 OldG) \qquad (6.4)$$

The estimates for this model do not provide support for the hypothesis that "old" public officials had any influence on network formation. Not only is the sign negative, suggesting that these actors were less attractive, but the parameter $(\hat{\theta}_6)$ was not statistically significant. The remaining parameters are not changed by the inclusion of this additional attribute. Current public officials still have a positive impact on the formation of ties, and the corresponding parameter $(\hat{\theta}_5)$ still remains significant at the 10 percent level.

Differentiating between current and old public officials may be too blunt an approach to examining the role of influential political actors. For instance, the previous chapter on political careers clearly established that public officials enjoyed long tenures. One would expect that the longer a career, the greater the ability of a public official to provide private enforcement. Hence, many of the "old" public officials (and indeed the current ones as well) could have extensive experience and information that would be very useful to protect property rights. To that effect, I ran a different model that did not differentiate between current and old public officials, but rather accounted for the political experience of corporate directors, as measured by the number of years they spent in public office during the Porfiriato. This attribute (experience) was added to the baseline model to derive a new specification:

$$Pr(X = x) = \frac{1}{\kappa} \exp(\theta_1 L + \theta_2 \textit{Two-Star} + \theta_3 \textit{Three-Star}$$

$$+ \theta_4 \textit{Triangle} + \theta_7 \textit{Experience}) \tag{6.5}$$

Using experience as the relevant attribute, we get similar results as for the model with current public officials (model 2). Regarding structural factors, the propensity for clustering continues to dominate, although with the latest model, the previously reported probabilities of 0.17 and 0.36 now increase slightly to 0.21 and 0.42 respectively. Regarding political actors, we find that the coefficient for experience has the same positive sign as $\hat{\theta}_5$, but exhibits more statistical significance; so in that sense, the attribute experience gets better support from the data than the G attribute.

The magnitude of $\hat{\theta}_7$ is much smaller than that of $\hat{\theta}_5$, apparently suggesting a lesser influence of political experience. However, unlike the previous variables that simply accounted for the presence of a public official, the experience variable captures the experience of both potential partners. Hence, experience can be high in two cases—if one node has a lot of experience or if both have moderate experience—but the sum is high. To get a better sense of the effects, consider the cases in which a tie involves twenty, thirty, or sixty years of shared experience in a social context in which both players are already well connected. In those cases, the probability of an additional tie would increase from 0.42 to 0.59, 0.70, and 0.90 respectively.

The added value of the last model is that enables us to understand further the influence and identity of important political actors within the network. The relatively smaller coefficient for experience does not imply that public officials (old and new) are any less important, but instead points to the importance of long-lived public officials. This model indicates that those actors with long political careers would be more attractive partners. If we connect this result to what we learned about political careers in Chapter 5, then it becomes clear who the more attractive network partners will be: governors and prominent legislators, especially senators, whose careers spanned several decades.

4   Concluding Remarks

In this chapter I conducted a network analysis of the private protection that major companies obtained during the Porfiriato. Identifying the structure of protection helped clarify the incentives of public officials who were motivated to offer private protection in exchange for direct economic benefits. Likewise, network analysis also allowed me to examine the network from the perspective of protected firms and their expectations that the network could serve to protect their individual property rights.

The network analysis showed that protected firms were closely allied with influential public officials with the ability and incentive to punish predatory behavior by the dictator. To be sure, the degree of private protection varied across industries, but the distribution of protection was consistent with my theory that domestic investors would seek private protection more so than foreign investors.

One notable feature of the industry distribution of private protection warrants additional comments. My analysis found a close connection between bankers and public officials. In addition, a large percentage of corporate board seats existed in industries that depended crucially on the existing financial system. Because the financial system was dominated by a small elite of financiers and prominent public officials, it is not surprising to see that cabinet members and state governors, many of whom were also bankers, dominated access to the corporate boards of banks and other industries, such as manufacturing, that needed credit from banks.

The analysis provides strong evidence that banking was the backbone of the Porfiriato political economy. What made commitments credible was the creation of a network in which not only governments committed to good policies, but economic actors themselves cooperated across industries within their elite network. Legislators were active participants in this political economy network. They played enforcement and monitoring roles to ensure that enhanced executive powers did not have a negative impact on economic activity.

In addition, I showed that public officials were part of a larger group of people interested in the preservation of an exclusive network of private protection. Private actors were relatively well organized and had dense connections, but they were otherwise disconnected across industries. Public officials not only provided private protection, they also played a critical role in bridging the interests of various industries, thus expanding the scope of encompassing interests to the whole network.[34]

Chapter 7

Conclusion

The motivating question for this study was to understand how dictators make credible commitments to investors. To answer this question, I developed a theory that addressed the issue of credible commitments in the absence of institutions of limited government.

My network theory of private protection makes two substantive contributions to the study of institutions and growth. First, I developed an organizational theory of selective credible commitments in which dictators offer private, rather than universal, protection to a limited set of actors.[1] My theory of selective credible commitments contributes to the extant literature by redefining the types of commitments that dictators can make, and the *private enforcement mechanisms* (or underlying political organization) that they rely upon to replace or complement political institutions.

Second, my theory also provides an institutional explanation for the encompassing interests espoused in Olson's (2000) theory of stationary banditry. To be sure, my theory posits the same general incentives as Olson—namely, that long-lived dictators will want to promote growth when they internalize the costs that their predatory behavior imposes on economic activity. But this internalization mechanism is actually more general and applies to all types of governments. For instance, in democratic settings, the internationalization occurs through political costs when prospects of removal from office or reelection incentives serve to discipline governments. Dictators will not, of course, subject themselves to the types of electoral mechanisms that democracies have, so one important question remains. How, exactly, do stationary bandits internalize the costs of predation? The answer lies in Olson's concept of encompassing interests, which needed further definition.

What defines encompassing interests is a *collection* of actors, organized or *related* in a particular way, rather than a single actor. More precisely, my theory posits that encompassing interests are embedded in social networks of private protection. The underlying incentive is the sharing of rents facilitated by special privileges. Dictators will engage systematically in the use of private rather than public policies, contrary to Olson's argument that the encompassing interest of stationary bandits leads to the provision of public goods to generate growth, presumably for the benefit of all of society.

I presented a series of models that demonstrated the underlying logic that enables private protection to scale up with the use of a simple network structure. Network configurations will, of course, differ from one case to another but, as a general proposition, my theory identifies the potential ability of informal networks to enable collective retaliation against predation, thus protecting the property rights of network participants.

The introduction of network analysis to the study of institutions is novel and offers various venues for subsequent research on the joint study of networks and institutions. One extension involves the development of better theories and network models. SNA has largely been developed within the discipline of sociology (Wellman and Berkowitz, 1997). A bulk of the literature has examined the mathematical properties of networks using graph theory (Scott, 2000; Wasserman and Faust, 1994). There has been less work on formal models of networks. The work by Dutta and Jackson (2003) is representative of an economic approach to modeling networks with a game–theoretic approach, but this highly technical literature largely focuses on examining the stability of abstract networks. There is a lot of potential in applying and extending these abstract models to problems of political economy, to formulate more detailed models that examine interesting instances in which networks arise from the interplay of politics and economics.

More empirical work cannot only inform theory and methods, but may itself illuminate other processes beyond collective retaliation and the propagation of predation risk, which I examined in this book. For example, there are clear connections to the study of patron–client relationships and corruption. Indeed, some of the countries that have long been heralded as exceptional cases of economic growth (under authoritarianism) are now derided as prominent examples of corruption. Some scholars recognize the relational aspects of corruption, but a systematic analysis involving networks of corruption remains to be done.[2]

Because of its focus on networks, however, the theory has important methodological implications regarding the type of data needed to assess it. At this point, we are not ready to engage in large-N comparative studies. Studying the impact of networks cannot be addressed solely with the addition of "network" variables to cross-country statistical studies.[3] As it turns out, such relational data are currently unavailable, and part of the reason is that we would not know exactly what to look for. As I noted earlier, references to social networks tend to be vague, so we need further guidance in identifying reliable and valid measurements of networks that directly address our research questions.

More important, network analysis also entails a *multilevel* analysis that examines the interaction between lower level processes (where social relations operate) as well as higher level processes (where social structures and aggregate outcomes are manifested). To date, quantitative studies of institutions tend to focus on aggregate outcomes, but remain incomplete accounts because they obscure the underlying microfoundations. Moreover, assuming we had the relevant data, we would also need to develop new methods.[4]

To evaluate my theory and illustrate how one may proceed to analyze networks and institutions, I analyzed the question of policy credibility in a particular setting to explain how the dictator Díaz was able to promote growth in late nineteenth-century Mexico. As part of the analysis, I showed how one can map the structure of private protection with the use of SNA tools. Identifying the structure of protection helped clarify the incentives of public officials who offered private protection in exchange for direct economic benefits.

The following section reviews my empirical findings as a preamble to an evaluation of the variable economic performance of dictatorships. I end with a discussion about the long-term implications of growth in nondemocratic settings.

1 Politics and Policy Credibility During the Porfiriato

The Porfiriato has received much attention during the last hundred years. Students of the Díaz dictatorship have brought to bear various questions and approaches. Before reviewing my own empirical contribution to what is a largely normative body of historical literature, I should make clear what this book is not. First, the fact that Mexico's early industrialization occurred under a dictatorship was approached as an outcome to be explained rather than justified. Hence, although this book explains how Díaz was successful in making credible commitments to some actors, it is not meant as an apology for the Díaz dictatorship. I have noted throughout the book that not everyone's rights were protected, and, as will become clear in my discussion, Díaz's economic model was flawed in several respects.

Second, I emphasize as well that Díaz's policies were evidently successful, but were not always premeditated, and took a long time to develop. This book should not then be misconstrued as a manual on how to run a successful dictatorship simply because retrospective analysis shows that Díaz performed relatively well in terms of narrow economic objectives. What is more, not only was the dictatorship eventually overthrown, but the long-term implications of making selective commitments are more pernicious. For one, this type of economic success is not sustainable in the long run; so, at best, success is short-lived. In addition, both the theory and evidence provide sobering lessons for developing countries like Mexico when they base their development on authoritarian government and the dispensation of special privileges.

To specify my contribution, my analysis focused on identifying the mechanisms that enhanced the credibility of Díaz's economic policies. My answer was that the network structure of special privileges that Díaz awarded created a critical mass of actors with the incentive to defend the system against predation. This is not to say that the existence of social networks alone facilitated economic growth, as not all social structures lead to collective retaliation. Moreover, unlike his predecessors, Díaz benefited from a particular point in time with increasing opportunities to attract foreign investment and to integrate into world markets (Glade, 1984, pp. 7–8, 39–46). These economic opportunities represented the prospect of high rents, which were unavailable to previous dictators like Itúrbide and Santa Anna during the early nineteenth century. But the prospect of rents alone does not automatically generate growth, so despite Díaz's unique situation, there remained the important question of how the dictator could induce actors to take advantage of these new economic opportunities.

I.I RENTS AND PRIVATE PROTECTION

My theory predicts that dictators can credibly commit only to private policies, or selective protection. Therefore, a testable implication of my theory is that the Díaz government should have relied heavily on private policies. To evaluate the private or public nature of Díaz's policies, I gathered three types of direct evidence regarding the question of policy definition at different levels of aggregation. First, I examined the general nature of authoritarian government by analyzing all known policies and decrees that were passed at the national level for relevant subperiods of the Díaz dictatorship. Second, I analyzed the types of policies that supported development in Mexico's major industries. Lastly, I evaluated whether particular firms that developed during the Porfiriato based the protection of their property rights on private or public policies—with a sample of more than 5000 firms, covering the period 1886 to 1911.

Taken together, the historical record provides overwhelming evidence that policy-making processes in Porfirian Mexico were dominated by private agreements between the executive government (sometimes in coordination with state governments) and affected economic actors. I also established that there was a systematic variation in the specific terms that enterprises obtained—even when located in the same industry. Firms with higher expected rents were more likely to obtain better concession terms.

1.2 AVAILABILITY OF PRIVATE ENFORCERS

Special privileges had economic implications, but also served political purposes. For instance, historians have long noted that Díaz maintained himself in power with the use of strategic concessions to officials at all levels of government. There was, therefore, room for public officials at the state and local levels to provide protection in exchange for rents from local economic activity. Katz (1984) aptly summarizes the incentives behind opportunities for private gain by state and local government officials as follows:

> ...Díaz encouraged or at least allowed...the *caciques* in power...to enrich themselves by acting as intermediaries for foreign investors who wished to settle in these regions or to acquire property there. In this way, Díaz gave the members of the local oligarchy...a powerful stake in the stability of the region. (p. 37)

In order for social networks to be the basis for sustained economic growth, it must be the case that selective credible commitments are perceived to be long-lived. This requirement, in turn, implies that there must be a steady source of private enforcers. I examined this testable implication with a study of political careers.

The evidence shows that there was a stable system of political careers. First, there is evidence of influential public officials who held offices for long periods of time, including governors as well legislative and executive officers. Second, my political mobility analysis showed stability at higher offices and opportunities for career advancement (of senators becoming governors, for example) that provided incentives for public officials to cooperate with the dictator.

In order for dictators to make selective credible commitments, there must be third parties with the incentive and collective ability to punish the dictator. To test this implication, I used SNA to map relevant connections in a network of economic and political actors. The testable implication is that influential political actors be at the center of the network, and that they be powerful enough to mitigate government opportunism.

The evidence showed that Díaz's network was not particularly dense, but did include a cadre of central players whose interests spanned the whole network. The evidence shows that the central players in Díaz's network were powerful enough to keep the dictator in check. The fragmented nature of the polity during the nineteenth century, and continuing regional autonomy, enabled some actors to accumulate political power, which enabled them to become private enforcers after Díaz came to power. From Roderic Ai Camp's extensive work on political recruitment and politicians in Mexico, one learns that many politicians were very influential (Camp 1982, 1991, 1992, 1995a, 1995b). Central political figures were likely to come from well-to-do families, with already existing political connections to relatives in government. In addition, the general profile of public officials indicated that public officials had experience at the local government, business sector, and in the Mexican army. Díaz could not have dispensed with social elites easily. In addition, he relied heavily on military officers to serve in various public offices, especially as state governors, to help pacify the country and to keep political opposition under control.

I.3 SOCIAL NETWORKS AND GOVERNANCE STRUCTURE

The core of my empirical analysis was a network analysis of connections between influential public officials and companies. But my theory also has implications about the coexistence of formal institutions with a network of private protection, which I discuss next.

If social networks were the main mechanism supporting Díaz's network of private protection, then one implication is that that there would be less dissension in Congress because policy differences could be dealt with within the network. To test this implication, I collected data to assess whether deputies or senators attempted to transform policies in the context of formal policy-making processes.

An analysis of executive–legislative relations during Díaz's dictatorship shows four interesting patterns that are consistent with my theory of networks as a complementary governance structure to formal political institutions in terms of policy formulation. First, the executive government was active in proposing policies to the legislative branch through cabinet proposals or a congressional permanent commission with close ties to the Díaz government. Second, congressional opposition to executive proposals decreased steadily over time. Third, Congress transferred legislative authority over to the executive government, to which it also awarded extensive executive decree authority. Lastly, the executive government, in turn, eventually delegated policy making to affected economic groups outside the legislative arena.

A second implication is that if there was a network in which public officials and economic actors came together to negotiate and craft policies, we would expect the Díaz government and other influential actors to work out their differences within the network, and not through open political conflict. In other words, as Díaz consolidated his dictatorship, and relied more on a private network for the exercise of government, we would also expect to see less conflict over time. The evidence shows that military expenditures decreased steadily during the period, reaching their lowest points during Díaz's period of consolidated dictatorship.

Thus, my empirical analysis finds strong support for my network theory of private protection in the case of the Porfiriato. I note that this conclusion is not based on finding support for a single hypothesis. Admittedly, some of the tests are more direct than others in terms of evaluating the role of networks. Weighing all the evidence, however, all hypotheses point the same way: demonstrating that I have identified with a high degree of plausibility the particular mechanism that enabled Díaz to make selective credible commitments.

My findings also call into question the conventional view that formal political institutions were unimportant during the Porfiriato. Katz (1984) notes, for instance, that "[b]y 1888, [Congress] had become for all practical purposes a rubber stamp institution" (p. 30). Weldon (1997) also notes that the "Congress fell into relative disuse under the Porfiriato, after Porfirio Díaz ... had placed loyalists in both chambers" (p. 229). If one focuses solely on formal legislative processes, it is clear why this conventional view has taken hold. My analysis of policy-making processes and legislative behavior shows that legislators did, in practice, defer to the executive power, especially after Díaz's dictatorship was consolidated during the early 1890s.

My analysis makes it clear, however, that legislators—and public officials more generally—remained active participants in the policy-making process, but they preferred to defer legislative powers to the executive government in exchange for access to a network of private protection that shared the fruits of economic growth.[5] What is more, public officials had direct influence on the private policies that were formulated, while also serving in many cases as sources of third-party enforcement. Their interaction as political actors was perhaps more informal, because they relied heavily on a social network that operated in conjunction with formal political institutions. The role served by social networks during the Porfiriato is similar to the role of political parties in Weldon's theory of *Presidencialismo* (presidentialism) (Weldon, 1997, pp. 227–228) in that it enabled the dictator to control which policies were enacted while maintaining discipline among network members. Formal political institutions, especially Congress, provided the necessary conditions for Díaz's network to be (indirectly) based on the participation of (constitutionally sanctioned) influential political players.[6]

Among other substantive issues, my empirical analysis finds two interesting results that warrant further empirical analysis of other cases. The first result involves the role of legislatures in maintaining dictatorships. The second result involves the prevalence of connections between politicians and banks.

In a sense, the study of the Porfiriato is a study about the making of a dictator. Díaz came to power during a situation in which the executive government was relatively weak with respect to Congress, as well as state governments. Over time, Díaz consolidated power and convinced Congress to delegate policy making to him, and to give him ample authority to govern by executive decree. Díaz, in turn, delegated policy formulation to private economic actors and used executive decrees to make policy agreements with private actors.

Why would the legislature want to give up so much power? My SNA indicates that they did it for money. The legislature realized that dictators can only make selective commitments, but that these commitments are often very profitable. The legislature was thus purposefully instrumental in creating a dictatorial government that could offer members of Congress, and politicians in general, selective access to lucrative economic opportunities. Although legislatures in authoritarian regimes are often portrayed as democratic façades or rubber stamp institutions, this interpretation of politics during the Porfiriato invites a more detailed analysis of the interests and strategies of legislators in nondemocratic settings.[7]

In addition, my analysis found a close connection between bankers and politicians. Given the type of economic activity that dictators can sustain (when appropriate enforcement is available), there is reason to believe that my findings would be replicated in other settings. Large-scale economic activity requires financial resources that entrepreneurs themselves may not be able to provide. If dictators want to maintain their ruling coalitions, they must secure access to finances for their protected economic interests. The testable implication is that we should expect dictators to have tight control of their banking sector, and that these banking sectors should be very concentrated. In other words, there cannot be a competitive banking sector that diffuses political control over finance, because it threatens the stability of the informal coalitions between governments and economic interests, and would not be able to coordinate against government opportunism (Maurer, 2002, p. 3).

2   Other Cases of Growth Under Dictatorships

I have shown that my network theory helps explain the ability of the Díaz dictatorship to make selective credible commitments. I will now discuss how the theory and evidence I have presented can inform our understanding of other relevant cases. In particular, my theory should be able to explain the so-called East Asian miracle (World Bank, 1993). I note that the goal here is not to engage in a detailed comparative study, which is beyond the scope of this book, but it is to propose that there is a common logic to the way that different authoritarian governments commit to growth-enhancing policies.

To a large extent, notably successful dictatorships have benefited from propitious conditions that facilitated fast rates of growth. Invariably, successful cases occurred in developing settings in which capital investments could produce significant increases in output simply because countries had a lot of catching up to do. In that context, a heavy reliance on rents had an immediate, positive impact, even without regard for efficiency (Khan, 2000). In the long run, as is evident now, the nature of industrial development caught up to reveal its vulnerability. Capital-intensive growth, mostly protected, would not generate incentives to innovate, would create inefficiencies, and would eventually collapse, as it did in the case of East Asia in the late 1990s. When this development model collapsed, however, it also revealed its underlying social foundations (Campos, 2002; Bhargava and Bolongaita, 2004).

The impressive economic performance of authoritarian governments, especially in East Asia, spurred a large body of literature seeking to apply lessons from these success stories to other developing countries.[8] The main lesson that emerged from these studies was that states could accelerate development by choosing the right economic policies, by having expert bureaucracies, and by enhancing state capacity. The right economic policies involved choosing a path of technological development that accelerated growth. Expert bureaucracies were needed to devise fast growth policies and to select the right industries to be developed. Lastly, states needed the capability to coordinate and manage conflict among different groups, especially among bureaucrats and business groups (Evans, 1995).

All things being equal, these conditions are likely to have a positive impact on rates of economic growth, so they can be used to explain variability along that dimension, but the literature has not placed much attention to the underlying mechanisms that enabled government to provide those conditions credibly in the first place. My network theory provides a rationale for the success of these countries. However, simply choosing the right policy is not enough to promote growth. I have argued that all policies, irrespective of their efficiency implications, must be deemed credible by investors. Thus, in a fundamental sense, the reason behind the success of authoritarian governments depends crucially on the credibility of proposed policies.

To assess the potential role of networks of private protection in bringing about policy credibility, we need to inquire about the organization of growth-promoting policies. Recent scrutiny of East Asian development in the aftermath of the financial crisis of the 1990s sheds some light on the specific ways that authoritarian governments went about promoting growth. Against the backdrop of impressive economic performance prior to the financial crisis, a closer look at these countries shows a high incidence of corruption, enrichment of the dictator and close allies, and favoritism in economic policies. In other words, policies were private as well as inherently relational. To be sure, MacIntyre (1994) notes a wide variation in the organization of business–government relations, as these do not always lead to corruption. For instance, the role of patronage and clientelism in public policy has varied over time in Thailand (Doner and Ramsay, 2000; Laothamatas, 1994).

Without formal political institutions to tie their hands, dictators have to rely on informal arrangements, so it is not surprising that East Asian economic development—mostly guided by authoritarian governments—is depicted from a relational perspective. Informal arrangements go by various names in the literature, including *crony capitalism* (Haber, 2002; Kang, 2002), *booty capitalism* (Hutchcroft, 1998), *capitalist dictatorships* (Olson, 2000), or *tin-pot dictatorships* (Wintrobe, 1998), among others. Although their names may differ from one case to another, all of these arrangements shared a common logic and social structure to enhance the credibility of dictatorial policies during earlier periods.[9] The common logic is that dictatorial policies were credible because concomitant encompassing interests were distributed and embedded within a social network that diffused political power and economic rents to selected political and economic actors. These social networks served to limit government opportunism, thus enabling dictators to become credible stationary bandits or limited dictators.

My argument is consistent with the explanation by Campos and Root (1996) for the success of East Asian countries. Clearly, there was the potential for rents through the promotion of high-technology and large-scale economic activity, there was vulnerability to social pressure evidenced by outside threats, and encompassing interests were widely dispersed through a strategy of shared growth. But policies remained private to generate rents, and the allocation and implementation of those policies depended heavily on connections, thus their recent depiction as crony capitalism. My network theory further clarifies that the outside threats emphasized by Campos and Root, although important, are not the only source of restraint on government abuses. Protected interests, which were densely connected, could have also punished the government. Political actors, like the generals in South Korea, had some ability to punish predation, and governments were also constrained because they depended on private actors for finance and investment.[10]

My theory thus serves to reconcile the impressive record of economic performance in some dictatorships with recent debates on crony capitalism. In fact, my theory predicts that credible commitments in those dictatorships could not have been sustained otherwise, but the availability of cronies must be accompanied by other conditions. As we know, despite apparently similar social arrangements, not all East Asian economies developed successfully (Kang, 2002; MacIntyre, 1994).

Crony capitalism is but one requirement toward the provision of selective property rights, and by itself does not always lead to good outcomes. Bad outcomes can occur for one of two reasons. First, the cronies may not be strong enough to inflict penalties on the dictators. Second, and most important, even when cronies are capable of providing private enforcement, selective protection must be accompanied by appropriate governance structures that facilitate the exercise of authoritarian government, that ensure a steady stream of rents, and that complement existing, formal political institutions.[11] In light of my theory, it was the combination of crony capitalism with a good political organization that enabled East Asian authoritarian countries to grow, but this is not an easy combination to obtain.[12]

3   Why Do Most Dictatorships Fail?

The theory of this book sought to resolve the paradox of growth in dictatorships. A more general understanding of the political economy of dictatorships would go beyond that paradox to explore the mixed economic performance of dictatorships. To be sure, the historical record shows a great deal of variation in the ability of dictatorships to sustain economic growth. The set of countries with dictatorships or authoritarian regimes includes most of the poorest nations in the world, along with a few countries with high standards of living. This evidence raises several fundamental questions for the study of the political economy of development. Why do some dictatorships have impressive economic records, but most remain poor? What are the political foundations of economic growth in dictatorships?

My network theory of private protection identifies three major factors that can be useful in explaining the variable performance of dictatorships. First, the distribution of wealth in society will be important in determining the availability of rents to help pay for private protection. If a typical investor cannot deploy assets that result in highly profitable investments, there will be no incentives for third parties to enforce private policies. Concentration of assets also enables asset holders to organize themselves more effectively to obtain better private policies. Foreign investors can, of course, substitute for domestic ones, but they are more mobile and may not be reliable long-term partners for the dictator.

Second, the distribution of power will be crucial in determining whether there will be a critical mass of influential political actors that can punish predatory governments. A third factor emphasized in this book is organization. For sustained growth to occur, it is required that there be a governance structure that allows the dictator to manage multiple commitments that arise from offering private policies to various actors. The more commitments there are, the greater the scope of economic activity that the dictator can sustain. Specifically, for this governance structure to encourage long-term selective credible commitments, it must ensure not only that the dictator stays in power for a long time, but it must also ensure the existence of a long-lived pool of private enforcers.

As explained in Chapter 2, the conditions necessary to make credible commitments are fairly stringent (see the small commitment regions in Figures 2.3 and 2.6). It does not suffice that there be profitable opportunities, so my theory is not about how awarding favors to cronies automatically generates commitments. The passage of private policies is actually a general feature of authoritarian government, and not all dictators are able to sustain large-scale economic development on the basis of special privileges. Mine is also not a general statement that social networks are always reliable sources of enforcement. As it turns out, social networks exist anywhere, and most will fail to meet the conditions of my theory. Ultimately what matters is that the private policies generate encompassing interests, and the creation of such interests does depend on particular social structures. The constitution of society will thus be an important variable, insofar as it affects how relevant actors relate to one another and how they distribute political power among themselves to enable collective retaliation.

To clarify how these conditions work in tandem, it will be helpful to have an empirical referent in which the exercise of authoritarian government did not translate into economic growth. Although this requirement may describe most of the developing world, the African continent, especially Sub-Saharan Africa, is a prime example of the necessity for good political institutions to encourage economic development. Dictators like Mobutu Sese Seko in Zaire, among others, represent the prototypical predatory government whose abuse of authority has led to continued underdevelopment (Guest, 2004).

Africa is also a continent where various types of relations permeate social and political life. Thompson (2004) notes that lineage, kin relations, and other affinities among individuals mediate all types of social interaction. Traditional values reinforce particular ways in which society relates to political authority. In many cases, in what are sometimes referred as *patrimonial states* (or a variant thereof), there is a cult of personality around political leaders with rigid social structures for political interaction that encourage abuses and corruption (Chehabi and Linz, 1998a, pp. 5–9; Martinussen, 1997, p. 250; Sawyer, 2005, pp. 6, 15–22; Thomson, 2004, pp. 10, 30–56, 115–121).

Driven by various types of social connections, African states have dispensed special privileges on the basis of ethnicity, kin relations, or through more impersonal patronage networks. Dalton (1965) illustrates the relevance of social connections for the case of Liberia in the second half of the twentieth century. He notes that social relations have been historically important in obtaining political influence. Through a series of sociograms, he shows that Liberian politics were dominated by a small number of families—a social and economic elite that excluded groups with inferior status. To understand Liberian political history, he argues, one must evaluate how the elites related to one another (Dalton, 1965, pp. 581, 587–590).

Africa is a continent of vast natural resources with the potential to generate high rents. If there were all sorts of networks, including crony networks, why has not Africa followed a similar path of development as in East Asia or the case of the Porfiriato? The answer I propose is twofold. First, the distribution of power did not lead to a supply of independent third-party enforcers, partly as a consequence of incipient institutional development.

And second, there were no social structures that could sustain national development. In other words, Africa has thus far has lacked the necessary political and social foundations to promote sustained development.

Regarding political conditions, the insights generated by my theory suggest that dictatorships that are unable to grow must have a distribution of power that is lopsided in favor of the dictator. In other words, the dictator is too powerful to be punished by anyone in society.[13] Unlike the case of the Porfiriato, where there were regional groups that remained influential even after Díaz came to power, a more typical pattern in Africa is one in which a victor comes to power through a violent struggle that weakens opponents at least temporarily (Sawyer, 2005, p. 27; Thomson, 2004, pp. 217–220). Individuals who populate the state are cronies who depend on the dictator for their own survival; hence, they do not have the necessary independence to fight off the dictator. If they do have the potential to restrain the dictator, the latter may find ways to weaken them, as was the case with Mobutu's rotation system that prevented significant political players in Zaire from attaining too much power.[14]

Along with the absence of reliable third-party enforcers, the distribution of assets has not been not conducive toward private investment. In fact, we cannot really speak of an independent class of asset holders or entrepreneurs interested in investing because economic activity has focused on the extraction of natural resources. A critical impediment, in terms of my theory, is that the state is the primary stakeholder in the exploitation of these resources. Because the state does not directly depend on domestic actors for the generation of rents, there is no incentive to offer lucrative private policies to other actors beyond the dictator's closest supporters.[15] Of course, there is a need to make credible commitments to foreign investors, but they have reliable sources of third-party enforcement, such as the intervention of their home government, that are not readily available to domestic actors.[16]

Lastly, there are no social structures that could create encompassing interests to promote national development. One salient reason in the literature has to do with the various cleavages that exist in African societies that prevent large-scale policy responses. Some authors actually see the constitution of society as a major impediment for development. Martinussen (1997, p. 246) discusses, for instance, the work of Göran Hydèn, who notes that African economies are dominated by peasant modes of production, embedded in a so-called "economy of affection." This economy of affection relates to the fact that economic decisions are embedded in social networks that do not have an industrial orientation that could bring about economic development. As described by Martinussen, the most important concern for

Hydèn is that these social networks are narrow-minded, not recognizing the opportunities for cooperation with other groups. Dalton (1965, p. 572) shares a similar view when he notes that social relations reflect a "traditional" type of organization that causes underdevelopment. Social relations are also seen as impediments to reform and, more specifically, as unreceptive to developmental policies prescribed by economists.

Although instructive, a naive approach to dispense with social relations in general is misguided. It is true that democracies do tend to set limits on these relations. Laws to fight nepotism, to manage conflicts of interest, and to abate corruption are explicit antirelational mechanisms. But the intent of these laws is not necessarily to dissipate social relations altogether or to atomize members of society completely, but rather to prevent these relations from leading to undesirable outcomes such as corruption. Perhaps because in democratic settings relations ought not to matter (a normative aspect of laws), we may think that they do not matter at all. Again, this line of thought may hold in some democratic settings, but is clearly unrealistic in nondemocratic settings.

My approach to social relations is not normative at all, and is guided by the pragmatism espoused by Rose-Ackerman's (1999) study of corruption and government (pp. 89–110). Instead of positing social relations as an essential impediment that need to be eradicated, I focus on analyzing incentives, taking the social context as given. For the problem of policy credibility, I therefore propose an alternate reason regarding social relations and underdevelopment. What matters, given my theoretical argument, is that there be a social structure that overlaps the interests of multiple participants to enable collective retaliation. I have already established that the scale of private protection in Africa appears to be mostly limited to cronies, but another distinction that needs to be made—because of more general applicability to other settings—has to do with the specific way in which special privileges are distributed. In very broad terms, what we see in African crony networks is a *radial* structure in which private policies emanate from the dictator, with minimal if any overlap among beneficiaries. Networks are thus not only low in density, but they also only have one central player—the dictator, and that player cannot be a third party to enforce private policies.

The elements missing in the African context are either political organizations or political entrepreneurs that are able span local networks into larger social structures with broader encompassing interests. To be precise, the radial nature of crony networks does not give cronies or potentially powerful third-party enforcers the incentives to defend the network beyond their own turf.[17] A prime example of these types of allocations occurred under the regime of Ferdinand Marcos in the Philippines. Basically, Marcos (and his wife, Imelda) created "islands of privileges" in which beneficiaries received exclusive privileges in specific industries, without interference from other actors.[18] Although Marcos was able to sustain some growth, we do not see the same type of progress as in other Asian countries, and eventually the system collapsed under the weight of corruption.[19]

Note that the organization of private protection encompasses both formal and informal governance structures. The former will be limited in dictatorships because, by definition, dictators are above the law and can manipulate laws, but this is not to say that political institutions are at all unimportant. I argue that formal political institutions complement networks by facilitating policy making and identifying reliable private enforcers. Formal political institutions may give the appearance of inaction or passivity, but this is a misconception because their contribution is kept out of the public eye.

To end this section, African dictatorships have not been able to become limited dictatorships. By limited dictatorship, I mean two things. First, there is the requirement that the dictatorship be constrained—perhaps not as much as in democratic settings, but with enough "limited pluralism" in Linz's (2000) parlance, that the dictator cannot engage in arbitrary behavior. The second aspect of a limited dictatorship relates more closely to the underlying enforcement mechanisms explored in this book, and it has to do with *vulnerability*. Díaz's power in Mexico was limited because his stay in power was contingent on the ability to deliver benefits continually to his supporters. This is a more general point that others have made (Przeworski and Limongi, 1993), but this book clarifies the source of that vulnerability. The dictator does not operate in a vacuum. A concurrent governance structure must be in place that keeps the dictator in continuous check. The actual form of this governance structure will most likely make use of formal institutions, not as a way to democratize, but as a way to impose barriers to entry to opponents.

To ensure exclusivity, formal institutions need to be somewhat functional—a condition that may perhaps require much more time and resources than many African societies have. Formal institutions do not become any less relevant in limited dictatorships, but their function differs from that of democracies. In the latter, representation is a key directive. More precisely, comprehensive representation of all citizens is expected, at least in principle. In contrast, formal institutions in dictatorships do not aim to represent in any comprehensive way additional interests beyond those of elites and ruling coalitions. There may be an element of representation to the extent that actors with political power are relatively heterogeneous, in which case there is a need for mutual monitoring. However, there is also a common interest in excluding others—that is, not being representative of what oftentimes will be the majority of the population.

4   Long-Term Implications for Political and Economic Development

I will end this book with two exploratory questions that invite further reflection on my network theory of private protection and that, I hope, may also stimulate further research. How does reliance on private protection affect subsequent political development? Under what conditions, if any, can countries that rely on selective commitments ever make a transition to more universal commitments? These questions are addressed in the context of twentieth-century Mexico, but their scope is more general. Both questions inquire further about the long-term implications of economic growth under dictatorships to ascertain whether regimes of private protection may plausibly trap societies along a path of concentrated political and economic power.

4.1   ORGANIZATIONAL REQUIREMENTS AND POLITICAL DEVELOPMENT

Although I have shown how Díaz was able to make selective credible commitments despite being a dictator, there remain some open questions regarding the specific governance structure that Díaz used. For instance, why didn't Díaz create a political party to organize political and economic interests? If there was a legislature, and I have noted that there were persistent regional differences, why didn't legislators organize around parties? My theory, and subsequent political development in Mexico, provide some answers.

Recall that my network theory of private protection requires only that there be private enforcers with mutual stakes in protected economic activity. The actual choice of governance structure to maintain those mutual stakes incurs both costs and benefits. The more economic activity the governance structure can sustain, the higher the rents available for sharing. A national party, therefore, appears to be an attractive candidate over social networks because it can increase the scale of protected economic activity. However, political parties have maintenance costs, and to the extent that political parties incorporate a wider range of preferences, these costs can be very high if there is a lot of policy dissension among members.

Having pacified the country during the first decade of his tenure, Díaz certainly had an incentive to decrease the costs of maintaining political stability. The recent history of violent conflict among political movements prior to Díaz's arrival clearly showed that political organizations or cohesive movements were difficult to maintain, and often led to increased political conflict when internal factions assumed confrontational stances. An informal social network therefore appeared to be the least expensive venue for Díaz to organize like-minded economic and political actors, after he had consolidated his dictatorship. As Chapter 5 showed, the economic and political elites of the period were a relatively homogenous group.

Subsequent historical development supports this theoretical argument. Haber et al. (2003) have shown that the economic elites who were protected during the Porfiriato survived the Revolution relatively intact and remained influential players afterward. However, after the Mexican Revolution of the 1910s, a new constitutional arrangement was brokered that incorporated two groups that had not previously been part of Díaz's coalition of protected political and economic interests: industrial workers and peasants.

The conflicting demands that labor and peasant movements imposed on the new postrevolutionary coalition made it difficult to reorganize solely with the use of informal networks, as had been the case during the Porfiriato. Indeed, there was a period of political instability after the enactment of the Constitution of 1917, which ended the Mexican Revolution. To manage conflict among diverse and sometimes diametrically opposed interests—like capitalists and workers—the Mexican government required more micromanagement and formal organization under the umbrella of a political party. Political stability was not restored until 1929, with the creation of a new national political party that was to be the predecessor of the modern-day Institutional Revolutionary Party (PRI). The PRI proved very adept at managing conflict, having remained in power for more than seventy years.[20]

In Mexico's case, the political legacy of Díaz's network of private protection was a regime that restricted political competition and inhibited democratic development for most of the twentieth century. One may be tempted to infer from Mexico's subsequent political development that networks of private protection are natural precursors to the establishment of single-party regimes or some type of authoritarian rule, but a comparative perspective suggests otherwise.

Strongmen (so-called *caudillos*, or regional leaders) were typical in newly independent nineteenth-century Latin America, including Mexico. Various *caudillos* established some type of authoritarian government throughout the region, but few were able to deal successfully with the twin problems of political instability—fueled by an ideological conflict similar to that described in Chapter 3 and economic stagnation that accompanied the end of the colonial period. Lewis (2006) identifies two cases of successful establishment of "national dictators": Mexico and Venezuela. The case of Mexico was studied in this book. A brief discussion of Venezuela, which saw the emergence of two national dictators (Antonio Guzmán Blanco and Juan Vicente Gómez) is instructive because it reveals relevant similarities in the mechanisms that brought about policy credibility.

From the 1920s to the 1970s, Venezuela was one of the fastest growing countries in Latin America, and the richest country in the region by 1977. Venezuela's economic success was coupled with remarkable political stability. This political stability is rooted is in the establishment of national dictatorships around the turn of the twentieth century (Rodriguez and Gomolin, 2006, pp. 4–5).

In many ways, the restoration of political stability and reactivation of economic growth in Venezuela was very similar to that of the Porfiriato. As argued by Rodriguez and Gomolin (2006), the same logic and mechanisms applied in both cases. The case of Venezuela lends support to the thesis that I have advanced in this book regarding the importance of networks of private protection to encourage economic growth and to bring policy credibility under authoritarian rule.

First, there was the role of independent foci of political power. Just like Díaz inherited a fragmented political system with powerful opponents, regional political bosses were also critical to the development of the Guzmán Blanco dictatorship from 1870 to 1888. Guzmán Blanco also sought to promote foreign investment. Like Díaz, he offered lucrative concessions to foreign investors, whose deployment of assets and market power led to the generation of rents. These rents were shared with the dictator, who in turn transferred resources to states governed by *caudillos* (Rodriguez and Gomolin, 2006, pp. 6–8).[21]

That these *caudillos* were powerful was to be demonstrated in 1888, when they deposed Guzmán Blanco. Lewis (2006) reports that there was a concern about the dictator's extended multiyear vacations and installment of puppet governments, which led the *caudillos* to rise up and overthrow Guzmán Blanco. In terms of my theory, this behavior was rational. While rents were distributed, and the permanence of the regime was not in question, *caudillos* had no incentive to revolt. When the durability of the arrangement was put into question with Guzmán Blanco's mixed signals about his ability to govern continuously, the profitability of the arrangement also became uncertain. Without the incentive of sustained rents, there was no need to support the regime anymore.

But reconstituting the previous system of privileges was no easy matter, and Venezuelan politics were then subject to a temporary period of instability as political interests realigned. Various governments, including some dictators, came to power, but none were able to restore the success of the Guzmán Blanco dictatorship until Gómez took over in 1908 (he would last twenty-seven years in power, until 1935). Gómez would refine Guzmán Blanco's original formula based on a network of private protection. With a more complex economic structure, which reflected the emergence of Venezuela as a leading oil exporter, the network accommodated a wider range of actors, not just key state politicians and bureaucrats. This was a time when the army was also modernized, so the incorporation of professional military officers was also necessary (Lewis, 2006, pp. 65–69).

Rodriguez and Gomolin (2006) note that the arrangement between economic and political actors could be characterized as a type of vertical political integration (VPI), given the blurring of distinctions between public and private actors. VPI in Venezuela entailed a complex web of social relations, with a prominent role for Gomez's family and friends, but the network did not include just cronies whose survival depended on the dictator. The network also incorporated other independent political powers, including state governors, *caudillos*, and army officers.

The Venezuelan case is perhaps more interesting, not because of its similarities to the Porfiriato, but because it invites reflection about the dynamics of exclusive networks. Just like Mexico, Venezuela had a very stable political system during most of the twentieth century, but the political organization could not have been any more different. If we agree on the premise that Mexico's and Venezuela's early industrialization had the same social and political foundations, it remains to explain the divergence in terms of subsequent political development. In Mexico, Díaz's dictatorship led to the eventual establishment of a single-party regime. Although there was a brief interruption during the revolutionary period, the system constructed under Díaz was reconstituted after the conflict was over, although it required a more formal type of organization, which would take the form of the once-dominant PRI party. In contrast, Venezuelans shifted from a dictatorship to a two-party regime.

The divergent development of Mexico and Venezuela raises important questions about the democratic prospects of limited dictatorships. Why didn't Mexico develop a multiparty system right after the Revolution? Rodriguez and Gomolin (2006) note that making a transition to the two-party system in Venezuela was difficult. The central government was extremely powerful and had access to oil revenues to support a vast patronage network.

They argue that the availability of high oil revenues nonetheless enabled the development of parties with broad membership. These parties became alternate sources of favors through their own system of loyalties (pp. 25–26). When resources started decreasing in the 1980s in Venezuela, Rodriguez and Gomolin argue that the system of patronage could not be scaled down, leading to the collapse of the political institutions in the 1990s (p. 32).

In both cases, political development was constrained, but apparently less so in Venezuela. In Mexico, there was one dominant party, the Institutional Revolutionary Party or PRI. In Venezuela, political stability was predicated on a civilian–military alliance that allowed competition between two populist parties, but retained the military as guardian of that arrangement. In other words, increased revenue allowed a strategy of shared growth with a relatively more competitive political environment, but one that did not threaten the regime. However, if Venezuela's development was predicated on the windfall from oil revenues, a condition that is not readily replicated in other settings, does this mean that Mexico's development is the more typical one? If so, does limited dictatorship (based on an exclusive network of private protection) inhibit long-term democratic development?

4.2 ROBUSTNESS OF EXCLUSIVE NETWORKS

Another concern with networks of private protection is that they may inhibit economic development for two theoretical reasons. First, by relying on protection, economic activity need not be organized in the most efficient way. At some point in the future, these inefficiencies, which may be reinforced by a lack of incentives to innovate, will kick in and bring down the system, especially when facing foreign competition. Second, a network of private protection is exclusive by nature, and it elongates time horizons precisely because protected interests expect that market power will be somewhat permanent.

Mexico's economic development after Díaz provides confirming evidence for both theoretical claims. Relying heavily on protectionism, the economic model that prevailed under the PRI would collapse in the 1980s, bringing about a series of economic and political reforms. Almost two decades of market reforms under two different political parties have failed, however, to restore sustained economic growth. I argue that one main reason behind the inability to reactivate sustained growth has been a relatively constant political economy based on the system first set in place by Díaz during the late nineteenth century.

Díaz's network of private protection has proved to be rather robust. Its first challenge came in 1910 to 1911 with the advent of the Mexican Revolution. As noted by Haber et al. (2003), however, the network survived this event relatively intact. This is not to say that the Revolution was inconsequential, because it came with a huge cost in terms of lost lives and displaced individuals. However, throughout the conflict and at the end of the Revolution, the interests that were protected under Díaz had no real reason to worry. To be sure, there was a new constitution in 1917 with revolutionary provisions like an agrarian reform and new labor laws attempted against the interests of capitalists. In practice, however, postrevolutionary governments deliberately chose to postpone or not fully implement policies that affected economic elites. Later, when the PRI was created, extreme demands would be placated easily with party controls.

More recently, the process of market reforms and financial crises in the mid 1990s called for drastic changes, including attempts at creating a more competitive environment that challenged protected interests. For the most part, recent reforms either did not take away protection or otherwise afforded new privileges in compensation, revealing the importance of social relations in the allocation of economic resources and the protection of special interests. Market reforms gave way both to corruption as well as to further concentration of economic resources.[22] In the 1990s, the Mexican government was also forced to rescue an insolvent banking sector in a controversial bailout process that greatly benefited well-connected bankers (Haber, 2005).

While reviewing the prospects of Mexican elites in the twenty-first century, Camp (2002) notes that networks and social relations have been and continue to be important pillars of Mexican politics and economics. Policy making was (and has been) constantly influenced by business during the twentieth and twenty-first centuries (p. 14). Although he notes the changing nature and dynamics of elite mentoring and networking patterns, Camp (2002) argues that there is a power elite network that maintains societal structures and shapes policy. Moreover, networking takes place mostly through informal channels, such as kinship networks. The social underpinnings and relational character of Mexico's economic system are especially highlighted. Camp notes that the banking and financial sectors are dominated by leading capitalist families, and that financial institutions have historically had very close ties to industrial groups with connections that persist to this day. Perhaps more striking are the figures he presents: in 1998, 15 percent of the Mexican gross domestic product (GDP) was controlled by ten capitalists, and an overwhelming percentage of Mexico's GDP is controlled by fewer than 500 individuals (pp. 51–54).

The general implications for development are mixed. Private protection and selective credible commitments provide a way out of poverty and stagnation—as they did in nineteenth-century Mexico. But they also embark countries on a path of economic and political development that may be incompatible with economic liberalization and greater competitiveness.

This tension suggests that perhaps the big question about development is not whether governments can make commitments or restrain themselves, because credibility is a matter of degree. Unless there is extreme instability (with no well-defined actor or entity who can dispense privileges), the prototypical way to develop will be based on some degree of exclusive privileges. These selective commitments can mimic the development of today's advanced economies in terms of bringing about industrialization and growth, and may even support some democratization process. However, as the experience of Mexico has shown, these systems of private protection do not benefit the whole population and can be difficult to reform.

We should not forget, however, that advanced countries embarked on a similar developmental path of selective property rights and concentrated economic activity during earlier stages of their development.[23] The Rise of the West was predicated on concurrent economic and political developments that enhanced economic and political rights gradually. Over the course of several centuries, advanced countries did become less restrictive, and their societies enjoyed more widespread opportunities and prosperity.

The big question is not, then, about the ability to sustain growth, but about the quality of economic development that can be supported without universal protection of property rights. As I argue in this book, an immediate jump to universal protection is unfeasible because it would not be deemed credible by all members of society, but intermediate steps can be taken on the basis of selective commitments. As this book has shown, countries can grow even when they lack democratic institutions. But are these selective commitments based on monopolies or highly concentrated markets a developmental trap? Can the Rise of the West be replicated to make an eventual transition from selective to universal commitments? What conditions enabled that transition in advanced countries? Are those conditions feasible for today's developing countries, especially those who have already experienced economic growth with incipient democratic institutions?

Appendix

Network Data

Sources

The relational data for this project were obtained from a combination of primary and secondary sources. The collection of relational data was done in two steps. First, I collected information on nodes (people or entities that could be related in many ways). Second, I coded for relevant connections among the previously identified nodes.

Sources on public officials are described in Chapter 5. My company sample of 149 companies was drawn from historical documents from three cross-sections, circa 1907 (México, Banco Central Mexicano, 1908; Mexican Year Book, 1908), and 1909 to 1910 (Mexican Year Book, 1910). The first source is an official document of the Mexican government, which includes information on seventy-five public corporations. The second and third sources were independently published as guides for foreign investors and contain information on Mexico's largest companies, including those in oil and agriculture, for example, which were not organized as public corporations.

Additional ties, including all personal ties, were identified in secondary sources. Secondary sources included a review of the historiography of the period, especially those works that directly dealt with elite networks. These historical studies contained in their narratives valuable information about personal connections and person-to-company connections, instances of which were coded and entered individually into a database of social network connections.

The list of secondary sources includes a rich collection of regional studies as represented in the works of Cerutti and Marichal (2003), Aguilar Aguilar (2003), Cerutti (2003), Gamboa Ojeda (2003), Gómez (2003), Ibarra (2003), Ludlow (2003), Olveda (2003), Rodríguez López (2003), and Marichal and Cerutti (2003).

Private Protection Network

My data collection led to the identification of an affiliation network with 3376 person-to-business ties between persons (some private, some in government) and various businesses. I transformed this affiliation network into a director-to-director network that I used to analyze overlapping protection, and a company-to-company network used for the ego network analysis, all of which are presented in Chapter 6. Tables A.1 and A.2 list the sample companies and public officials analyzed in Chapter 6.

TABLE A.1
List of Major Companies for Network Analysis

Company	Industry
Banco Nacional de México	Banking
Banco de Londres y México	Banking
Banco Central Mexicano	Banking
Banco Internacional e Hipotecario de México	Banking
Banco Agrícola e Hipotecario de México	Banking
Banco Mexicano de Comercio e Industria	Banking
Almacénes Generales de Deposito de México y Veracruz	Banking
Banco Minero de Chihuahua	Banking
Banco Yucateco	Banking
Banco Mercantil de Yucatan	Banking
Banco de Durango	Banking
Banco de Zacatecas	Banking
Banco de Nuevo Leon	Banking
Banco del Edo. de México	Banking
Banco de Coahuila	Banking
Banco de San Luis Potosi	Banking
Banco de Sonora	Banking
Banco Occidental de México	Banking
Banco Mercantil de Veracruz	Banking
Banco de Jalisco	Banking
Banco Mercantil de Monterrey	Banking
Banco Oriental de México	Banking
Banco de Guanajuato	Banking
Banco de Tabasco	Banking
Banco de Chiapas	Banking

Company	Industry
Banco de Hidalgo	Banking
Banco de Aguascalientes	Banking
Banco de Michoacán	Banking
Banco de Tamaulipas	Banking
Banco de Oaxaca	Banking
Banco de Morelos	Banking
Banco de Querétaro	Banking
Banco de Campeche	Banking
Banco de Guerrero	Banking
Banco Comercial Refaccionario	Banking
Cia. Bancaria de Obras y Bienes Raices	Banking
Descuento Español	Services
Cia. Bancaria de Orizaba	Banking
Soc. Financiera para la Industria en México	Banking
FC Mexicano México a Veracruz	Transportation
FC de Toluca a Tenango y Juan	Transportation
FC de Campeche a Lerma	Transportation
Cia. de Tranvías, Luz y Fuerza de Guadalajara	Transportation
Cia. Naviera del Pacífico	Transportation
Cia. de Seguros La Mexicana	Services
La Nacional Cia. de Seguros	Services
La Fraternal Cia. de Seguros	Services
Cia. Minera Fundidora y Afinadora de Monterrey	Mining
Cia. Fundidora de Fierro y Acero de Monterrey	Manufacturing
Cia. Eléctrica e Irrigadora	Manufacturing
Cia. Industrial de Orizaba	Manufacturing
Cia. Nacional Mexicana de Dinamita y Explosivo	Manufacturing
La Unión Cia. Benef. de Metales	Manufacturing
La Tabacalera Mexicana	Manufacturing
Cervecería Moctezuma	Manufacturing
San Idelfonso Tejidos de Lana	Manufacturing
Cia. Cigarrera Mexicana	Manufacturing
Cia. Carbonifera "Agujita"	Mining
La Casa Colorada Refinadora de Alcoholes	Manufacturing
Cia. Agrícola y Ganadera del Río de San Diego	Agriculture
Cia. de Cemento Privilegiado	Manufacturing
Fábrica de Vidrio de Apizaco	Manufacturing
Cia. Ind. de Atlixco	Manufacturing
Cia. Minera "Natividad"	Mining
Cia. Minera La Providencia, San Juan de la Luz	Mining
Cia. Minera La Reina	Mining
Cia. Minera el Carboncillo	Mining
Negoc. Minera de San Rafael	Mining
Cia. Minera Ignacio Rodríguez Ramos	Mining
Cia. Minera Asturiana	Mining
Cia. Minera Dos Estrellas	Mining
Cia. Harinera y Manufacturera Nacional	Manufacturing
Cia. Ind. de San Antonio Abad	Manufacturing
Cia. Manufacturera Buen Tono	Manufacturing
Caja de préstamos	Banking
Banco Hipotecario de Crédito Territorial Mexicano	Banking
Centro Bancario de Liquidaciones	Banking

TABLE A.1
Continued

Company	Industry
United States Banking Co.	Banking
Mexico City Banking Co.	Banking
Mercantile Banking Co., Ltd.	Banking
The Central Mexican Railway	Transportation
Cia. del FC Nacional de México	Transportation
Mexican International Railway Co.	Transportation
Cia. del FC Nacional de Tehuantepec	Transportation
Mexican Southern Railway	Transportation
Kansas City, México and Orient	Transportation
Chihuahua and Pacific Railroad	Transportation
Chihuahua Mineral Railway	Transportation
Mexican Northern Railway	Transportation
Parral and Durango Railway	Transportation
Durango Central	Transportation
Sonora Railway, Cananea, Río Yaqui and Pacific	Transportation
Occidental Railway of México	Transportation
Mexican Pacific Railway Co.	Transportation
Hornos Railway	Transportation
Potosi and Río Verde Railway Co.	Transportation
Pan-American Railway	Transportation
United Railways of Yucatan	Transportation
Merida to Peto Railway	Transportation
Mapimí Railway	Transportation
El Oro Mining and Railway Co., Ltd.	Mining
The México Mines of El Oro, Ltd.	Mining
The Peñoles Mining Co.	Mining
Cia. Minera de Real del Monte y Pachuca	Mining
Maravillas y Anexas Mining Co.	Mining
American Smelting and Refining Co.	Mining
Cia. de Tranvías, Luz y Fuerza de Puebla	Manufacturing
Mexican Light and Power Co., Ltd.	Construction
Cia. de Tranvías y fuerza de Guadalajara	Transportation
Guanajuato Power and Electric Co.	Construction
Sta. Gertrudis Jute Manufacturing Co., Ltd.	Manufacturing
Cia. Industrial La Aurora	Manufacturing
Cia. Linera de México	Manufacturing
Cia. de las Fábricas de Papel de San Rafael	Manufacturing
Mexican National Packing Co.	Agriculture
Banco Refaccionario de La Laguna, SA	Banking
Banco Refaccionario de Michoacán	Banking
Banco Peninsular Mexicano	Banking
Veracruz and Isthmus Railroad Co.	Transportation
Mexican Railway Co., Ltd.	Transportation
Matehuala Railway	Transportation
México Northwestern Railroad Co.	Transportation
The Mexican Northern Power Co.	Manufacturing
Mexican Telephone and Telegraph Co.	Communications
The México Tramways Co.	Transportation
Veracruz Terminal Co., Ltd.	Transportation
Zitácuaro and Soconusco Railroad	Transportation
Chapala Hydro-eléctrica é Irrigadora de Chapala	Manufacturing
Batopilas Mining Co.	Mining

TABLE A.I
Continued

Company	Industry
Cananea Central Copper Co.	Mining
Cananea Consolidated Copper Co.	Mining
Cia. Minera Del Tiro General	Mining
Mazapil Copper Co., Ltd	Mining
Cia. Metalúrgica de Torreón, SA	Manufacturing
Cia. Mexicana de Petróleo "El Aguila"	Oil
Mexican Coal and Coke Co.	Mining
Mexican Petroleum Co., Ltd.	Oil
Oil Fields of México Co.	Oil
Teziutlán Copper Mining and Smelting Co.	Mining
Cia. Ind. Jabonera de La Laguna, SA	Manufacturing
Banco de La Laguna, SA	Banking
Cervecería Cuauhtémoc, SA	Manufacturing
Cementos Hidalgo, SA	Manufacturing
Vidriera Monterrey	Manufacturing
Cia. Metalúrgica México, SA	Manufacturing
Servicios de Agua y Drenaje de Monterrey	Construction
Cia. Telefónica Mexicana	Communications
Federal Banking Co	Banking
La Owens de Mexico	Manufacturing

TABLE A.2
List of Political Actors for Network Analysis

Network Code	Last Name	First Name
Aguirre.C	Aguirre	Carlos
Alcazar.R	Alcázar	Ramón
Aldasoro.A	Aldasoro	Andrés
Alfaro.F	Alfaro	Francisco
Aspe.J.R	Aspe	José
Azcue.P	Azcué	Pedro
Baranda.P	Baranda	Pedro
Barcena.M	Bárcena	Mariano
Beck.EL	Beck	Eman
Bulnes.F	Bulnes	Francisco
Burgoa.I	Burgoa	Ignacio
Camacho.S	Camacho	Sebastián
CantuTreviño.M	Cantú Treviño	Manuel
Cardenas.A	Cárdenas	Amador
Carreon.J	Carreón	Juan
Casasus.C	Casasús	Carlos
Casasus.JD	Casasús	Joaquín
CastañedaPalomar.R	Castañeda y Palomar	Ramón
Castelazo.J.B	Castelazo	Juan
Castello.J	Castellot	José
Cervantes.J.M	Cervántes	Julio
Chazaro.J	Cházaro Soler	Juan
Creel.E.C	Creel	Enrique

TABLE A.2
Continued

Network Code	Last Name	First Name
CuestaGallardo.M	Cuesta Gallardo	Manuel
Curiel.L.C	Curiel	Luis
DiazJr.Porfirio	Díaz, Jr.	Porfirio
Dominguez.M	Domínguez	Manuel
Donde.S	Dondé	Salvador
Duret.F	Duret	Fernando
Elizaga.L	Elizaga	Lorenzo
Enriquez.G	Enríquez	Gumersindo
Escandon.P	Escandón y Barrón	Pablo
Esperon.A.G	Esperón	Antonio
Espinosa.F	Espinosa	Francisco
Espinosa.U	Espinosa	Urbano
Fernandez.Jus	Fernández	Justino
Garcia.C	García	Canuto
Garcia.G	García	Genaro
Garcia.J.G	García Gual	José
GarzaAldape.M	Garza Aldape	Manuel
Gomez.J	Gómez	José
Gonzalez.A.R	González	Agustín
Gonzalez.Man	González	Manuel
GonzalezC.M	González Cosío	Manuel
Henkel.E	Henkel	Eduardo
Hernandez.A.V	Hernández	Antonio
Herrera.C	Herrera	Carlos
Landa.G	de Landa y Escandón	Guillermo
LanderoCos.J	de Landero y Cos	José
Lanz.M	Lanz	Miguel
LaPeña.P	De la Peña	Prágedis
Liceaga.E	Licéaga	Eduardo
Limantour.J.M	Limantour	Julio
Limantour.J.Y	Limantour	José Y.
Lujan.J.E	Lujan	Jesus
Macedo.M.S	Macedo	Miguel
Macedo.P	Macedo	Pablo
Macera.T	Mancera	Tomás
Madero.Ern	Madero	Ernesto
Mancera.G	Mancera	Gabriel
Marroquin.M	Marroquín Rivera	Manuel
Martinez.Ang	Martínez	Angel
Martinez.C	Martinez	Carlos
Martinez.Pablo	Martínez del Río	Pablo
Mendez.S	Méndez	Santiago
Molina.R	Molina	Ricardo
Moral.N	del Moral	Nicolás
Muñoz.F	Muñoz	Francisco
Núñez.R	Núñez	Roberto
Obregon.G	Obregón	Guillermo
Ortega.Man	Ortega Reyes	Manuel
Pardo.E	Pardo	Emilio
Pardo.Rafael	Pardo	Rafael
PardoJr.E	Pardo, Jr.	Emilio
Parra.Man	Parra	Manuel

TABLE A.2
Continued

Network Code	Last Name	First Name
Pazos.E	Pazos	Enrique
Peon.C	Peón	Carlos
PeonC.J	Peón Contreras	Pedro
Pimentel.F.F	Pimentel y Fagoaga	Fernando
Pineda.R	Pineda	Rosendo
Pliego.Antonio	Pliego Pérez	Antonio
Rabasa.R	Rabasa	Ramón
Ramos.Jo	Ramos	José
Riba.L	Riba y Cervantes	Luis
RincónG.F	Rincón Gallardo	Francisco
Rivas.F	Rivas Gómez	Francisco
Robleda.F	Robleda	Felipe
Romero.Fran	Romero	Francisco
Sagredo.C	Sagredo	Carlos
Sanchez.J.M	Sánchez	José
SantaMarina.J	Santa Marina	Juan
Septien.Ju.A	Septien	Juan
Terrazas.Ab	Terrazas	Abraham
Terrazas.Al	Terrazas	Alberto
Terrazas.Lu	Terrazas	Luis
Uriarte.Jes	Uriarte	Jesús
Urquidi.M	Urquidi	Manuel
Valenzuela.P	Valenzuela	Policarpo
Veraza.A	Veraza	Alonso
Vidal.L	Vidal y Flor	Luis
Villarreal.V	Villarreal	Viviano
Villegas.J	Villegas	Juan
Zamacona.M	Zamacona e Inclán	Manuel

NOTES

CHAPTER I

1. Throughout this book, I use the Northian definition of *institutions* as "the rules of the game in a society" that constrain individual behavior. Institutions may take the form of formal or informal rules, but unless noted otherwise, I reserve the term to denote formal institutions. The importance of institutions does not mean, of course, that proximate causes are inconsequential for economic growth, but rather that capital accumulation requires prior good rules and incentives. See North (1994), North and Thomas (1973), North and Weingast (1989), Weingast (1997b), and World Bank (2001, pp. 99–115).

2. In reality, governments face various types of credible commitments. In what follows, I will use the term *credible commitment* to refer to the credible commitment problem of economic growth that arises when a government makes promises to encourage investment and to protect property rights that it can later abrogate or prey upon. Of course, credible commitment problems can arise in noneconomic contexts, which I do not explore in this book. For example, ethnic conflict can occur among groups that cannot commit to peace or between people who do not trust one another.

3. This commitment problem is also known as the *sovereign dilemma*. See Weingast (1995, 1997a).

4. The term *limited government* has a broader meaning in democratic theory and political philosophy, but I use the term here much more narrowly to identify a set of formal political institutions that constrain the government from preying on economic activity. Discussions of the broader philosophical definition of limited government, which encompasses both economic and political liberties, can be found in Brennan and Buchanan (1985), Hayek (1960), Gordon (1999), and Schedler and Plattner (1999).

5. To facilitate the presentation, I will make a common distinction between two types of regimes: *democracies* and *dictatorships* (see Przeworski et al. [2000], for example). The latter term will also be used interchangeably with the related terms of *nondemocracies, autocracies,* or *authoritarian governments.*

6. In political science, students of comparative politics have long been interested in the link between political regimes and their relationship to economic development.

197

See Huntington (1968) for a classic account and Przeworski (1991) for a more recent treatment. Detailed country or regional studies of political and economic development include those by Oi and Walder (1999) and Oi (1999) for the case of China, Amsden (1989) and Jones and SaKong (1980) for the case of South Korea, and Wade (1990) for the case of Taiwan and East Asia. See Islam and Chowdhury (2000, pp. 1–42), Akyüz (1999), Campos and Root (1996), Haggard (1990), and World Bank (1993) for an overview of East Asian development. See Olson (2000, pp. 111–134), for an explanation of the political economy of the Soviet Union. See World Bank (2001, pp. 99–115) for a discussion of various success stories of economic development. See Evans (1979, 1995) for accounts of developmental states in Latin America. For an economic view of development in Latin America, see Dornbusch and Edwards (1991) and Reynolds (1970). See Collier et al. (1979) for related literature on bureaucratic–authoritarian regimes in Latin America. Chehabi and Linz (1998b) also include various cases from developing countries that combined capitalistic development with restricted political liberties.

7. Przeworski et al. (2000) classify countries by their annual growth rates during the postwar period (1950–1991). Of thirteen countries with annual growth rates of seven percent or more, twelve countries were dictatorships. See their Table 3.9.

8. My dependent variable is a dictator's ability to make credible commitments (or policy credibility in nondemocratic settings). Although credible commitments ought to increase levels of economic development in the long run, my theory makes no specific predictions about levels or rates of growth.

9. Among these traits, one finds discussions of "visionary leadership," as in Gray and McPherson (2001). Along with vision, authoritarian leaders can also be the source of a developmental ideology aimed at improving the welfare of society (Vatikiotis, 1998).

10. I use Olson (2000) as the main reference for the theory of stationary banditry, but this theory has been developed in several works. An earlier statement of this theory can be found in Olson (1993). McGuire and Olson (1996) is a related article that formalizes some of the arguments in Olson (1993). Olson (2000) further develops the theory, and also includes discussions of the rise of democracy, legal institutions, and communism.

11. Wintrobe (1998) offers a different rationale for economic growth, although his framework focuses mostly on survival rather than economic development. Dictators get utility from power and consumption, and have two instruments—loyalty and repression—that they can use to maximize their utility. The choice of loyalty and repression depends on the objective function of governments, but the basic means of obtaining loyalty is by providing economic rewards. According to Wintrobe, dictators promote growth to encourage loyalty to their regime.

12. Thousands of years ago, Plato advanced the notion of a philosopher–king as a basis for better government, especially to avoid the pitfalls of democracy. Presumably,

because the king would be wise and bring reality closer to an ideal state, the outcomes would be optimal from a societal perspective. See Plato and Cornford (1945, pp. 175–176, 189–192, and 205–209). Related arguments favoring the political insulation of technocrats follow a similar logic in terms of allowing experts to enact optimal policies without political pressures. For critical reviews, see Przeworski and Limongi (1993, p. 55–57) and Collier (1979).

13. It may also be that concentration is needed, not for efficiency reasons, but simply to reach a decision. From social choice theory, Arrow's impossibility theorem (Arrow, 1951) indicates the potential need to restrict preferences or choices to achieve consistent group choices.

14. Incidentally, dictatorships are not always analyzed as unitary actors. Evans' (1995) focus, for instance, is on the state and its capacity to promote development within a polity that accommodates other actors.

15. This literature does not necessarily see bureaucratic–authoritarianism as a desirable outcome, but does note the importance of authoritarianism in facilitating the implementation of policies that promoted growth, albeit without benefiting all members of society.

16. See, in Lewis (2006), the introductory chapter and Chapters 2 and 3 on Latin American *caudillos* (leaders) and charismatic actors who were able to undertake national development projects. See also the account by Vatikiotis (1998) of how Suharto used Javanese cultural values to rule Indonesia as a king would to implement his "New Order" program.

17. To be sure, some of these studies have other types of questions, especially sociological concerns about bureaucratic administration. For instance, Evans (1995, 1997), and more recently Evans and Rauch (1999), have studied how the quality of government affects economic growth, which has important political implications. But the quality of government is the outcome of political choices, so there still remains the question of why countries choose governments with different qualities. For an explanation of how political institutions affect choices regarding reforms in the public sector, see Geddes (1994).

18. In the most complete analysis to date of the comparative performance of democracies and dictatorships, Przeworski et al. (2000) show that there is a wide variation in the performance of dictatorships. Only a small subset of dictators are able to sustain economic growth.

19. In the broader empirical literature on growth theory, Barro (1997, pp. 50–51) notes that there is nothing in principle that prevents autocracies from providing growth-enhancing policies, although he does not explain why only some autocracies choose those policies.

20. Two notable exceptions include Campos and Root (1996), who address the question of how (strong) authoritarian governments are able to commit and not abuse

their authority to sustain growth; and Haggard (1990), who studied how political institutions affected the choice of import–substitution and export–orientation policies.

21. The absence of political considerations is an important omission in Olson's (2000) theory of dictators who choose to become stationary bandits. In a related article, McGuire and Olson (1996) allude to other political groups, but these authors only discuss the base of political support for consensual democracies, not dictatorships. The stationary bandit's base of political support will likely determine the dictator's ability to deliver on his promises to provide public goods, so politics cannot be ignored.

22. We do understand, generally, that dictators need to institutionalize their regimes to stay in power for a long time (see Wintrobe, 1998, p. 30). What we do not fully understand is which types of institutions are most conductive toward this goal. In addition, there is no typical institutional setup for dictatorships, because they exhibit great variability in terms of institutions and political organization (Linz, 2000).

23. MacIntyre (1991) makes exactly this argument to account for the success of Suharto's policies in Indonesia. Also, although Campos and Root (1996) emphasize various institutional mechanisms that made growth in East Asia credible, they also rely heavily on a nondomestic explanation behind the ability of regional governments to make credible commitments: the threat of communism. (Or, more generally, it was the threat of foreign armies that kept East Asian governments in check.) Monaldi (2002) advances a related argument in the case of export-oriented developing countries, in which external enforcement via a hostage—rather than domestic political institutions—has been the dominating mechanism to enable credible commitments.

24. Haggard (1990) provides a political explanation of policy choice in some of these countries. He also shows that some of the East Asian countries that have been noted for their economic success—and export orientation (see World Bank, 1993)—had in the past pursued import–substitution strategies. Wintrobe (1998) notes that many so-called newly industrialized countries relied on interventionist policies that "do not fit the free market model" (p. 148).

25. See also Solís (1970), Reynolds (1970), and Collier et al. (1979) for other protectionist cases among Latin American military regimes, including Mexico's authoritarian one-party political system.

26. See Haber et al. (2003, pp. 18–40) for a discussion of various commitment mechanisms.

27. This is not to say that scholars have not attempted to draw general lessons from specific cases. Before financial crises became the focus in East Asia, there was a cottage industry trying to extract lessons from East Asian development applicable to other regions. See World Bank (1993), Aoki et al. (1997), Akyüz et al. (1999), Evans (1999), and Wade (1990), among others.

28. However, see Levitsky and Helmke (2004) for a recent effort at framing the study of informal institutions.

29. My use of Olson's (2000) theory addresses the general question of how dictators can commit to make credible commitments to any type of economic activity. Hence, I do not require the dictator to promote economic growth solely via industrialization. The same logic would apply if a dictator wanted to encourage growth based on more traditional economic activity like agriculture, as long as it is very profitable.

30. Although my focus is on dictatorships, it is important to have a comparative perspective with respect to democratic systems, which are better known. Moreover, I make a sharp distinction between dictatorships and democracies, but my argument does not depend on a dichotomous typology of regimes. One can easily extend the argument to more gradated regime classifications by allowing each of these dimensions to vary along a continuum. The advantage of that extension would be to generalize the argument to regimes—regardless of whether they are democratic—where formal political institutions cannot guarantee policy credibility. In fact, I develop my theory along those lines (see "General Assumptions" in Chapter 2).

31. In terms of their motivation, I assume dictators are self-interested and care primarily about the benefits they obtain from their authority.

32. An example of a public enforcement mechanism is the existence of independent judicial powers that can punish transgressions by an executive government. Moreover, that mechanism is accessible to the general public.

33. The term *rent* is used to denote an excessive benefit, like a monopoly profit, that would not have been obtained if an individual or firm operated in a competitive market. More generally, Khan and Jomo (2000a) define rents as "income which is higher than the minimum which an individual would have accepted given alternative opportunities" (p. 5).

34. A similar argument is made by Weingast (1997b), who argues that in the absence of the rule of law and democratic constraints, governments have strong incentives to engage in favoritism.

35. My focus is on dictatorships that want to promote private investment; thus, I do not address cases of command economies, for which there is no private ownership of assets and factors of production.

36. These encompassing interests are similar to the notion of a *winning coalition*, or a government's set of essential supporters (Bueno de Mesquita et al., 2001). My theory does not preclude, however, that members of the "selectorate" (a larger group of supporters) also be part of the encompassing interests.

37. See Knox et al. (2006) for a critical review of various network approaches in the social sciences.

38. I adhere here to the view that economic, as well as political, activities are embedded in various social structures. Moreover, to the extent that these social structures define informal institutions, social structures are likely to be more relevant in countries with nonexistent or incipient formal political institutions.

39. Given this definition, a network should not be confused with a group of nodes or people. For example, in a group in which people have both kin and business ties, there would effectively be two distinct networks: one network involving kin relations alone and a second network that tracks business relations.

40. Overlapping protection characterizes a situation in which firms hire multiple enforcers, and these enforcers have a stake in multiple firms. The empirical chapters will address other relations that may be relevant, but the critical relation presented here is the one that I formalize in Chapter 2.

41. This is a bare bones theory that lays out the general logic by focusing solely on the incentives of hired private enforcers. The propagation of predation risk diminishes expected rents for connected firms and their enforcers. Clearly, if there are additional ties that further propagate risk, the response to predation could be even more extensive and effective at punishing the dictator.

42. It is for this reason that the cases of authoritarianism and growth are small in number. In many other cases, dictators have enough power to offer private lucrative deals to investors, but otherwise lack a politically competitive environment in which they can be punished by others. The cases of authoritarianism in which we see growth are cases in which the government is not too powerful relative to members of the ruling coalition. In other words, these are cases of "limited" dictators.

43. Indeed, in my case study, political institutions were extremely important in allowing and extending Díaz's stay in power. For example, the dictators needed senators to approve presidential appointments, nullify state governments, grant executive decree authority, and pass important legislation. See Barragán Barragán et al. (1987, pp. 297–310). See also Díaz–Cayeros (1998) and Carmagnani (1994, pp. 101–190).

44. See McCubbins and Noble (1995), Rosenbluth (1989), Mainwaring and Shugart (1997), and Weldon (1997) for related discussions about the influence of legislatures and political institutions through governance structures such as political parties, behind the public scene.

45. This period in Mexican history (1876–1911) is also referred to as the *Porfiriato* or *Porfirian Mexico.*

46. See Garner (2001, pp. 1–17), and Benjamin and Marcial (1984) for an overview of the historical literature. As Garner (2001) noted, literature on the Porfiriato is extensive and has gone through at least three phrases. During the Porfiriato, political assessments were largely favorable to the dictator (see, for example, Reyes [1903] and Velasco [1889]). Negative assessments of the Porfiriato followed the Mexican Revolution of 1910, which Garner characterizes as anti-Porfirismo literature. More revisionist views of the period have been informed by Cosio Villegas and collaborators based at El Colegio de México, who led a project on Mexican history, which provided a reassessment of the period (Gómez Galvarriato, 2000).

47. This is not say that nineteenth century Mexican history does not have actors with dictatorial ambitions, but previous dictatorships were short-lived and not able to solve the problem of instability.

48. To be sure, there were electoral challenges to Díaz's stay in the presidency, especially from the anti-reelectionist parties that sprang up right before the Revolution. These organizations were not modern parties with a history of reliability and responsibility, but rather were vehicles for personal advancement that rallied support for prominent public figures in their quest to attain political power. Madero, who was to replace Díaz in the presidency, led such an organization (nominally known as a party) as a vehicle of elite dissatisfaction with the regime, but one that lacked national resonance as a political organization.

49. The edited volume on the Mexican economy by Bortz and Haber (2002) includes an impressive collection of recent studies on these questions. Gómez Galvarriato (2000) reviews the recent literature on the economic history of the Porfiriato.

50. Garner (2001) provides a critical assessment of Díaz's positivism as "patriarchal liberalism" (pp. 70–72). Gómez-Quiñones (1981) characterizes the ideology of the Porfiriato as authoritarian positivism (pp. 55–60, 206–207).

51. Díaz had to wait a long time to build a good reputation, and, in fact, that reputation was contingent on honoring earlier commitments. See Marichal (2002).

52. For a related study of interlocking directorates in 1908 and the role of elite networks in Latin American economic history, see Read and Musacchio (2001).

53. The selection of the period 1907 to 1910 was based on the availability of corporate information. Clearly, the available information reflects the state of affairs toward the end of the Porfiriato. One limitation of this analysis is the inability to trace the development of the political economic network over time. Notwithstanding this limitation, there are two reasons why this analysis is appropriate for the question at hand. First, the political economy of the Porfiriato circa 1907 reflects a mature system. That is, the information I analyze with my 1907 to 1910 sample clearly reflects persistent rules of the game affecting political and economic behavior, and it directly addresses the question of how a dictator was able to make credible commitments to investors. Second, we know from historical analysis that the system in 1907 does not look particularly different from that instituted in the late 1890s (Haber et al., 2003, pp. 41–79). That is, to the extent that we lack network data on the development and creation of these arrangements, we are only missing the dynamics of the system from the time Díaz arrived in power in 1876 to the 1890s, when the major institutional changes that governed economic activity in 1907 came to pass. Analyzing the latter period starting in 1907 thus gives a rough approximation of how the system worked during the second half of the Porfiriato.

54. In other words, SNA provides a method to characterize and measure the institutional mechanisms of stationary banditry.

CHAPTER 2

1. The purpose of this section is to characterize the interaction between government and economic actors that leads to the credible commitment problem of economic growth. I take as given that there is already a government in place, so I am not assuming that the government (or state) gets created with this purpose. See Hardin (1997) for a criticism of economic theories of the state as a social contract to solve some social problem or provide some public good.

2. See Watson (2002, pp. 191–209) for a brief overview of the strategy of contracts.

3. These resources may take the form, inter alia, of votes, political support, campaign contributions, and bribes.

4. In chapter 7 of his book, Wintrobe (1998) makes a related argument that all types of dictatorships have an incentive to redistribute.

5. I use the term *social networks* to denote a specific relation for a set of people or organizations, rather than specific social relations such as friendships and family ties. The critical relation studied in this chapter is *private protection*. Private protection entails a connection or affiliation between a public official that provides private protection to a particular firm.

6. This is Olson's (2000) basic assumption about revenue-maximizing stationary bandits, and is a standard assumption in economic studies of government behavior driven by the pursuit of some self-interested goal. See also North (1981).

7. My two assumptions draw heavily on Wintrobe's theory of dictatorship (1998), in which "dictators maximize utility, which depends on consumption and power" (p. 107). In addition to the standard assumption of consumption, Wintrobe (1998) introduces the concept of power to formulate a general model that can accommodate not just tin-pot dictators motivated by greed, but also totalitarian regimes with the main objective of controlling society. Wintrobe (1998) does not discuss in detail the nature of power and how it enhances the utility of a dictator, because the analysis focuses not so much on the objective function of dictators, but on the constraints that dictators face. My assumptions make it clear that power is conceptually different from consumption because it can be used for noneconomic purposes.

8. Individual actors in society behave similarly to the private actors in Gambetta's (1993) analysis of mafias. Private protection may not generate as good an aggregate outcome than public protection, but individual actors may still find it rational to buy private protection for their own benefit.

9. From an institutional perspective, for example, the study of political institutions has been driven by students of American politics. See a summary of this literature in Mueller (1997). Comparative political economy also focuses on democratic, industrialized nations. See, for example, Hall and Soskice (2001).

10. To date, Wintrobe (1998) provides the most systematic analysis of these two questions, with some limitations. Although he develops a behavioral theory of dictatorships based on various political constraints that is closely related to questions of political institutions, he does not directly address relevant topics such as legislatures and political parties. Wintrobe (1998) also provides rich examples of dictatorships and the particular mechanisms and organization that these dictators relied upon to accomplish their goals, but he does not posit a general argument to account for organizational variation among dictatorships. Despite the limitations, Wintrobe's theory, as well as this book, point to ways in which the study of dictatorships can be extended along these two lines of research: institutional and organizational theories of dictatorships.

11. To make my assumptions as general as possible, I refrain from making assumptions about types of political organization in dictatorships, but this is not to say that I ignore organizational questions altogether. I address issues of political organization, which are central to this book, later in my discussion of social networks and throughout the rest of the book. The concluding chapter also provides some remarks about political organizations in dictatorships.

12. In his work, Linz (2000, pp. 67–69) advances a distinction between authoritarian and totalitarian regimes that goes beyond the scope of my book. Briefly stated, the main difference between authoritarian and totalitarian regimes is that the former regimes lack an ideology and have less control over all aspects of society. In particular, totalitarian regimes are characterized by an ideology, a single mass party, and concentration of power in a small group, unaccountable to the rest of society.

13. The literature on authoritarianism offers a variety of typologies and descriptions, which even experts find difficult to evaluate. For a relevant discussion, see Linz (2000, pp. 171–183).

14. In other words, authoritarian governments cannot totally disregard the preferences of their supporters (Geddes, 1999, p. 121).

15. I actually do not ignore Linz's third and fourth dimensions, because they share the mechanisms affecting the two dimensions on which I focus. A third dimension is limited or political mobilization, which effectively translates into limited pluralism in terms of the political interests that are taken into account in policy-making decisions. The remaining dimension is a distinctive *mentality*, which Linz contrasts with the *ideology* of totalitarian governments. Mentality is an elusive concept by Linz's own admission, so I was unsure about how it would affect government behavior regarding policy commitments. But if we think that mentality reflects a policy directive, then mentality is really the output of a bargaining process that takes limited pluralism and discretion as inputs. Hence, the two dimensions on which I focus already accommodate this fourth dimension.

16. In this sense, the most authoritarian regime would be one of a personalistic type, as in Geddes' classification (1999, p. 121). Also in this category, we can include Chehabi and Linz's (1998a) sultanistic regimes, which are "based on personal ruler-ship...with loyalty to the ruler based not on tradition,...or on charismatic qualities, but on a mixture of fear and rewards to his collaborators" (p. 7). Linz (2000, p. 151) argues that what distinguishes sultanistic regimes from authoritarian regimes is that the former are not subject to bureaucratic rules and thus are subject to the arbitrary rule of their leader. My theoretical framework studies the impact of discretion on government behavior. In that respect, I have no need for a third category of non-democratic regimes. In my framework, a sultanistic regime can be thought of as an authoritarian government with ultimate discretion.

17. It is more difficult to say how other dimensions of authoritarianism, such as military rule or political parties, affect discretion. If we assume that a greater number of decision makers reduces discretion, then we could say that authoritarian governments under military rule would act less arbitrarily than personalistic types, whereas party-controlled authoritarian governments would have even more constraints than military rule. See related typologies in Geddes (1999) and Huntington and Moore (1970).

18. Arguably, in some situations this separation of powers may only be apparent when different political parties are in charge of the legislative and executive branches of the government. I don't ignore this possibility altogether, but I note that it is too specific for my purposes of distinguishing the prerogatives of democratic and dictatorial governments. The purpose of my comparison is simply to say that we often see formal distinctions between legislative and executive powers, and these powers are attributed to different groups that may or may not work in tandem.

19. This is not to say that there won't be other actors that engage in such activities. By definition, however, the dictator has a monopoly on political power, including legislative and executive powers. These powers can be delegated to other actors, but, in principle, can be easily taken back at the dictator's discretion.

20. This statement implies that there would be a public enforcer, such as an independent judiciary, to punish the government. In practice, the actual form of punishment may be different, although ultimately sanctioned by formal institutions. For instance, McCubbins and Schwartz (1984) differentiate between more formal monitoring mechanisms and informal ones in which affected political interests have it in their interest to monitor government behavior. Even in this latter case, informal political monitoring is based on electoral constraints or other formally based political mechanisms that enable citizens to demand certain political rights, hold public officials accountable, and remove officials whose performance is deemed unacceptable.

21. Przeworski et al. (2000) also note that investors' economic and political interests were closely intertwined because "only the propertied enjoyed political rights" (p. 209).

22. There is a clear analogy here to price discrimination by monopolies. If a monopoly is able to segment consumers into various groups, the monopoly can increase profits by charging a different price to each group. In a similar way, if a dictator can offer protection selectively, it can increase its income by "selling private protection" at different prices to different economic actors.

23. This argument is implicit in Weingast (1997a) and North and Weingast (1989), for example, in which parliament is a public institution that serves to protect the interests of society by constraining government opportunism. Most notably for the question of credible commitments in dictatorships, Olson (1993, 2000) and Clague et al. (1996) explicitly view property rights being offered as a matter of public policy.

24. A more general argument is also made in economics regarding incentives for rent seeking and the capture of government by special interests. See Krueger (1974) and Khan et al. (2000).

25. Subsequent chapters identify elite networks and the beneficiaries under the Díaz dictatorship, but the more general problem of selecting recipients of special privileges is beyond the scope of this book.

26. A binary choice setup can only be justified by either alluding to a representative agent or noting that public policies are meant to be anonymous and nondiscriminatory. Hence, in that context, it suffices to see how policies affect an arbitrary economic actor.

27. See Haber et al. (2003, pp. 18–40) for a more detailed description of enforcement options.

28. For an overview of Chinese networks in Asia, see Clarke et al. (1999).

29. It may be the case that the firm has access to an external third-party enforcer, such as a foreign government. Alternatively, the firm could rely on some private technological know-how that makes its assets unprofitable if taken over by the government. As long as these alternative protection mechanisms are available, this firm may be able to engage in production without fear of explicit government predation. However, as discussed later, unless this firm eventually recruits government officials, it will suffer an informational loss that will affect the private policies that it obtains from the dictator. The dictator can exploit these informational asymmetries to prey on the asset holder in a subtle way, by not offering the best possible policy in the asset holder's best interests.

30. Vulnerability can be defined in terms of expected predation gains. Ironically, large firms with more resources to buy private protection are also more vulnerable: very profitable investment projects make predation very attractive.

31. My discussion focuses on the incentives of G to respond—that is, to attempt unilaterally to protect these two firms. As a matter of fact, the dictator is affecting a larger set of interests, including government officials who protect only one of these two firms, along with the two asset holders. The whole collection of economic and

political interests represented in these two firms would have incentives for collective retaliation against the dictator.

32. As I discuss later, the social networks that develop in dictatorships can be very dense, so there is, in fact, a lot of communication among network members. Moreover, entry to the network is determined politically, so there is much coordination among key members, which will affect the actual nature of the social network in terms of the types of economic activity and the distribution of public officials that it permits. Nonetheless, the point here is that asset holders have an incentive to devise networked protection strategies even in the absence of coordination or previous communication.

33. A network structure with a density equal to one identifies a sufficient but not necessary condition to deter predation. The basic requirement is that there be a critical mass of private enforcers with interests that span the whole network. Two general network structures that can meet this requirement are: (1) highly dense networks or (2) networks with central players who have widespread connections and are sufficiently strong to punish the dictator.

34. I use the terms *predation* and *reneging* interchangeably, although they are not generally equivalent. *Predation* refers to the confiscation or destruction of property, expropriation, and other abuses of authority. *Reneging* is a more general concern about policy credibility. In this book, the two terms are closely related due to the sequential nature of the credible commitment problem of growth. Predation—if it occurs—entails reneging on a prior promise to provide secure property rights.

35. See Osborne and Rubinstein (1994, pp. 87–116) for the definition and derivation of SPNE.

36. I make the following indifference assumptions: (1) If indifferent between protecting or not, the dictator chooses to protect; (2) If indifferent between investing or not, the asset holder chooses to invest; and (3) if indifferent between enforcing or not, the third party chooses to enforce.

37. All things being equal, higher rents increase the critical tax value as $(\partial t_1^*/\partial R)=v_1/(R)^2>0$. More important, higher reservation values allow A_1 to demand lower rates because $(\partial t_1^*/\partial v)=-1/R<0$. Indeed, if the reservation value is sufficiently high, such that $v_1 > R(1-b)$, there is no tax rate that could induce A_1 to participate.

38. For simplicity, I assume that the same protection fee b applies to both firms because they have the same protector. Also, the change in payoffs reflects relative changes in utility when D decides to go after A_2. If T enforces, there is no predation risk, and thus the other firm is unaffected. But when D acts as a predator, what was a sure gain (bR_2) has now become a loss.

39. The vertical distance between these two lines is equal to the gains from preying on A_2: $(1 - t_2)R_2$.

40. The value $\hat{\rho}_1$, defined by the intersection of lines ρ_1^* and R_1^*, represents the minimum effective penalty that can induce credibility.

41. The logic of private protection requires an affiliation between an enforcer and a protected firm. With multiple enforcers and multiple firms, these affiliations constitute a two-mode network (see Wasserman and Faust [1994, pp. 29–30]). For purposes of my theory, however, what matters for enforcement and commitments is overlapping protection (or how enforcers relate to one another), rather than the identity of protected firms.

42. The implication of a common tax rate given different rents is that A_2's reservation value is higher than that of the first firm: $v_2 > v_1$. This result follows from equating the corresponding participation constraints as defined in condition (2.3).

43. This probability, an exogenous parameter, can be interpreted as the probability that ρ_1 is located in the credible commitment region of the parameter space of Figure 2.3. That is, G_1 can take on D by itself.

44. By assumption, $\rho_2 > \rho_1$, and G_2 is able to punish the dictator effectively.

45. This result follows from the assumption that $R_2 \leq R_2^*$ and $R_1 < R_2$. R_2 is at most equal to $c/(2b)$ and $sR_1 < sc/(2b)$.

46. By the assumption that the firms are subject to the same tax rate, and the government's budget constraint, it follows that $t = C_D/(R_1 + R_2)$.

47. The horizontal axis in Figure 2.6B now corresponds to total rents, not just the rents from A_2. The line for ρ_N^* would be just below ρ_2^* for small s.

48. Clearly, if asset holders have some flexibility in recruiting enforcers, unreliable enforcers are likely to be substituted with more reliable ones, so combinations when ρ_i is much lower than ρ_j $(i \neq j)$ are not likely to persist.

CHAPTER 3

1. See, for example, Lewis (2006, pp. 49–74) and Meyer and Sherman (1995, pp. 453–466, 483–497).

2. As will be clear in Chapters 5 and 6, the fact that Díaz eventually became a dictator—and the country was pacified—does not imply that he eradicated all opposition to his regime, for the members of his network included highly influential economic and political actors that could not be easily manipulated.

3. For a political history of Central America, see Skidmore and Smith (2005, pp. 356–395).

4. For an account of political development during this period, see Sinkin (1979).

5. Ironically, the call for private property (as opposed to corporate or communal land holdings) would provide a legal basis for the latter usurpation of Indian laws, as explained in the next chapter.

6. For that reason, it is possible that the amendment to add a senate chamber to the congress in 1874 could have been an attempt by Díaz's predecessor, Sebastian Lerdo de Tejada, to diffuse legislative power.

7. Juárez is a major figure in Mexican history for several reasons. Not only did he help drive out the French, he also promoted laws aimed at mitigating the problem

of land concentration, an endemic problem in Mexican society. Moreover, his life had the elements of a legendary rags-to-riches story that remains popular to this day. Juárez was a Zapotec Indian, who had managed to attend law school, married into an influential family, and eventually become a leading promoter of democracy and defender of indigenous rights.

8. Ironically, it is for this pronouncement that Díaz would be eventually overthrown. The call to arms made by leading revolutionary, and future president, Francisco I. Madero, touched on this very point. Madero's famous phrase of "*sufragio efectivo, no reelección*" (effective suffrage, no reelection) spoke directly to Díaz's earlier democratic promises.

9. While describing the independence movement of the early nineteenth century, Reyes (1903, p. 10), talks about the "sketch" of two parties—a republican party and a monarchist party—to differentiate competing movements, but there was no formal creation of a party structure to sustain them.

10. Duclós Salinas (1904) highlights the repressive tactics of the Díaz government, and notes that there were continuous attempts to depose Díaz as late as the late 1890s, which were met with repression.

11. Díaz–Cayeros (1998) notes that state governors were very influential. Carmagnani (1994) also notes that there were important state and regional interests in the congress that were initially in opposition to Díaz's policies.

12. I used these aggregate data as an indirect measure of latent political opposition. The data do not permit disaggregation to check the exact purposes for which monies were allocated. It is conceivable that some of these "military" expenditures were distributed for patronage purposes. That is, their purpose was to buy loyalty rather than to fight or repress. But even if that was the purpose, increases in military expenditures would signal that the dictator is more insecure, and has found it worthy to spend more resources to curtail the opposition.

13. Carmagnani (1994, pp. 69–80) also notes that there was a great deal of policy conflict between the states and the central government.

14. With the exception of the term served by Manuel M. González, a puppet president who ruled from 1880 to 1884, Díaz was president of Mexico from 1876 to 1911.

15. Initially, Article 51, which established Congress, provided for one assembly (deputies) to exercise this right. Subsequently, the constitutional amendments of November 13, 1874, modified Article 51 (regarding the composition of Congress) and Article 65 (regarding legislative activity) to accommodate a second congressional body, the Senate.

16. Mexico's Constitution of 1857, Article 71.

17. Coupled with instability, one recurrent problem in nineteenth century Mexican politics had been the propensity of new governments to establish authoritarian

governments or otherwise engage in measures that concentrated power in the executive branch.

18. Article 72 of Mexico's Constitution of 1857 gave the Chamber of Deputies exclusive rights to ratify the federal budget.

19. At this time in history there were twenty-nine states and three territories. The latter included Baja California Sur and Nayarit on the Pacific Coast, and the eastern state of Quintana Roo (in the Gulf of Mexico). Despite not being states, federal territories did have representatives in the federal Congress, albeit probably appointed in consultation with the dictator.

20. In counting the number of terms served, Benjamin and Marcial (1984, p. 325) note that Díaz actually served eight presidential terms, although the last one was cut short by the start of the Mexican Revolution. Díaz went into exile in Paris, where he died in 1915.

21. A clause against reelection would be added on November 7, 1911, shortly after Díaz's overthrow at the start of the Mexican Revolution.

22. To be sure, these cooperative schemes occur in all successful dictatorships, so I am not suggesting that networks cause this cooperation. In the particular case of the Porfiriato, I have established that there were no political organizations that could have mitigated conflict outside of formal institutions, so it must have been the case that differences were being mediated elsewhere. The following chapter will make it clear that policies were private rather than public.

23. Roll call data for the Porfiriato were extracted from a series of congressional diaries found in México, Congreso, Cámara de Senadores (1876–1911).

24. I take the prevalence of unanimity in senatorial votes after 1890 as evidence that the executive branch and senators were defining policy outside of the realm of formal political institutions. Hence, it only makes sense to check for coalitions before 1890. See Razo (2003, pp. 120–145), for a statistical analysis of roll calls.

25. The Constitution of 1857 granted the executive government veto power over policies approved by both the Chamber of Deputies and the Senate. Because the approval of the budget did not involve the Senate, the executive branch could not veto the final budgets approved by deputies (see Díaz–Cayeros [1998, p. 4]). This is not to say that senators were out of the loop altogether. The same author notes that the executive government eventually became very adept (using its national party, the Institutional Revolutionary Party [PRI], and political incentives) at using senators to affect financial transfers from the federal to state governments (Díaz–Cayeros, 1998, p. 12).

26. The executive government was required to send a budget initiative to Congress for planning purposes. It was up to the Chamber of Deputies to amend the executive initiative and pass a federal budget.

27. The conventional view is that Díaz overwhelmingly dominated the whole Porfiriato period. For example, Meyer and Sherman (1995) note: "Porfirio Díaz

controlled the destiny of the Mexican nation for a third of a century" (p. 431). That Díaz was the dominant figure of the Porfiriato is clear in retrospect. A closer analysis of his early years, however, makes it clear that it was unknown how long he was going to remain in power.

28. Original data are in nominal pesos for the period 1867 to 1911. I converted all these figures to real values using the price index developed by Razo and Haber (1998) for the period 1850 to 1933.

29. This pattern is confirmed by statistical analysis. Nonparametric and regression analysis in Razo (2003) indicates that although deputy constraints changed from one period to another, they were relaxed over time. In other words, the Chamber of Deputies was not attempting to transform budget policy systematically at any time during the Porfiriato.

30. Carmagnani (1994) does provide a more disaggregated analysis of the federal budget. He also mentions various key personalities and deputy coalitions involved in budget politics, but he does not specify budget preferences for legislators.

31. Carmagnani (1994, pp. 145–148, 155–156) provides historical detail that would diminish the possibility of a collective action problem. He notes that there is an institutional change within the Chamber of Deputies in which the composition of the internal Budget Commission becomes very stable when it becomes populated by the same group of people for long periods of time, as opposed to the early years of the Porfiriato, when commission members were replaced annually (p. 129).

32. See Carmagnani (1994, pp. 101–121) for a more detailed analysis of three main coalitions organized along federal, regional, and central government preferences.

33. To be sure, this is not a comprehensive test of all potential divisions. The relevant division here whether the Budget Commission was representative of the rest of the Chamber. If the Chamber suffered from multiple cleavages, we would expect to see major differences between the Committee's proposal and the final revised budget approved by the whole Chamber.

34. Alternatively, members of Congress realized that they could reliably demand more resources, without opposition from other legislators, with the end result that the final budget was inflated with respect to the original one. For this budget inflationary process to work, however, there must have been an expansionary fiscal policy. But that fiscal policy was unlikely given the central government's borrowing constraints.

35. According to Carmagnani (1994, pp. 145–147), Budget Commission members—at least after 1890—certainly shared the expansionary preferences of the Díaz government. What remains unknown is how representative the Budget Commission was relative to the whole Chamber. We know that state governors had a stake in the budgets that the Chamber approved and Díaz–Cayeros (1998, p. 4) notes that there

was an internal rule that guaranteed parity among states. The implication is that states that were not represented in the Budget Commission would not necessarily defer to the commission's proposal.

36. Using a Kruskal-Wallis test, the H statistic for the comparison between the period before the Porfiriato and the Porfiriato (1876–1911) was 0.500, which was well below the critical value of 3.8418 corresponding to a 0.05 significance level if the underlying distribution is χ^2 with 1 degree of freedom. In the second alternate test comparing the early years of the Porfiriato with the latter years of consolidated dictatorship, the statistic H was equal to 0.710, which was also well below the critical value of 3.8418.

CHAPTER 4

1. See, for example, Beatty (2001).

2. My interest in this chapter is restricted to identifying the type of policies that Díaz passed. I will address the question of how these policies were enforced in Chapters 5 and 6.

3. See also Marichal and Cerutti (1997) and Haber (1989).

4. Coatsworth's (1978) estimates are similar, with an annual growth rate of GDP of roughly 2.5 percent between 1895 and 1910 (pp. 80–81). According to the Mexican government, GDP grew at a higher annual rate of 7.7 percent between 1895 and 1910 (México, INEGI, 1994, pp. 401–402). In general, there is limited macroeconomic evidence to accurately measure all economic activity during this period, but available evidence suggests that the Porfiriato was indeed a period of intensive economic activity (Razo and Haber, 1998).

5. I used an official compilation of these published laws, found in Azpiroz (1890–1898).

6. Certainly, Díaz relied on a combination of repression and favors while attempting to consolidate this dictatorship. These favors included appointments to governorships and access to political influence. Before 1890, there were limited economic opportunities to offer rents.

7. In fact, the "Other" category includes items that could be either private or public policies, so I am biasing the results against me.

8. My argument in Chapter 2 was that the prevalence of private policies should be higher in dictatorships than in democracies. This argument is consistent with the view that dictatorships engage in more redistribution. We do not yet have a theory, however, that gives more precise estimates for the differential rates of private protection across regimes.

9. See Haber et al. (2003, pp. 285–341). This favoritism affected future regional development because export-oriented agriculture was not distributed uniformly

throughout the country. Current problems with poverty partly reflect the incipient development of rural communities, especially in Central and Southern Mexico. A modest agrarian reform implemented in the mid-1930s neither ameliorated regional disparities nor significantly improved the livelihood of peasants.

10. For more detail, see Haber (1989) and Haber et al. (2003, pp. 124–189).

11. Table 6.2 provides direct evidence of political influence on economic concessions.

12. Subsoil rights would later be reversed to become exclusive national patrimony ever since President Lázaro Cardenas nationalized the oil industry in 1938.

13. See "Structure of Private Enforcement" in Chapter 6.

14. Recall that I placed the beginnings of Díaz's dictatorship circa 1890, and thus his dictatorship lasted roughly two decades, instead of the traditional period of the thirty-five-year dictatorship (1876–1911).

15. The company registry includes the universe of all commercial and industrial enterprises by various corporate types, including not just corporations, but also partnerships and other types of small enterprises. It is possible that there may have been other types of economic activity not included in this report. However, given the detail of this company registry, it is clear that the government was willing to invest resources to get the most accurate record of its tax base. Hence, it is doubtful that the economic activity occurring outside this sample was of major significance, especially for tax purposes. I also note that this registry recorded a single value for each firm in Mexican pesos, but does not identify the base year. This omission does not affect my statistical analysis, however, because all firms are valued with the same measurement rule.

16. Each of these enterprises was authorized to function for a given period of time, denoted here as *length of concession*. The actual figure captured in my data set is the expected length of operation granted by the Mexican government. For many firms, the length greatly exceeded the Porfiriato, and there were some enterprises with concessions that had no terminal date.

17. This classification does not imply that these enterprises did not have domestic investors at all. In fact, as I will show in the following section and the next chapter, all corporations relied on connections to influential public officials. My classification is based on company registry information that indicated that a given enterprise was dependent on a corporation or economic group headquartered abroad.

18. In 1900 pesos, the average capital stock was 265,875, with a standard deviation of 2,169,285! The minimum capital stock was 90 (A. Villanta y Cia., a firm involved in trading services) and the maximum capital stock was 100,000,000 (American Smelting and Refining Co.). The capital stocks corresponding to the 25th, 50th, and 75th percentiles were 3306 pesos, 12,000 pesos, and 66,660.50 pesos respectively.

19. I use capital stock as a proxy for these (expected) rents, but it is possible that the capital stock may itself be determined by the terms of the concession that an en-

terprise gets. For example, in the case of mining companies, the size of investments would probably depend on the number of years that companies expected to exploit their concessions. The company registry does not specify which comes first, capital or concessions, and it does not include time series to evaluate how capital stocks varied over time. It is thus possible that the error term of a regression equation with concession (as the dependent variable) and capital stock (as the independent variable) may be correlated with the capital stock, which violates one of the assumptions of ordinary least squares regression analysis. I ran a parallel set of regressions using corporate type as an instrumental variable for capital to circumvent this endogeneity problem. The results indicate a larger effect for the capital stock, but are qualitatively similar to those shown in Table 4.4.

20. This does not mean that the property rights of Indian communities were respected, but the Reform laws that would have ended those rights were not implemented.

21. Coatsworth (1981, p. 155) notes that concessions were published in the *Official Gazette (Diario Oficial)*, which could be consulted prior to construction.

22. For a discussion of the *encomienda* system of land grants, see Lockhart and Schwartz (1983, p. 69).

23. Clearly, these enterprises with long or perpetual concessions, such as Banamex, were expected to be around for a long time.

24. Ideally, one would want to check directly for the affiliation of influential public officials (or private enforcers) to evaluate the benefits of network protection. Unfortunately, this industrial census did not have systematic data on ownership or boards of directors.

25. The estimated coefficients are hazard ratios, which indicate the relative risk of dissolution, depending on whether the coefficient is greater or less than one. A coefficient $\hat{\beta} < 1$ indicates that a unit increase in a given explanatory variable makes it $(1 - \hat{\beta})\%$ less likely that the company will dissolve. In contrast, a coefficient $\hat{\beta} > 1$ indicates that it is $(\hat{\beta} - 1)\%$ more likely that the company will dissolve.

26. The corresponding coefficients for capital in models 2 and 3 are 0.445 and 0.463 respectively. The statistical significance level for these coefficients is 0.05 and 0.10 respectively.

CHAPTER 5

1. Acemoglu and Robinson (2006) make a similar argument regarding the sharing of political power by elites to make credible commitments to the poor. My argument here is slightly different because the dictator is simply trying to reach out to other political elites rather than the whole population; thus, required institutional changes need not include a process of democratization.

2. Most of this section is based on Camp (1995b), but see also Camp (1982, 1991, 1992, 1995a).

3. Velasco (1889) notes that many cabinet members not only had similar backgrounds, but were connected directly through various social and economic relations.

4. But see Camp (1992) for a notable exception.

5. Indeed, the prominent political institution that permeates studies of modern Mexican political history is the dominant political party (the PRI), which dominated politics for most of the twentieth century. In the shadow of the PRI, the army has had a more limited role than other countries in Latin America.

6. Eventually, some elites did rebel against the dictator, calling for a revolution in 1910 to 1911. The success of their rebellion was predicated not solely on the support of other network players, but on a larger segment of the population—especially peasants—who had not shared the fruits of economic growth during the Porfiriato. Indeed, those Díaz supporters who did not go into exile, were divided in their support of various revolutionary figures. If influential members did not switch sides after Díaz' had been weakened (and later exiled), it is doubtful that they would have considered rebellion when Díaz had greater political control.

7. This caveat applies strictly to this particular network analysis. One can make a more definite statement about the important role of elites by examining the historical literature, as well as by the other bodies of evidence analyzed in this book. Clearly, elites had much influence. (Indeed, as I claim, they effectively made Díaz a dictator of their own choosing.) However, studying relational aspects of these elites is hampered a bit by the lack of information sources.

8. My database also allowed for the identification of political allies and opponents, but this type of information was not readily available. This is not to say that there were no such antagonistic relationships. Indeed, I noted in Chapter 3 that there were alliances as well as conflicts and disagreements among influential political actors. But reading the historical literature, most of the references to personal relations were either to some kind of family relation or friendship, rather than explicit political connections to the effect that actor X provided political support to actor Y. But even while coding strictly for social relations, I also coded whether any of the parties was in government, thus capturing an element of political connections.

9. See Cerutti (2003) and Gamboa Ojeda (2003).

10. Note that this is a different type of relation than that of private protection. In the former, I identified company directors who received some partial payment for their services. The affiliation in that case was made from one person to a company. Here, the affiliation is made directly between two people and must have a business character, distinct from other social relations, in the sense that the two people have a shared stake in their common property or assets.

11. Note that the ties in this diagram require that at least one of the partners have a public office. Brittingham did not have public office, but he had a close personal

friendship and business relationship with members of the Terrazas, whom he had met while in college in the United States.

12. See, for example, the edited volumes by Altamirano (2000) and Meyer Cosío (1999).

13. My main source of career information was by Camp (1991), which included information for most offices for the period 1884 to 1911. Before 1884, systematic career data were only available for members of Congress. I consulted México, Congreso, Cámara de Diputados (1876–1911) and Barragán Barragán et al. (1987) to get rosters of deputies and senators for the period 1876 to 1884.

14. As far as I know, this sample includes all positions for the categories I examined. Other than governorships and federal legislative positions, however, the sample does not include information on lower levels of government. For instance, the sample does not include state offices such as state cabinets and state legislatures. The omission of these lower level offices does not affect the results of this chapter. Even if there was a lot of mobility at these lower levels, my sample includes all other higher offices. The analysis shows that careers did not go much higher beyond a certain point (the legislative branch).

15. All these governors participated actively in Díaz's social network of private protection, especially as it concerned the direction of state banks (see Chapter 6).

16. Additional analysis in Razo (2003), not shown here, does not show major differences in position length by region, although central regions around and just north of Mexico City appear to show a bit more variability than other regions.

17. The fact that career lengths exceed thirty-five years (the number of years in the Porfiriato) indicates that these officials (with names in bold type in Table 5.8) often held multiple positions at the same time.

18. The previous section does analyze actual lengths and seniority (cumulative length) rather than transitions.

19. The claim that the time interval does not affect the transition analysis is valid because I am ultimately interested in evaluating political mobility over periods of time that are longer than this interval. In principle, smaller time intervals provide the added advantage of a larger number of potential transitions to analyze during this first stage. A larger number of transitions may lead to more precise time averages during the second stage, provided that most careers are not too long relative to the interval. Finding the appropriate time interval is ultimately a practical question depending on particular samples. In my sample, it did not make sense to use daily time intervals because for a one-year position, for example, I would have obtained transition probabilities of 1.0 for 365 subsequent days. This result would be very accurate in that the probability of changing positions from one day to the next is practically nil, but it is not very informative when positions last for years, not days.

20. In actuality, I am only interested in careers extending up to 1911, when the Díaz dictatorship collapsed. The Porfiriato includes only seventeen congresses proper, with the Twenty-Fourth Congress being the last one held before the Mexican Revolution. However, the Twenty-Fifth Congress was already underway when Díaz was overthrown at the onset of the Mexican Revolution, so it made sense to include the Twenty-Fifth Congress in my transition analysis to account for the mobility of the last cohort of the Porfiriato. The Porfiriato would not outlast the Twenty-Fifth Congress, but this fact was unknown when this Congress started.

21. By construction, there is an underlying assumption that this matrix is time invariant within subperiods. In other words, by looking at all political careers for the whole Porfiriato, I am, in a sense, obtaining time averages of the underlying transition probabilities. This is a fairly strong assumption in that it describes a system in a steady state in which the rules of the game regarding political mobility are fixed. Clearly, these rules were not in place when Díaz arrived to power, but it is reasonable to assume that the rules were fairly fixed after Díaz consolidated power midway through his tenure.

22. The multinomial logit model is a generalization of the binary logit model, used with dependent variables that have more than two categories (Greene, 1993, pp. 664–668).

23. Public officials constituted a relatively homogenous group, populated by social and economic elites. The implications for my statistical analysis was to dispense with the need to model unobserved heterogeneity, or the need to model some unobserved characteristic that differentiated public officials. Public officials were not selected randomly. For the most part, the major exception some individuals with military prestige, they came from well-to-do families.

24. Additional tests in Razo (2003) included adding covariates that accounted for regional differences (in terms of the states or entities that a particular office or position represented). The results shown here were unaffected by the inclusion of regional variables—an important result in and of itself. Political careers do not appear to have been affected by regional biases.

25. Alternatively, one can subtract or add one to the relative risk ratios to make comparisons in percentage terms. For this case, a relative risk ratio of 0.06 indicates that the odds of deputies becoming senators are equal to 1–0.06, or 94 percent less than continuing as deputies. A year of experience, on the other hand, increases the odds of becoming senators by 1.09–1, or 9 percent, all things being equal.

26. These conditional plots are derived from an estimated multinomial logit model with similar results to those of Table 5.9, but measuring time in terms of congresses rather than major periods.

27. By governance structures I refer to both stable formal and informal mechanisms affecting policy-making processes.

28. See Haber et al. (2003, pp. 41–79), and Meyer and Sherman (1995, pp. 483–568), for a more detailed discussion of the revolutionary period.

CHAPTER 6

1. The network analysis should be interpreted as an analysis of political connections operating under a mature set of institutional arrangements between government officials and corporations. It is possible that some of the 1907 board of directors did not change much from previous years during the early 1900s, in which case the board analysis would be representative of a longer time period. We know from Chapter 5 that public officials enjoyed stable and long careers, so it is plausible that they were offering protection well before 1907. However, it is difficult to verify continuity for private actors, given the lack of data.

2. Indeed, eventually these elites would depose the dictator at the advent of the Mexican Revolution, but for political reasons unrelated to the protection of property rights.

3. See the Appendix for data sources.

4. More precisely, this chapter analyzes four distinct networks. The first network is composed of industry nodes that share private protection. The second network is composed of companies that share private protection. The third one, and the one that relates directly to the theory of Chapter 2, is a network of public officials providing common protection to multiple firms. Finally, I analyze a network of interlocking directorates, including both private actors and public officials with shared membership in boards of directors.

5. Indeed, banking policy during the Porfiriato expressly prevented foreign investors from entering the financial sector. Manufacturing was heavily protected as well. The industries in which foreign investors were concentrated had fewer restrictions and a greater potential for higher profits.

6. Given the prominence of the public officials who participated in the network, this type of association captures the notion that industries are protected by a powerful public official who could influence sectoral policy in their favor. In actuality, however, there were multiple links from one industry to another.

7. The importance of governors is somewhat driven by particular features of the Mexican political system in which governors in a federalist system had varying levels of independence from the federal government. Had Mexico not been a federal republic with some fairly strong governors, the connections to elites discussed in Chapter 5 suggest that state-level government officials would not have been excluded from participation in Díaz's network of private protection.

8. In fact, virtually all companies had several private enforcers in common, so this measure does not bias the measure in my favor; it does the contrary. If companies A and B have twenty directors in common, and companies C and D have five directors

in common, this measure would not differentiate between the pairs A-B and C-D in terms of the intensity of their connections.

9. It is quite possible that some government actors may own part of the enterprises and thus have a greater stake in the rents they produce, even when these actors may not themselves serve as directors. State governors, for example, often received rents from protected economic groups even when these latter groups were not always organized as corporations with boards of directors, as was the case among some agricultural enterprises.

10. To be sure, my theory does not make behavioral predictions for this company network because asset holders are assumed to be passive (except for investing). It is the public officials that provide protection, and that enforcement mechanism is embedded a separate network of public officials to be examined in the following section. Nonetheless, this interpretation is warranted if asset holders readily call upon their affiliated public officials to provide protection.

11. Thinking of density in terms of the probability of collective retaliation, as I do here, actually requires a uniform distribution of public officials across companies. We know that there were more connections in certain industries. In those more dense industries, the probability of retaliation would be more than 7 percent. In contrast, in industries with fewer connections, the probability of retaliation would be less than 7 percent.

12. For the network that traces shared private protection among corporations, we can construct 149 different networks.

13. The maximum number of ties is $(103 \times 102) \div 2$, or 5253 distinct ties. The number of actual ties was 400.

14. See Scott (2000, pp. 82–99) for a discussion of various centrality measures.

15. These nobility terms came from the Fagoaga family's connections to Spain's Basque region. The Fagoaga family, along with others, was able to position itself in high places during Spain's colonial period in Spanish America, which culminated with Mexico's independence in 1821, after which the Fagoaga family remained loyal to conservative movements that wanted to restore a monarchy. This family was able, however, to align itself with new factions, including the liberals who dominated Mexico during the late nineteenth century. Thus, by the time Díaz came to power in 1876, prominent members of the Fagoaga family were able to find themselves influential niches in the new government.

16. Camp (1991) provides club membership information for most biographical entries.

17. Note that the Porfiriato (1876–1911) lasted for thirty-five years.

18. See the discussion of the oil industry in Haber et al. (2003, pp. 190–234). See also Read and Musacchio (2001, p. 15).

19. I made a single exception in coding Díaz, Jr. as a public official for the evident and direct connection that he had with the dictator.

20. José Y. Limantour had a long legislative career from the early 1880s to the late 1890s. See Tables 5.7 and 5.8 for a list of public officials with the longest positions and political careers, respectively.

21. The national bank, or Banamex, was the most important bank during this period and remains important today. See also Maurer (2002) and Haber et al. (2003, pp. 80–123).

22. The encompassing interests behind Díaz's exclusive network of private protection included at least the people analyzed in this network. In fact, because shareholder information was unavailable in a systematic way, the network analyses here may greatly underestimate the number of stakeholders in this system of private protection.

23. Some of the analyses were performed with statnet 1.0 (Handcock et al., 2003).

24. See Pollock (2006, pp. 179–202) for a nontechnical introduction to logistic regression. For a more advanced treatment, see King (1998, pp. 97–132).

25. To illustrate, suppose that a network had two nodes and we allow ties to be directed (e.g., one node can relate to a second one in a particular way, but that relationship need not be reciprocated). Excluding loops involving the same node, then there would be four possible network configurations represented by the following sociomatrices: $\begin{pmatrix} & 1 \\ 0 & \end{pmatrix}, \begin{pmatrix} & 1 \\ 1 & \end{pmatrix}, \begin{pmatrix} & 0 \\ 0 & \end{pmatrix}, \text{ or } \begin{pmatrix} & 0 \\ 1 & \end{pmatrix}$. These configurations would represent the four possible outcomes for the random variable X. If any of these configurations is the actual datum, we denote it by x, and then the quantity of interest becomes $Pr(X = x)$ rather than the independent probabilities of individual cells being equal to one.

26. Each tie would be determined by an independent probability. See Wasserman and Robins (2005, p. 151).

27. Another example that illustrates these considerations is the case in which two people establish a tie if the connection enables them to join an elite clique within a larger network.

28. This probability model also goes by the name of a *Markov random graph*. The first term, κ, is a normalization coefficient to ensure a proper probability function with values between zero and one. For a complete specification of Markov random graphs and technical details on the Hammersley-Clifford theorem that justifies this approach, see Anderson et al. (1999) and Wasserman and Robins (2005).

29. These are the structural variables used to model nondirected Markov random graphs. All the networks analyzed in this book assume nondirected ties. Nondirected implies a two-way relationship, as opposed to an asymmetric or directed connection

that can only go in one direction (e.g., for fatherhood—the binary relation "is the father of," if we establish that X *is the father of* Y, then it cannot be that Y is also the father of X).

30. To recover probabilities, note that these equations can be rewritten in log-odds form as $\log\left[Pr(X_{ij}=1|x)/Pr(X_{ij}=0|x)\right]=\theta_1 L+\cdots$. If a proposed tie connects two otherwise disconnected nodes, there is an additional tie so $\Delta L = 1$. The log-odds of that tie are equal to $\hat{\theta}_1 \times \Delta L = -0.2173 \times 1$. Hence, the probability that $X_{ij} = 1$ equals $\exp(\hat{\theta}_1)/(1+\exp(\hat{\theta}_1))$. Similar calculations can be done when adding other network statistics or explanatory variables $z_k(x)$: $Pr(X_{ij}=1|x)=\exp(\sum_k \hat{\theta}_k \Delta z_k(x))/(1+\exp(\sum_k \hat{\theta}_k \Delta z_k(x)))$.

31. Other attributes included the level and type of public office, and the regional basis for representative offices, but these additional attributes were not found to be significant.

32. The corresponding P value is 0.07, which implies that the estimate is almost significant at the more conventional level of 0.05.

33. This probability is lower in absolute terms than in the baseline case because that model does not account for the types of potential players, and thus overestimates the probability of generic ties.

34. Coatsworth (1981) makes a more general point about how regional elites became more connected by the end of the Porfiriato. Ironically, the construction of railroads (a keystone of Díaz's economic policies) lowered the costs of communication among elites, and made it easier for them, eventually, to challenge the government.

CHAPTER 7

1. Scholars do recognize that property rights regimes are not always efficiently produced and do not benefit everyone (North, 1990). However, the degree and implications of inefficient property rights *under* various political regimes have not been systematically analyzed.

2. Recent research has begun to recognize this link. For example, see McMillan and Zoido (2004) for the case of Peru's corruption network during the Fujimori administration (1990–2000).

3. See Aron (2000) for a review of this empirical literature.

4. My purpose here is not to criticize a particular approach to the study of institutions and growth. Ideally, we want cross-country studies to complement detailed country studies, but we are not ready to engage in such studies because of data and methodological limitations. Among the methodological limitations, we have not just the reliance on single-level aggregate studies, but the need to dispense at lower levels of aggregation with the common assumption that observations are independent.

5. This is not to say that legislators did not have any say in important matters. For instance, Díaz required the cooperation of the Senate to ratify, among other decisions, political appointments and to remove unwanted public officials.

6. My findings are consistent with recent evaluations of the Senate and state governors as key players during the Porfiriato. See Díaz-Cayeros (1998, pp. 3–4).

7. For example, to what extent do theories of executive decree delegation in presidential systems as found in Carey and Shugart (1998) carry over to authoritarian regimes?

8. Before financial crises became the focus in East Asia, there was a cottage industry that tried to extract lessons from East Asian development that were applicable to other regions. See Amsden (1989), Aoki et al. (1997), Akyüz et al. (1999), Evans (1999), Evans et al. (1992), and Wade (1990), among others.

9. It seems that these social networks may also have a role in determining levels and types of corruption, but the question of corruption is beyond the scope of this book.

10. Networks may also have played an informational role, not just to deliberate on the formulation of optimal policies as Campos and Root argue, but to help political and economic actors monitor each other to avoid holdup problems because of an asymmetric distribution of political and economic resources.

11. This statement is clearly related to issues regarding the quality of bureaucracies, which apparently played a major role in East Asian economic development. Evans (1995) has argued strongly in favor of expert bureaucracies within the larger literature of developmental states. My theory does not dispute the fact that good bureaucracies can help dictators deal with an increasing number of selective commitments. In fact, a bureaucratic structure can ameliorate the dictator's governability dilemma. Unlike the developmental literature, however, the governance structure that my theory proposes not only solves bureaucratic problems but also aligns the incentives of all relevant actors. The implication is that bureaucrats themselves must have obtained private benefits from selective commitments and that other actors be constrained from preying on the bureaucracy. (Bureaucrats themselves need a credible commitment from the dictator that the time they spend developing expertise will not go to waste if the dictator acts arbitrarily and disregards expert advice.)

12. It is also the case that many of these countries adopted export-oriented strategies after some period of time, so there were additional disciplining mechanisms that worked to enhance the credibility of dictators, even if cronies were not strong enough or their organizational capability was limited.

13. Alternatively, even if there is a critical mass of influential political actors, economic activity may not be of such a scale that will make it profitable for third parties to enforce private policies.

14. Thomson (2004, p. 220) describes this rotation and notes also that the number of influential players was deliberately set to a maximum of eighty individuals.

15. For example, Sawyer (2005, p. 27) notes that the Liberian state's monopoly on natural resources did not lead to independent sources of economic activity. The

government was therefore not vulnerable to social pressure and it did not need private economic activity to generate its own revenue. Although elites retained political influence as Dalton (1965) had noted, there were no viable contenders. Even the military was unable to retain its independence and became, instead, an instrument of the state.

16. Dictators may be constrained by the need for diplomatic recognition and foreign aid, among other incentives.

17. A radial structure limits the propagation of predation risk, and hence induces economic and political actors to only care about themselves. Evans (1995) advances a similar argument regarding the conditions that enable successful developmental states. Evans' concern is how to prevent the disintegration of the state into atomistic predatory actors, rather than to prevent predation from a dictator. His argument implies that it is critical for development that the state enhance various social networks as an embedded, rather than an independent, heavy-handed actor (as would be the case with a radial structure where the state engages in the exclusive dispensation of favors and resources). The ability of the state to perform this bridging role, however, will depend on the quality and structure of its bureaucracy, according to Evans.

18. Thompson (1998) refers to the Marcos regime as a "conjugal dictatorship," where even at the highest level Ferdinand and Imelda offered separate privileges. Thompson (1998) notes that the Philippines had a patrimonial state well before Marcos came to power, and that its "traditional socio-economic order…has shown itself to be particularly resistant to change" (p. 216).

19. See Kang (2002) for a comparative study of the Philippines and South Korea.

20. See Díaz-Cayeros (1997) for an explanation of the political incentives that allowed the PRI to stay in power for such a long time.

21. Rodriguez and Gomolin (2006) also highlight a particular institutional innovation by Guzmán Blanco that survives to this day: the "Situado Constitucional, a rule for the allocation of a fixed fraction of government revenues among regional governments" (pp. 8–9).

22. This situation was not unique to Mexico. See Tulchin and Espach (2000) for a regional perspective.

23. Przeworski et al. (2000) note that property rights were selectively provided to those with economic resources, so early development favored only a small number of citizens.

REFERENCES

Acemoglu, Daron, Simon Johnson, and James A. Robinson. 2001. The colonial origins of comparative development: An empirical investigation. *American Economic Review* 91 (5):1369–1401.

Acemoglu, Daron, and James A. Robinson. 2006. *Economic origins of dictatorship and democracy.* Cambridge: Cambridge University Press.

Aguilar Aguilar, Gustavo. 2003. "El sistema bancario en Sinaloa (1889–1916). Su influencia en el crecimiento económico." In *La Banca Regional en México (1870–1930)*, ed. Mario Cerutti and Carlos Marichal, 47–100. Mexico City: Fondo de Cultura Económica.

Akyüz, Y. Imaz, ed. 1999. *East Asian development: New perspectives.* London: F. Cass.

Akyüz, Y. Imaz, Ha-Joon Chang, and Richard Kozul-Wright. 1999. "New perspectives on East Asian development." In *East Asian development: New perspectives*, ed. Y. Imaz Akyüz, 4–36. London: F. Cass.

Alston, Lee J., Tráinn Eggertsson, and Douglass Cecil North. 1996. *Empirical studies in institutional change.* Cambridge: Cambridge University Press.

Altamirano, Graziella, ed. 2000. *Prestigio, riqueza y poder: Las élites en México, 1821–1940.* San Juan, Mixcoac, México: Instituto Mora.

Amsden, Alice H. 1989. *Asia's next giant: South Korea and late industrialization.* New York: Oxford University Press.

Anderson, Carolyn J., Stanley Wasserman, and Bradley Crouch. 1999. A p* primer on logit models for social networks. *Social Networks* 21:37–66.

Anna, Timothy. 1984. "The independence of Mexico and Central America." In *The Cambridge History of Latin America*, ed. Leslie Bethell, 51–94. Cambridge: Cambridge University Press.

Aoki, Masahiko, Hyung-Ki Kim, and Masahiro Okuno. 1997. *The role of government in East Asian economic development: Comparative institutional analysis.* Oxford: Clarendon Press.

Aron, Janine. 2000. Growth and institutions: A review of the evidence. *World Bank Research Observer* 15 (1):99–135.

Arrow, Kenneth Joseph. 1951. *Social choice and individual values.* New York: Wiley.

Azpiroz, Manuel, comp. 1890–1898. *Recopilacion de leyes, decretos y providencias de los poderes legislativo y ejecutivo de la Union.* Vol. 56–71. Mexico City: Imprenta del Gobierno en Palacio.

Barragán Barragán, José, Jaime del Arenal Fenochio, Manuel González Oro-
peza, and México, Congreso, Cámara de Senadores. 1987. *El Senado
mexicano: Por la razón de las leyes.* Mexico City: Senado de la República.

Barro, Robert J. 1997. *Determinants of economic growth: A cross-country empirical
study.* Cambridge, MA: MIT Press.

Barro, Robert J., and David Gordon. 1983. Rules, discretion, and reputation in a
model of monetary policy. *Journal of Monetary Economics* 12 (1):101–121.

Bazant, Jan. 1984. "Mexico from independence to 1867." In *The Cambridge
History of Latin America,* ed. Leslie Bethell, 423–470. Cambridge: Cambridge University Press.

Beatty, Edward. 2001. *Institutions and investment: The political basis of industrialization in Mexico before 1911.* Stanford, CA: Stanford University Press.

Beatty, Edward. 2002. "Commercial policy in Porfirian Mexico: The structure
of protection." In *The Mexican economy, 1870–1930: Essays on the economic
history of institutions, revolution, and growth,* ed. Jeff L. Bortz and Stephen H.
Haber, 205–252. Stanford, CA: Stanford University Press.

Benjamin, Thomas, and Ocasio Melendez Marcial. 1984. Organizing the
memory of modern Mexico: Porfirian historiography in perspective,
1880s–1980s. *Hispanic American Historical Review* 64 (2):323–364.

Bhargava, Vinay Kumar, and Emil P. Bolongaita. 2004. *Challenging corruption in
Asia: Case studies and a framework for action.* Washington, DC: World Bank.

Bortz, Jeff, and Stephen H. Haber, eds. 2002. *The Mexican economy, 1870–1930:
Essays on the economic history of institutions, revolution, and growth.* Stanford,
CA: Stanford University Press.

Brennan, Geoffrey, and James M. Buchanan. 1985. *The reason of rules: Constitutional political economy.* Cambridge: Cambridge University Press.

Bueno de Mesquita, Bruce, James D. Morrow, Randolph Siverson, and Alastair
Smith. 2001. Political competition and economic growth. *Journal of Democracy* 12 (1):58–72.

Camp, Roderic A. 1982. *Mexican political biographies, 1935–1981.* 2nd ed., rev.
and expanded. Tucson, AZ: The University of Arizona Press.

Camp, Roderic A. 1991. *Mexican political biographies, 1884–1935.* Austin, TX:
University of Texas Press.

Camp, Roderic A. 1992. *Generals in the Palacio: The military in modern Mexico.*
New York: Oxford University Press.

Camp, Roderic A. 1995a. *Mexican political biographies, 1935–1993.* 3rd ed. Austin, TX: University of Texas Press.

Camp, Roderic A. 1995b. *Political recruitment across two centuries: Mexico, 1884–
1991.* Austin, TX: University of Texas Press.

Camp, Roderic A. 2002. *Mexico's mandarins: Crafting a power elite for the twenty-
first century.* Berkeley, CA: University of California Press.

Campos, J. Edgardo, ed. 2002. *Corruption: The boom and bust of East Asia.* Manila:
Ateneo de Manila University Press.

Campos, José Edgardo L., and Hilton L. Root. 1996. *The key to the Asian miracle: Making shared growth credible.* Washington, DC: Brookings Institution.

Carey, John M., and Matthew Soberg Shugart. 1998. *Executive decree authority.* Cambridge: Cambridge University Press.

Carmagnani, Marcello. 1994. *Estado y mercado: La economía pública del liberalismo mexicano, 1850–1911.* Mexico City: Fondo de Cultura Económica.

Carrington, Peter J., John Scott, and Stanley Wasserman, eds. 2005. *Models and methods in social network analysis.* Cambridge: Cambridge University Press.

Cerutti, Mario. 2003. "Empresariado y banca en el norte de México (1870–1910). La fundación del Banco Refaccionario de La Laguna." In *La Banca Regional en México (1870–1930),* ed. Mario Cerutti and Carlos Marichal, 168–215. Mexico City: Fondo de Cultura Económica.

Cerutti, Mario, and Carlos Marichal, eds. 2003. *La Banca Regional en México (1870–1930).* Mexico City: Fondo de Cultura Económica.

Chehabi, Houchang E., and Juan J. Linz. 1998a. "A theory of sultanism 1: A type of nondemocratic rule." In *Sultanistic regimes,* ed. Houchang E. Chehabi and Juan J. Linz. Baltimore: Johns Hopkins University Press.

Chehabi, Houchang E., and Juan J. Linz, eds. 1998b. *Sultanistic regimes.* Baltimore: Johns Hopkins University Press.

Clague, Christopher, Philip Keefer, Stephen Knack, and Mancur Olson. 1996. Property and contract rights in autocracies and democracies. *Journal of Economic Growth* 1:243–276.

Clarke, Linda, Ming Yue, and Mary Ann Von Glinow. 1999. "Chinese family business networks and regional economic development in Asia." In *Business networks in Asia: Promises, doubts, and perspectives,* ed. Frank-Jürgen Richter, 171–207. Westport, CT: Quorum Books.

Coatsworth, John H. 1978. Obstacles to economic growth in nineteenth century Mexico. *American Historical Review* 83 (1):80–100.

Coatsworth, John H. 1981. *Growth against development: The economic impact of railroads in Porfirian Mexico.* Dekalb, IL: Northern Illinois University Press.

Coatsworth, John H. 2005. Structures, endowments, and institutions in the economic history of Latin America. *Latin American Research Review* 40 (3):127–145.

Collier, David. 1979. "The bureaucratic–authoritarian model: Synthesis and priorities for future research." In *New Authoritarianism in Latin America,* ed. David Collier, 363–398. Princeton, NJ: Princeton University Press.

Collier, David, Fernando Henrique Cardoso, and the Joint Committee on Latin American Studies. 1979. *The new authoritarianism in Latin America.* Princeton, NJ: Princeton University Press.

Connolly, Priscilla. 1997. *El contratista de don Porfirio: Obras públicas, deuda y desarrollo desigual.* Mexico City: Fondo de Cultura Económica.

Dalton, George. 1965. History, politics, and economic development in Liberia. *The Journal of Economic History* 25 (4):569–591.

Díaz-Cayeros, Alberto. 1997. *Political responses to regional inequality: Taxation and distribution in Mexico*. PhD diss., Duke University, Durham, NC.

Díaz-Cayeros, Alberto. 1998. *Federalism and endogenous institutional change in the Mexican Senate*. Mexico City: CIDAC.

Do, Quy Toan, and Andrei A. Levchenko. 2006. *Trade, inequality, and the political economy of institutions*. Washington, DC: World Bank.

Doner, Richard F., and Ansil Ramsay. 2000. "Rent-seeking and economic development in Thailand." In *Rents, rent-seeking and economic development: Theory and evidence in Asia*, ed. Mushtaq H. Khan and Kwame S. Jomo, 145–181. Cambridge: Cambridge University Press.

Dornbusch, Rudiger, and Sebastian Edwards. 1991. *The macroeconomics of populism in Latin America*. Chicago: University of Chicago Press.

Duclós Salinas, Adolfo. 1904. *Méjico pacificado: El progreso de Méjico y los hombres que lo gobiernan: Porfirio Díaz-Bernardo Reyes*. St. Louis, MO: Imprenta de Hughes.

Dutta, Bhaskar, and Matthew O. Jackson. 2003. *Networks and groups: Models of strategic formation*. Berlin: Springer.

Elster, Jon. 1989. *Nuts and bolts for the social sciences*. Cambridge: Cambridge University Press.

Evans, Peter B. 1979. *Dependent development: The alliance of multinational, state, and local capital in Brazil*. Princeton, NJ: Princeton University Press.

Evans, Peter B. 1995. *Embedded autonomy: States and industrial transformation*. Princeton, NJ: Princeton University Press.

Evans, Peter B., ed. 1997. *State–society synergy: Government and social capital in development*. Berkeley, CA: University of California International and Area Studies.

Evans, Peter B. 1999. "Transferable lessons? Re-examining the institutional prerequisites of East Asian economic policies." In *East Asian development: New perspectives*, ed. Y. Imaz Akyüz, 66–86. London: F. Cass.

Evans, Peter B., Claudio Frischtak, and Paulo Bastos Tigre. 1992. *High technology and third world industrialization: Brazilian computer policy in comparative perspective*. Berkeley, CA: University of California International and Area Studies.

Evans, Peter B., and James E. Rauch. 1999. Bureaucracy and growth: A cross-national analysis of the effects of "Weberian" state structures on economic growth. *American Sociological Review* 64 (5):748–765.

Gambetta, Diego. 1993. *The Sicilian Mafia: The business of private protection*. Cambridge, MA: Harvard University Press.

Gamboa Ojeda, Leticia. 2000. "Redes de Parentesco y de Negocios en el Empresariado Español. Angel Solana Alonso, entre el Porfiriato y la Pos Revolución." In *Prestigio, riqueza y poder: Las élites en México, 1821–1940*, ed. Graziella Altamirano, 180–191. San Juan, Mixcoac, México: Instituto Mora.

Gamboa Ojeda, Leticia. 2003. "El Banco Oriental de México y la formación de un sistema de banca, 1900–1911." In *La Banca Regional en México (1870–1930)*, ed. Mario Cerutti and Carlos Marichal, 101–133. Mexico City: Fondo de Cultura Económica.

Garner, Paul H. 2001. *Porfirio Díaz*. Harlow, UK: Longman.

Geddes, Barbara. 1994. *Politician's dilemma: Building state capacity in Latin America*. Berkeley: University of California Press.

Geddes, Barbara. 1999. What do we know about democratization after twenty years? *American Review of Political Science* 2:115–144.

Glade, William. 1984. "Latin America and the international economy, 1870–1914." In *The Cambridge History of Latin America*, ed. Leslie Bethell, 1–56. Cambridge: Cambridge University Press.

Gómez, Mónica. 2003. "El crecimiento de la banca local de emisión en México, 1897–1910." In *La Banca Regional en México (1870–1930)*, ed. Mario Cerutti and Carlos Marichal, 321–345. Mexico City: Fondo de Cultura Económica.

Gómez Galvarriato, Aurora. 2000. Porfiriato, Vida Económica ¿Qué sabemos de nuevo? Paper presented at the XXII international congress of the Latin American Studies Association. March 15–19, in Miami, FL.

Gómez-Quiñones, Juan. 1981. *Porfirio Díaz, los intelectuales y la Revolución*. Mexico City: Ediciones El Caballito.

Gordon, Scott. 1999. *Controlling the state: Constitutionalism from ancient Athens to today*. Cambridge, MA: Harvard University Press.

Gray, Clive, and Malcolm McPherson. 2001. The leadership factor in African policy reform and growth. *Economic Development and Cultural Change* 49 (4):707–740.

Greene, William H. 1993. *Econometric analysis*. 2nd ed. New York: Macmillan Publishing Company.

Guerra, François-Xavier. 1988. *México: Del Antiguo Régimen a la Revolución*. Vol. I. Mexico City: Fondo de Cultura Económica.

Guest, Robert. 2004. *The shackled continent: Power, corruption, and African lives*. Washington, DC: Smithsonian Books.

Gutiérrez Alvarez, Coralia. 2000. "Las Elites Porfirianas del Centro de México: Puebla, de 1885 a 1914." In *Prestigio, riqueza y poder: Las élites en México, 1821–1940*, ed. Graziella Altamirano, 54–63. San Juan, México: Instituto Mora.

Haber, Stephen H. 1989. *Industry and underdevelopment: The industrialization of Mexico, 1890–1940*. Stanford, CA: Stanford University Press.

Haber, Stephen H. 1997. *How Latin America fell behind: Essays on the economic histories of Brazil and Mexico, 1800–1914*. Stanford, CA: Stanford University Press.

Haber, Stephen H., ed. 2002. *Crony capitalism and economic growth in Latin America: Theory and evidence*. Stanford, CA: Hoover Institution Press.

Haber, Stephen. 2005. *Why institutions matter: Banking and economic growth in Mexico*. Unpublished paper. Stanford, CA: Stanford University, Department of Political Science.

Haber, Stephen, Armando Razo, and Noel Maurer. 2003. *The politics of property rights: Political instability, credible commitments, and economic growth in Mexico (1876–1929)*. Cambridge, UK: Cambridge University Press.

Haggard, Stephan. 1990. *Pathways from the periphery: The politics of growth in the newly industrializing countries*. Ithaca, NY: Cornell University Press.

Hall, Peter A., and David W. Soskice. 2001. *Varieties of capitalism: The institutional foundations of comparative advantage*. Oxford, UK: Oxford University Press.

Handcock, Mark S., David R. Hunter, Carter Butts, Steven M. Goodreau, and Martina Morris. 2003. "statnet: An R package for the statistical analysis and simulation of social networks." Funding support from NIH grants R01DA012831 and R01HD041877. Online: www.csde.washington.edu/statnet.

Hardin, Russell. 1997. "Economic theories of the state." In *Perspectives on public choice: A handbook*, ed. D.C. Mueller, 21–34. Cambridge: Cambridge University Press.

Hayek, Friedrich A. 1960. *The constitution of liberty*. Chicago: University of Chicago Press.

Huntington, Samuel P. 1968. *Political order in changing societies*. New Haven, CT: Yale University Press.

Huntington, Samuel P., and Clement Henry Moore. 1970. *Authoritarian politics in modern society: The dynamics of established one-party systems*. New York: Basic Books.

Hutchcroft, Paul D. 1994. "Business–government relations in the Philippines." In *Business and government in industrialising Asia*, ed. Andrew MacIntyre, 216–243. Ithaca, NY: Cornell University Press.

Hutchcroft, Paul D. 1998. *Booty capitalism: The politics of banking in the Philippines*. Ithaca, NY: Cornell University Press.

Ibarra, Romero. 2003. "El Banco del Estado de México (1897–1914)." In *La Banca Regional en México (1870–1930)*, ed. Mario Cerutti and Carlos Marichal, 216–253. Mexico City: Fondo de Cultura Económica.

Islam, Iyanatul, and Anis Chowdhury. 2000. *The political economy of East Asia: Post-crisis debates*. Melbourne: Oxford University Press.

Jones, Leroy P., and Il SaKong. 1980. *Government, business, and entrepreneurship in economic development: The Korean case*. Cambridge, MA: Harvard University Press.

Kang, David C. 2002. *Crony capitalism: Corruption and development in South Korea and the Philippines*. Cambridge, UK: Cambridge University Press.

Katz, Friedrich. 1984. "Mexico: Restored republic and Porfiriato, 1867–1910." In *The Cambridge history of Latin America*, ed. Leslie Bethell, 3–78. Cambridge: Cambridge University Press.

Katz, Friedrich. 1998. *The life and times of Pancho Villa.* Stanford, CA: Stanford University Press.

Khan, Mushtaq H. 2000. "Rents, efficiency, and growth." In *Rents, rent-seeking and economic development: Theory and evidence in Asia*, ed. Mushtaq H. Khan and Kwame S. Jomo, 21–69. Cambridge: Cambridge University Press.

Khan, Mushtaq H., and Kwame S. Jomo. 2000a. "Introduction." In *Rents, rent-seeking and economic development: Theory and evidence in Asia*, ed. Mushtaq H. Khan and Kwame S. Jomo, 1–20. Cambridge: Cambridge University Press.

Khan, Mushtaq H., and Kwame S. Jomo. 2000b. *Rents, rent-seeking and economic development: Theory and evidence in Asia.* Cambridge: Cambridge University Press.

King, Gary. 1998. *Unifying political methodology.* Ann Arbor, MI: University of Michigan Press.

Knox, Hannah, Mike Savage, and Penny Harvey. 2006. Social networks and the study of relations: Networks as method, metaphor and form. *Economy and Society* 35 (1):113–140.

Krueger, Anne. 1974. The political economy of the rent-seeking society. *American Economic Review* 64:291–303.

Kuntz Ficker, Sandra. 2002. "Institutional change and foreign trade in Mexico, 1870–1911." In *The Mexican economy, 1870–1930: Essays on the economic history of institutions, revolution, and growth*, ed. Jeff L. Bortz and Stephen H. Haber, 161–204. Stanford, CA: Stanford University Press.

Laothamatas, Anek. 1994. "From clientelism to partnership: Business-government relations in Thailand." In *Business and government in industrialising Asia*, ed. Andrew MacIntyre, 192–215. Ithaca, NY: Cornell University Press.

Levitsky, Steven, and Gretchen Helmke. 2004. Informal institutions and comparative politics: A research agenda. *Perspectives on Politics* 2 (4):725–740.

Lewis, Paul H. 2006. *Authoritarian regimes in Latin America: Dictators, despots, and tyrants.* Lanham, MD: Rowman & Littlefield.

Linz, Juan J. 1964. "An authoritarian regime: The case of Spain." In *Cleavages, ideologies, and party systems*, ed. Erik Allard and Yrjo Littunen. Helsinki: Westermarck Society.

Linz, Juan J. 1975. "Totalitarian and authoritarian regimes." In *Handbook of Political Science*, ed. Fred Greenstein and Nelson Polsby, 175–411. Reading, MA: Addison-Wesley.

Linz, Juan J. 2000. *Totalitarian and authoritarian regimes.* Boulder, CO: Lynne Rienner Publishers.

Lockhart, James, and Stuart B. Schwartz. 1983. *Early Latin America: A history of colonial Spanish America and Brazil.* Cambridge, UK: Cambridge University Press.

Ludlow, Leonor. 2003. "El Banco Mercantil de Veracruz (1898–1906)." In *La Banca Regional en México (1870–1930)*, ed. Mario Cerutti and Carlos Marichal, 134–167. Mexico City: Fondo de Cultura Económica.

Lynch, John. 1984. "The origins of Spanish American independence." In *The Cambridge History of Latin America*, ed. Leslie Bethell, 3–50. Cambridge, UK: Cambridge University Press.

MacIntyre, Andrew J. 1991. *Business and politics in Indonesia*. North Sydney, Australia: Allen & Unwin.

MacIntyre, Andrew. 1994. "Business, government and development: Northeast and Southeast Asian comparisons." In *Business and government in industrialising Asia*, ed. Andrew MacIntyre, 1–28. Ithaca, NY: Cornell University Press.

Mainwaring, Scott, and Matthew Soberg Shugart. 1997. *Presidentialism and democracy in Latin America*. Cambridge: Cambridge University Press.

Marichal, Carlos. 2002. "The construction of credibility: Financial market reform and the renegotiation of Mexico's external debt in the 1880's." In *The Mexican Economy, 1870–1930: Essays on the economic history of institutions, revolution, and growth*, ed. Jeff L. Bortz and Stephen H. Haber, 93–119. Stanford, CA: Stanford University Press.

Marichal, Carlos, and Mario Cerutti, eds. 1997. *Historia de las grandes empresas en México, 1850–1930*. Mexico City: Fondo de Cultura Económica and Universidad Autónoma de Nuevo León.

Marichal, Carlos, and Mario Cerutti. 2003. "Estudio Introductorio." In *La Banca Regional en México (1870–1930)*, ed. Mario Cerutti and Carlos Marichal, 9–46. Mexico City: Fondo de Cultura Económica.

Márquez, Graciela. 2001. *Protección y cambio institucional: La política arancelaria del Porfiriato a la Gran Depresión*. Mexico City: El Colegio de México.

Martinussen, John. 1997. *Society, state, and market: A guide to competing theories of development*. London: Zed Books Ltd.

Maurer, Noel H. 2002. *The power and the money: The Mexican financial system, 1876–1932*. Stanford, CA: Stanford University Press.

McCubbins, Mathew D., and Gregory W. Noble. 1995. "The appearance of power: Legislators, bureaucrats, and the budget process in the United States and Japan." In *Structure and policy in Japan and the United States*, ed. Peter F. Cowhey and Mathew D. McCubbins, 56–80. Political Economy of Institutions and Decisions series. Cambridge: Cambridge University Press.

McCubbins, Mathew D., and Thomas Schwartz. 1984. Congressional oversight overlooked: Police patrols versus fire alarms. *American Journal of Political Science* 28:165–179.

McGuire, Martin C., and Mancur Olson. 1996. The economics of autocracy and majority rule: The invisible hand and the use of force. *Journal of Economic Literature* 34:72–96.

McMillan, John, and Pablo Zoido. 2004. "How to subvert democracy: Montesinos in Peru." Stanford Research Paper No. 1851. Stanford, CA: Stanford Graduate Business School.

Mexican Year Book. 1908. *The Mexican year book: A financial and commercial handbook, 1908.*Vol. 1. London: McCorquodale.

Mexican Year Book. 1910. *The Mexican year book: A statistical, financial and economic annual, 1909–1910.*Vol. 2. London: McCorquodale.

México, Banco Central Mexicano. 1908. *Las sociedades anónimas en México.* Mexico City: Banco Central Mexicano.

México, Congreso, Cámara de Senadores. 1876–1911. *Diario de los debates.* Mexico City: Imprenta de Irineo Paz.

México, Dirección General de Estadística, and Antonio Peñafiel. 1908. *Noticia del movimiento de sociedades mineras y mercantiles habido en la Oficina del Registro Público de la Propiedad y de Comercio durante los años de 1886 a 1907.* Mexico City: Impr. y Fototipia de la Secretaría de Fomento.

México, Instituto Nacional de Estadística, Geografía, e Informática (INEGI). 1994. *Estadísticas Históricas de México.* Aguascalientes, México: INEGI.

Meyer Cosío, Rosa María, ed. 1999. *Identidad y prácticas de los grupos de poder en México, siglos XVII–XIX: Seminario de formación de grupos y clases sociales.* Mexico City: Instituto Nacional de Antropología e Historia.

Meyer, Michael C., and William L. Sherman. 1995. *The course of Mexican history.* 5th ed. New York: Oxford University Press.

Miller, Gary J. 1992. *Managerial dilemmas: The political economy of hierarchy.* Cambridge: Cambridge University Press.

Monaldi, Francisco. 2002. *Rent seeking, institutions, and commitment: The political economy of foreign investment in the Venezuelan oil industry.* PhD diss., Stanford University, Stanford, CA.

Mueller, Dennis C. 1997. *Perspectives on public choice: A handbook.* New York: Cambridge University Press.

North, Douglass C. 1981. *Structure and change in economic history.* New York: Norton.

North, Douglass C. 1989. Institutions and economic growth: An historical introduction. *World Development* 17 (9):1319–1332.

North, Douglass C. 1990. *Institutions, institutional change, and economic performance.* Cambridge, UK: Cambridge University Press.

North, Douglass C. 1994. Economic performance through time. *American Economic Review* 84 (3):359–368.

North, Douglass C., and Barry R. Weingast. 1989. Constitutions and commitment: The evolution of institutions governing public choice in seventeenth-century England. *The Journal of Economic History* 49 (4):803–832.

North, Douglass Cecil, and Robert Paul Thomas. 1973. *The rise of the western world: A new economic history.* Cambridge: Cambridge University Press.

Oi, Jean C., and Andrew G. Walder. 1999. *Property rights and economic reform in China.* Stanford, CA: Stanford University Press.

Oi, Jean Chun. 1999. *Rural China takes off: Institutional foundations of economic reform.* Berkeley, CA: University of California Press.

Olson, Mancur. 1993. Dictatorship, democracy, and development. *American Political Science Review* 87 (3):567–576.

Olson, Mancur. 2000. *Power and prosperity: Outgrowing communist and capitalist dictatorships*. New York: Basic Books.

Olveda, Jaime. 2003. "Banca y banqueros de Guadalajara." In *La Banca Regional en México (1870–1930)*, ed. Mario Cerutti and Carlos Marichal, 291–320. Mexico City: Fondo de Cultura Económica.

Osborne, Martin J., and Ariel Rubinstein. 1994. *A course in game theory*. Cambridge, MA: MIT Press.

Plato, and Francis MacDonald Cornford. 1945. *The Republic of Plato*, trans. Francis MacDonald Cornford. London: Oxford University Press.

Pollock, Phillip H., III. 2006. *Essentials of political analysis*. 2nd ed. Washington, DC: CQ Press.

Polsby, Nelson W. 1975. "Legislatures." In *Handbook of political science*, ed. F. Greenstein and N. Polsby. Reading, MA: Addison-Wesley.

Przeworski, Adam. 1991. *Democracy and the market: Political and economic reforms in eastern Europe and Latin America*. Cambridge: Cambridge University Press.

Przeworski, Adam, Michael H. Alvarez, and Jose Antonio Cheibub. 2000. *Democracy and development: Political institutions and material well-being in the world, 1950–1990*. Cambridge: Cambridge University Press.

Przeworski, Adam, and Fernando Limongi. 1993. Political regimes and economic growth. *Journal of Economic Perspectives* 7 (3):51–69.

Razo, Armando. 2003. *Social networks and credible commitments in dictatorships: Political organization and economic growth in Porfirian Mexico (1876–1911)*. PhD diss., Stanford University, Stanford, CA.

Razo, Armando, and Stephen H. Haber. 1998. The rate of growth of productivity in Mexico, 1850–1933: Evidence from the cotton textile industry. *Journal of Latin American Studies* 30 (3):481–517.

Read, Ian, and Aldo Musacchio. 2001. *Bankers, industrialists and their cliques: Elite networks in Mexico and Brazil, 1890–1915*. Unpublished paper. Stanford, CA: Stanford University, Department of History.

Reyes, Bernardo. 1903. *El general Porfirio Díaz: Estudio biográfico con fundamento de datos auténticos y de las memorias del gran militar y estadista, de las que se reproducen los principales pasajes*. Mexico City: J. Ballescá y Compañía.

Reynolds, Clark W. 1970. *The Mexican economy*. New Haven, CT: Yale University Press.

Robins, Garry, and Philippa Pattison. 2005. "Interdependencies and social processes: Dependence graphs and generalized dependence structures." In *Models and methods in social network analysis*, ed. Peter J. Carrington, John Scott and Stanley. Wasserman, 192–214. Cambridge: Cambridge University Press.

Rodriguez, Francisco, and Adam J. Gomolin. 2006. *Anarchy, state and dystopia: Venezuelan economic institutions before the advent of oil.* Unpublished paper. Middletown, CT: Wesleyan University, Department of Economics.

Rodríguez López, María Guadalupe. 2003. "Paz y bancos en Durango durante el Porfiriato." In *La Banca Regional en México (1870–1930)*, ed. Mario Cerutti and Carlos Marichal, 254–290. Mexico City: Fondo de Cultura Económica.

Roeder, Ralph. 1981. *Hacia el México moderno: Porfirio Díaz.* Vol. I. Mexico City: Fondo de Cultura Económica.

Root, Hilton L. 1989. Tying the king's hands: Credible commitments and royal fiscal policy during the old regime. *Rationality and Society* 1 (2):240–248.

Root, Hilton L. 2001. Do strong governments produce strong economies? *The Independent Review* V (4):565–573.

Rose-Ackerman, Susan. 1999. *Corruption and government: Causes, consequences, and reform.* Cambridge, UK: Cambridge University Press.

Rosenbluth, Frances McCall. 1989. *Financial politics in contemporary Japan.* Ithaca: Cornell University Press.

Sanchiz, Javier. 2000. La Familia Fagoaga: Apuntes Genealógicos. *Estudios de Historia NovoHispana* 23:129–167.

Sawyer, Amos. 2005. *Beyond plunder: Toward democratic governance in Liberia.* Boulder, CO: Lynne Rienner Publishers.

Schedler, Larry Diamond, and Marc F. Plattner, eds. 1999. *The self-restraining state: Power and accountability in new democracies.* Boulder, CO: Lynne Rienner Publishers.

Scott, John. 2000. *Social network analysis: A handbook.* 2nd ed. Thousands Oaks, CA: Sage Publications.

Shepsle, Kenneth. 1991. "Discretion, institutions, and the problem of government commitment." In *Social theory for a changing society*, ed. Pierre Bourdieu and James Coleman, 245–263. Boulder, CO: Westview Press.

Sinkin, Richard N. 1979. *The Mexican Reform, 1855–1876: A study in liberal nation-building.* Austin: The University of Texas Press.

Skidmore, Thomas E., and Peter H. Smith. 2005. *Modern Latin America.* 6th ed. New York: Oxford University Press.

Solís, Leopoldo. 1970. *La realidad económica mexicana: Retrovisión y perspectivas.* Mexico City: Siglo XXI Editores.

Thompson, Mark R. 1998. "The Marcos regime in the Philippines." In *Sultanistic regimes*, ed. Houchang E. Chehabi and Juan J. Linz, 206–229. Baltimore: Johns Hopkins University Press.

Thomson, Alex. 2004. *An introduction to African politics.* 2nd ed. London: Routledge.

Tulchin, Joseph S., and Ralph Espach, eds. 2000. *Combating corruption in Latin America.* Washington, DC: Woodrow Wilson Center Press.

Vatikiotis, Michael R. J. 1988. *Indonesian politics under Suharto: The rise and fall of the new order.* 3rd ed. London: Routledge.

Velasco, Alfonso Luis. 1889. *Porfirio Díaz y su gabinete: Estudios biográficos.* Mexico City: E. Dublan y Cia.

Wade, Robert. 1990. *Governing the market: Economic theory and the role of government in East Asian industrialization.* Princeton, NJ: Princeton University Press.

Wasserman, Mark. 1984. *Capitalists, caciques, and revolution: Elite and foreign enterprise in Chihuahua, Mexico, 1854–1911.* Chapel Hill, NC: University of North Carolina Press.

Wasserman, Stanley, and Katherine Faust. 1994. *Social network analysis: Methods and applications.* Cambridge: Cambridge University Press.

Wasserman, Stanley, and Garry Robins. 2005. "An introduction to random graphs, dependence graphs, and p*." In *Models and methods in social network analysis*, ed. Peter J. Carrington, John Scott and Stanley Wasserman, 162–191. Cambridge: Cambridge University Press.

Watson, Joel. 2002. *Strategy: An introduction to game theory.* New York: W. W. Norton.

Weingast, Barry. 1995. The economic role of political institutions: Market-preserving federalism and economic development. *Journal of Law, Economics, and Organization* 11 (1):1–31.

Weingast, Barry. 1997a. "The political foundations of limited government: Parliament and sovereign debt in 17th- and 18th-century England." In *The frontiers of the new institutional economics*, ed. John N. Drobak and John V. C. Nye, 213–246. San Diego, CA: Harcourt Brace Academic Press.

Weingast, Barry. 1997b. The political foundations on democracy and the rule of law. *American Political Science Review* 91 (2):245–263.

Weldon, Jeffrey. 1997. "The political sources of Presidencialismo in Mexico." In *presidentialism and democracy in Latin America*, ed. Scott Mainwaring and Matthew S. Shugart, 225–258. Cambridge: Cambridge University Press.

Wellman, Barry, and Stephen D. Berkowitz. 1997. *Social structures: A network approach.* Greenwich, CT: JAI Press.

Wintrobe, Ronald. 1998. *The political economy of dictatorship.* Cambridge, UK: Cambridge University Press.

Wintrobe, Ronald. 2001. How to understand and deal with dictatorship: An economist's view. *Economics of Governance* 2:35–58.

World Bank. 1993. *The East Asian miracle: Economic growth and public policy.* New York: Oxford University Press.

World Bank. 2001. *World development report 2002: Building institutions for markets.* Oxford: Oxford University Press.

Page numbers preceded by a *t* or *f* indicates tables or figures.

for influential Mexican industries, 87
of investors, security of, 101–2
in mining industry, 98–99
in Porfirian Mexico, 87–88
propagation of predation risk and, 32
protection of, 28
  by private enforcers, 139–40
  tax rate and, 36–37
rural populations and, 94, 96
selective, 176
Protection
overlapping, 12
  of companies, 137–38, 137f
  definition of, 137, 202n40
  of public officials, 144, 144f
private, social network enhancement of, 11
selective, 12
  exclusion and, 8
  in Porfiriato, 18
  selective predation and, 23, 27
universal, 28
Protectionism, 186
Public corporations, Mexican, 90t, 91, 92
Public officials, 128–30, 165. *See also specific*
  public officials or positions
accumulated seniority of, 115–17, 116t
on boards of directors, 142, 143t
businessmen, 106–7, 107t
centrality, measures of, 144–45, 145t
collusive behavior of, 133
company affiliations, 142, 150t–51t
connections to elite networks, 109–13,
  111f–112f, 111t
on corporate boards, 132
dictatorial power of Díaz and, 129–30
durability of industry agreements and, 134
family occupations of, 106, 106t
family political ties of, 105–6, 105t
general profile of, 104–13
importance, assessment of, 155–56
incentives, 35, 142
military experience of, 107–8, 108t
military positions of, 107–8, 107t, 108t
occupational experience of, 106–8, 107t,
  108t
overlapping protection from, 137–38, 137f,
  144, 144f
political careers of, 114
political mobility, 117
  definition of, 117

of deputies, 122t, 123–24, 124f
executive positions and, 122t, 123
gubernatorial positions and, 122t, 123
legislative positions and, 121, 122t, 123
long-term, 122t, 123, 128
measuring, factors in, 117–18
  by position, 121, 122t
prospects of, 113–14
relative frequency of position changes,
  118–19, 119t
positions of, 114–15, 115t
as private enforcers, 128
recruitment incentives (*See* Private policies)
relationship with economic elites, 109–13,
  111f, 111t, 112f
socioeconomic background of, 104–6, 105f,
  106f
sources on, 189
state governors (*See* Governors, state)
Public policy, 29–30

Quijano-Rivero family, 110, 111f

Railroads. *See* Transportation industry
Regional power holders, 154
Rent
definition of, 201n33
deterrence of predation and, 11
dictatorships and, 12, 30
higher
  company dissolutions and, 96–99, 97t
  concessions and, 89–94
for private protection, 142
Republicans (Mexican federalists), 56–57
Reputation, of dictator, 5
Reservation value, 36
Romano, Leopoldo, 115t
Royal land grants *(encomienda)*, 95
Royalists (Mexican conservatives), 56–57
Rubio, Romero, 153

Santa Anna, General Antonio López de, 57–58
Secondary sources, 189–90
Selective commitments. *See* Commitments,
  selective
Senators, political mobility of, 119t, 120, 122t,
  123–25, 124f, 125f
Sese Seko, Mobutu, 178
Single-party regimes, establishment of, 183,
  185